The Poetry of Han-shan

SUNY Series in Buddhist Studies

Kenneth K. Inada, Editor

The Poetry of HAN-SHAN

A Complete, Annotated Translation of *Cold Mountain*

Robert G. Henricks

STATE UNIVERSITY OF NEW YORK PRESS

Published by
State University of New York Press, Albany

©1990 State University of New York

For information, address State University of New York
Press, State University Plaza, Albany, NY 12246

Library of Congress Cataloging-in-Publication Data

Henricks, Robert G., 1943–
    The poetry of Han-shan: a complete, annotated
translation of *Cold Mountain*/by Robert G. Henricks.
        p.   cm.—(SUNY series in Buddhist studies)
    Bibliography: p.
    Includes index.
    ISBN 0-88706-977-0.—ISBN 0-88706-978-9 (pbk.)
    1. Han-shan, fl. 627-649—Translations, English. I. Title.
II. Series.
PL2677.H3A244   1990
895.1'12—dc20   89-4452
                                                                                       CIP

10 9 8 7 6 5 4 3 2

Contents

Preface / vii

INTRODUCTION / 1

Problems of Dating and Authorship / 3

On the Life of Han-shan / 7

The Poetry of Han-shan / 12

Translator's Note / 20

Notes / 21

TRANSLATIONS / 27

Preface to the Ch'üan T'ang Shih Edition
of Han-shan's Poems / 29

Poems No. 1–No. 311 / 31

APPENDICES / 417

I. The Dates of Han-shan: The Internal Evidence / 419

II. Previous English Translations / 423

III. An Index to Themes / 433

v

IV. Buddhist Terms, Metaphors, and Stories / 439

Bibliography / 457

Index / 469

Preface

For many years I have used Burton Watson's *Cold Mountain* as a textbook in my Buddhism in China course by way of introducing students to the way in which Zen Buddhist ideas might be put into verse. In the summer of 1983, I decided to spend some time reading the Han-shan poems in the original, and I discovered to my delight that there were many good poems in the Han-shan collection that had never before been translated into English, whether by Watson (who did one hundred of the poems), Arthur Waley (twenty-seven), Gary Snyder (twenty-four), or Wu Chi-yu (forty-nine). Moreover, in the extant English translations, very little had been done in terms of annotating allusions or explaining background information or providing the reader with analysis of what individual poems might mean in terms of the symbolism and/or literary structure of the verse. I decided, therefore, that a complete, annotated translation of the Han-shan collection of 311 poems would indeed be a worthwhile project, one that would make a significant contribution to the body of Chinese literary works available in English in providing a text that would be appealing and useful to specialists and general readers alike.

The project has taken four years to complete. My work has been aided tremendously by having an excellent, annotated Japanese edition of the poems to use—Iritani and Matsumura's *Kanzanshi*. Iritani and Matsumura not only document Han-shan's many allusions to works in the Chinese classical, literary tradition; they also locate with accuracy allusions to Buddhist texts (though they have been helped in this by the earlier work of Hakuin).

As my work progressed on the translation, I learned from others that the author "Red Pine" had just recently published a complete English translation of the poems (Copper Canyon Press, 1983), so my complete translation would not be the first. However, given that Red Pine's text is not a thorough scholarly edition of the poems, there is still a great deal the present work has to add; moreover, we translate in quite different styles. I also learned only last year that a complete, annotated French translation had appeared in 1985 (Patrick Carré, *Le Mangeur de Brumes*). Having read through this translation, I can say that the virtue of this book is that Carré is more concerned than I with exploring and explaining the Buddhist dimensions of Han-shan's verse; his annotation is often incomplete and imprecise.

Let me be clear at the outset that I do not offer the present translation as an improvement on all previous attempts at translating Han-shan. Arthur Waley and Burton Watson stand as two of the great all-time translators of Chinese things into English, and Gary Snyder has a feel for the colloquial nature of some of Han-shan's poems that is still enjoyed by a great many readers. It is not my hope or expectation that readers will enjoy my translations even more, though I certainly hope that my translations are smooth, readable, and accurate—even sometimes poetic; I strive throughout to maintain something of the balance and rhythm that we find in each line in the original.

My aims in the present work are three: (1) To provide a complete English translation of the Han-shan poems so that readers will at last know all of Han-shan's poems and in this way realize, if nothing else, just how varied his poetic interests were. (2) To make available to specialists on the T'ang (618–906) and to specialists on Chinese poetry and literature an important source of data for the work they do in their fields. (3) To make available to Buddhist scholars an important source of materials for understanding the spread and development of Buddhist texts and ideas in China during the T'ang, and an important source of materials on early Zen (Ch'an).

By way of conclusion, let me note that I think many readers will be struck, as I have been, by a number of things that such a translation reveals. For example, I am surprised by the wide variety of themes on which Han-shan writes, by the cleverness of his observations and the sharpness of his wit, and by his technique as a poet: quite a few of Han-shan's poems are only understood and appreciated through close line-by-line poetic analysis. Moreover, I think the reader will see that Han-shan was well acquainted with the classical Chinese literary tradition, alluding as he does to well-known people and events and anecdotes in the Confucian and Tao-ist classics, the dynastic histories, and so on. He shows special interest in using lines and themes from the "Nineteen Old Poems" of the Han and the collected *Yüeh-fu* (Music Bureau) ballads and songs. Finally, though we have known for some time that Han-shan knew of and used the *Nirvāṇa-sūtra* more than any other Buddhist text in his poems, my translation will reveal precisely which stories and metaphors caught his eye, and it will reveal that many of the fresh, strikingly graphic metaphors Han-shan employs in his po-ems—something for which he is known—stem, in fact, from Bud-dhist texts in general and the *Nirvāṇa-sūtra* in particular.

There are many people and organizations to thank for their help with this work. Much of the productive labor on this volume was completed at the Stanford Center in Taipei, where I enjoyed an IUP-CSCC Fellowship from January to June 1986: thus let me begin by expressing my thanks to that fellowship committee for selecting me as a fellow and to Dartmouth College for granting me sabbat-ical leave during that time. At the Stanford Center I was able to read through all of the poems with Wen An-p'ing and discuss with her meanings, allusions, and interpretations—I am deeply in-debted to her for her help with many poems and lines. I was also fortunate to have, as two of my fellow Fellows at the Stanford Center, Bill Nienhauser of the University of Wisconsin, an expert on T'ang poetry, and Bob Borgen of the University of Hawaii, a specialist in Japanese language and literature. Bill kindly agreed to read through my first draft translation and made many valuable suggestions; Bob willingly helped me with the Japanese of Iritani and Matsumura when I was unsure of what they might mean. Back at Dartmouth I was able to work with Professor Li Kai, a special-ist on Chinese literature from Beijing Normal University, who was in residence here for two years. Professor Li shared with me his views on a number of problematic interpretations, ably quoting similar lines from other poets off the top of his head. Pamela Cross-ley, my colleague at Dartmouth in Chinese history, helped me at the end with background on a number of Chinese institutional issues. Finally I want to thank Chen Zengyin, who served as my research assistant in the fall and spring terms of last year, Scott Abernathy, who checked the accuracy of Buddhist terms and allusions, and my typist Deborah Hodges, who conscientiously checked my grammar and helped with final improvements, as she typed the final draft.

My wife's delight in the poems—she was forced to read them nine or ten times—and the enthusiastic reception of my translations by students, colleagues, and friends over the past two or three years have added greatly to my own enjoyment of this work and kept me highly motivated.

INTRODUCTION

This is a complete, annotated translation of the poetry of Han-shan, Han-shan being a T'ang Dynasty (618–907) recluse who lived alone, apparently much of his life, in the T'ien-t'ai mountains in southeast China, and wrote many poems about his life alone in the hills. We know very little about this man other than what we can glean from the three hundred-odd poems that still survive in the collection of verse that bears his name. We do not know his real name[1]—a number of different accounts affirm that "Han-shan" (Cold Mountain) or "Han-yen" (Cold Cliffs) is a name that he took from the place where he lived.[2] We do not know his dates: opinions on that vary from early T'ang or even Sui (605–618) to mid and even late T'ang.

Everyone seems to agree that the place to begin looking into these matters is the "Lü-ch'iu Yin Preface" to the poems, a record whose existence is attested by at least the end of the tenth century in Tsan-ning's *Sung Kao-seng chuan* (comp. 982–988).[3] I will not cite here a complete translation of the Preface: an abridged version stands at the head of the *Ch'üan T'ang shih* edition of Han-shan's poems and is translated below (the reader might want to look ahead). Suffice it to say by way of summary that the Preface claims to be written by an official named Lü-ch'iu Yin who, having assumed his post as Prefect of T'ai-chou (modern day Lin-hai County in Chekiang), went to visit two oddball Buddhists named Han-shan and Shih-te at Kuo-ch'ing Temple in the nearby T'ien-t'ai mountains, such a visit having been recommended by the common master of the two, a monk named Feng-kan. Lü-ch'iu Yin tells us that Han-shan lived on Cold Cliff, located seventy li west of the town of T'ang-hsing, and that he—Lü-ch'iu Yin, that is—asked the monk Tao-ch'iao to copy down the three hundred-odd poems that Han-shan had spread about the countryside, written on trees and walls.[4]

The Preface is undated, and it is not until 1189, when Chih-nan wrote a postscript to the poems (entitled *T'ien-t'ai-shan Kuo-ch'ing-ssu san-yin-chi chi*), that we are told that these events took place in the early years of the T'ang. Chih-nan says, "The Zen mas-

ter Feng-kan lived at Kuo-ch'ing Temple on T'ien-t'ai in the early
years of the *chen-kuan* period (627–649) of the T'ang.[5]

There are problems with this preface, and the biggest problem
is that we can find no contemporary information on any Lü-ch'iu
Yin who was a Prefect of T'ai-chou at the beginning of the T'ang.
Lü-ch'iu Yin *is* listed as a Prefect of T'ai-chou during the *chen-kuan*
period of the T'ang in the Prefectural Gazetteer of T'ai-chou, published in 1722,[6] but that is very late. There is a Lü-ch'iu Yin mentioned in early sources, but that Lü-ch'iu Yin, who was in fact a
Prefect in early T'ang, was a Prefect in Li-chou, not T'ai-chou.

We cannot simply dismiss as irrelevant this "second" Lü-ch'iu
Yin, for Wu Chi-yu, in a well-known article on Han-shan, argued
persuasively that this *was* the man who visited Han-shan and that
"Han-shan," therefore, was a man named Chih-yen, a man who
had served with *this* Lü-ch'iu Yin in the army before becoming a
Buddhist and going off to live in the hills.[7] Our record on these two
men does in fact say that Lü-ch'iu Yin, while serving as Prefect of
Li-chou—which was apparently sometime in early *chen-kuan*[8]—did
pay his former colleague a visit at his mountain retreat. Thus there
are elements in the story that seem to accord with what we know
about Han-shan, especially since he too appears to have held some
minor government jobs before he became a recluse (poem 7 is important in Wu's argument). And Wu Chi-yu is certainly right in
pointing out that it is highly unlikely that there were two men with
the same, uncommon name (Lü-ch'iu Yin) holding much the same
post at this time.

Nonetheless, there are problems with the proposed identification. To begin with, there is no record that Chih-yen wrote any poems at all, and secondly, the Lü-ch'iu Yin of our Preface clearly did
not know who Han-shan was before making his visit, while this
Lü-ch'iu Yin was Chih-yen's former colleague.

To return to the Preface, the great Sinologist Hu Shih doubted
its authenticity as early as the 1920s. For a number of reasons he
suggested the dates 700–780 for the dates of Han-shan, noting, for
example, that the place mentioned in the Preface, T'ang-hsing, did
not go by that name before 675 (the second year of the reign period
shang-yüan) and that therefore the Preface could not have been written in early T'ang.[9] Hu Shih failed to note that in reality there were
two *shang-yüan* reign periods in the T'ang—the first running from
674–675, the second from 760–761—and the general consensus now
is that the change in this place's name from its original name of

Shih-feng to T'ang-hsing was made in 761, not 675, thus presumably pushing the date of the Preface back further into mid or late T'ang.[10] But all this scholarship may be in vain, since two of our early sources on the life of Han-shan say that he lived seventy li to the west of Shih-feng county—not T'ang-hsing—and Shih-feng was the name of this county from the time it was established back in the Chin (i.e., from about 300 A.D.) until it was changed in, apparently, 761 in the T'ang.[11]

If we set the "Lü-ch'iu Yin Preface" aside and turn to other sources to look for a date for Han-shan, we find little agreement. Tu Kuang-t'ing (850–933), whose *Hsien-chuan shih-i* (cited in *T'ai-p'ing kuang-chi* 55) is our earliest record on the life of Han-shan, says that Han-shan retired to the T'ien-t'ai Mountains during the reign period *ta-li* (766–779).[12] Tsan-ning, on the other hand, felt that Han-shan, Shih-te, and Lü-ch'iu Yin all lived during the reign of Jui-tsung (710–712), since it was around that time that Feng-kan died.[13] And looking further into Sung and Yüan sources, Hu Shih notes that the meeting of Lü-ch'iu Yin and Han-shan is variously placed in 633, 642, 643, 712–713, and right around 800.[14]

There are other ways to approach the problem of dating, of course. For example, we ought to be able to date the poems through analysis of their contents. And since Han-shan's poems are filled with Zen symbols and themes, and since we normally date the beginnings of creative developments in the Zen school to the early eighth century and the teachings of Hui-neng (638–713), the Sixth Patriarch of the Zen school, we might readily conclude that Han-shan lived in mid-T'ang, a point already made by V. T. Yang in his review of Burton Watson's translation.[15] But Han-shan does not use any of the technical terms that become part of Zen jargon with Hui-neng's Southern School of Zen (such as *chien-hsing* ["realize" or "see your own nature"], *wu-nien* ["absence of thought"], and *tun-wu* ["sudden enlightenment"]), as we might expect if he lived and wrote after this period.[16] Moreover, recent studies of the beginnings of Zen/Ch'an in China continue to note important developments in the school in early T'ang and before.[17]

Another point made by V. T. Yang on the problem of dating is that Han-shan's disdain for "regulated verse" *(lü-shih)* reflected the attitude of late T'ang.[18] Iritani and Matsumura also approve of a mid or late T'ang date, based on the author's knowledge of, and familiarity with, the *Wen-hsüan* (comp. 501–531) and the fact that his poems reveal common mid-T'ang literary concerns—e.g., he uses many *yüeh-fu* themes; he writes on the plight of the poor; and he delights in nature poetry.[19] Iriya Yoshitaka sees Han-shan as a Buddhist layman living sometime after mid-T'ang, since his conviction that "this very mind is the Buddha" reflects the subjective emphasis in Zen that we find after Ma-tsu (707–786); moreover, his admonishments to common folk and his criticism of Buddhist monks are also characteristic of this late time.[20]

In the poems themselves there are a number of datable references, and I have listed these in summary form in Appendix I. While the evidence is not unanimously in favor of early, mid, or late T'ang, there are a number of things that point to a time around or after mid T'ang (e.g., see items 1, 2, 3, 5, and 11). But the whole issue of dating Han-shan and/or his poems is complicated—perhaps hopelessly so—by the fact that the Han-shan poems probably do not all come from one hand. Iriya Yoshitaka, in 1958, argued for multiple authorship of the poems based on the varied attitudes and concerns we find in them.[21] But most important in this regard is E. G. Pulleyblank's article on the "Linguistic Evidence for the Date of Han-shan."[22]

Pulleyblank analyzes the rhyme combinations in the 311 poems and concludes that "while a portion of the poems must clearly be of late T'ang date, another considerably larger portion shows rhyming which points very strongly to an early T'ang or even Sui date."[23] Pulleyblank distinguishes these two groups of poems by calling the early T'ang group "Han-shan I" and the later T'ang group "Han-shan II," and he correctly notes that most of the vibrant Han-shan poems belong to group I, while some of the Han-shan II poems (but certainly not all of them) read like dry "didactic sermons."[24] (Of course to the specialist on Buddhism, *all* of the poems are of interest for what they can tell us about the state of affairs in Buddhism at the time. Poems distinguished by Pulleyblank as Han-shan II are noted in this translation by a single asterisk following the number of the poem.) Thus our assumption would be that the real Han-shan lived and wrote at the end of the Sui or in early T'ang, and that later on in mid or late T'ang, a number of poems were added to his collection by one, or several, fellow Buddhist devotees.

The linguistic evidence is persuasive, and I think most literary scholars these days assume the truth of this thesis as a working position; it is certainly possible that counter-theses will be argued later on. There are a number of very good, and very interesting, poems which unfortunately fall into Pulleyblank's Han-shan II group (see poems 56, 106, 119, 160, 161, 170, 182, 186, 248, and 256). But then Pulleyblank cautions that we cannot know for sure, in individual cases, when a particular poem was written, since "In individual cases . . . poems from the later period might by chance show a narrower range of rhyming than was theoretically possible at the period and hence give a false impression of being earlier." And he adds, "Conversely, since we know that even in court poetry occasional fringe rhymes occur, one cannot insist that every poem that violates the strictest canons of Han-shan I rhyming has to be from the later period."[25]

I still remain troubled by poems like 120 and 179, which are by rhyme words Han-shan I poems, and which in style and theme correspond to that group, but which seem to contain—clearly in the case of 120—references to things in mid-T'ang (c. 750 A.D.).

On the Life of Han-shan

Legends concerning Han-shan recorded in Buddhist biographical sources tell us nothing about the main events of his life. They focus instead on conversations Han-shan had with his friend and fellow monk Shih-te and their common master Feng-kan, the three understood as incarnations, respectively, of the bodhisattvas Mañjuśrī and Samantabhadra and the buddha Amitābha.[26] In these accounts, the three men are invariably portrayed, in good Zen fashion, as poor but happy recluses, bordering on the crazy, who constantly do and say nonsensical things, gaily clapping, laughing, singing, and dancing when they are misunderstood. A number of these stories read like *kōans*.

For example, the following story is told of an encounter between Han-shan and Shih-te while the latter was sweeping:[27]

> Shih-te was one day sweeping the ground when the head of the monastery, passing by, questioned him: 'You are called a foundling, because you were found by Feng-kan. However, what is your real name? And where do you live?' Shih-te put down the broom and stood with his hands crossed. When asked once more, he took the broom again and resumed his sweeping. At the sight of this, Han-shan beat his own breast and repeated: 'Good heavens! Good heavens!' Shih-te was

quite amazed. 'Why are you doing this?' he asked. Han-shan replied, 'Don't you know, when a man dies in the east house, the west house neighbors should show their sympathy by groaning.' Both burst into laughter, danced, cried, and left.

With anecdotal literature presenting Han-shan, Shih-te, and Feng-kan as close friends who frequented Kuo-ch'ing Temple, it seems odd that in the 311 poems in the Han-shan collection, Shih-te and Feng-kan are mentioned only once (in poem 40) and Kuo-ch'ing Temple only twice (in poems 40 and 274), one of those poems (274) being by rhyme late. Moreover, even though Han-shan repeatedly laments that people do not understand him, and even though his poems and themes are often quite odd, he notes that others call him a "crackpot" or a "nut" in only four poems—poems 180, 186, 220, and 236—all of them, by Pulleyblank's criteria, belonging to Han-shan II. The Han-shan who left us these poems seems only obliquely related to the Han-shan of later Buddhist tradition.

While it is admittedly dangerous to reconstruct the life of a poet using his poems—and perhaps absurd when "his poems" probably come from more than one hand—what we know about the life of our poet really depends on this one source alone. I will attempt here no more than an outline or sketch of his life, relying entirely on Han-shan I poems (except where noted).

We know next to nothing about Han-shan's early years—was his family rich or poor? He opens poem 102 by saying "From birth I've been a farmer," and he says in poem 111 that, when he was young, he would "take the classics along when I hoed." So it might appear that his parents were peasant farmers and he knew only the hardships of that kind of life. But the claim that you take the classics along when you hoe is a stylized claim that shows devotion to study and a commitment to eventually succeed in the realm of scholars and officials, so it is unclear just how much stock we can put in these words.

He does say of his parents, "Father and mother left me plenty of books," and he continues, "Fields and gardens—I long now for nothing more" (poem 15). These words, I think, suggest someone raised in an educated family (not by peasants) who was probably groomed for the life of an official, but who—like the father of "Field and Garden" poetry T'ao Ch'ien (365–427)—chose at some point the life of the gentleman farmer over working at some lowly government job (note also the comments below on poem 5).[28]

There are a couple of poems that might suggest that Han-shan's parents were not all that poor. In poem 101 he talks of hunting in his youth—"On and on I'd race my white horse; Shout out the hares, release the green hawks." This sounds more like the activity of a young aristocrat than some poor farm boy. Also, in poem 177 he talks of travelling all over China as a young man to visit famed spots of scenic beauty.

Some scholars feel that Han-shan was originally from northern China and that he moved at some point to the south, and Pulleyblank feels there is linguistic evidence to support this.[29] I think the *literary* evidence on this is questionable, since it seems to consist of the fact that in some poems Han-shan mentions the northern cities Lo-yang and Ch'ang-an. Ch'ang-an, after all, was the capital of China in the early T'ang, and Lo-yang was a secondary capital for both the Sui and the T'ang. Moreover, the mention of Lo-yang and the royal cemetery there (Pei-mang) are common enough in Chinese poetry of any age and hardly need tell us anything about the home of the author.[30]

Han-shan was married. He mentions his wife and son a number of times: in poem 5 he alludes to a story in which a wife counseled her talented husband to turn down an offer of official appointment and says, "In turning down the king's carriage, I followed the words of my virtuous wife; For my officer 'Lord of the Cart,' I have my filial son"; in poem 15, as he delights in his "fields and gardens," he observes, "My wife works the shuttle—her loom goes 'creak! creak!' Our son is at play—his mouth babbles 'wa! wa!'" So he clearly indicates a period of time when he farmed and enjoyed country life with his family. Eventually he was to leave his family (though poem 111 implies that it was his wife who left him). He speaks of returning home—having lived in the mountains alone for a while, engaged in his long life and enlightenment pursuits— but claims that when he returned, his wife no longer recognized him.[31]

Did Han-shan take the examinations to become an official? His poetry reveals that he was clearly conversant in the classics and in pre-T'ang literature, as the reader will see. And in at least one poem he speaks of having studied the classics and the histories— even though it was all in vain. There are three poems that speak to the issue of the official exams: they are poems 80, 113, and 120. In 80 he says:

> In vain I labored to explain the Three Histories;
> Wasted my time, reading through the Five Classics.

As old age comes on, I examine the Imperial Records;
As before, I live as a common man.

Here he seems to hold a position as a clerk or scribe in some government office, but his being a "common man" (*pai-ting*) would normally mean that he held no degree and had no official appointment.

The evidence from poem 113 is somewhat different. There he begins with the words:

My writing and judgment were perfect—they were not weak;
But they detested my looks, so I did not receive an appointment.

And ends by saying:

Certain it is that it's all related to fate;
Still this winter again I'll try and see.

Here Han-shan seems to allude to a "second" examination that was given to men who already held degrees, to determine who in that pool would actually receive appointment as an official (see the notes to this poem below). In this second examination the candidates were examined in terms of their "writing" (*shu*), "judgment" (*p'an*), "appearance" (*shen*), and "speech" (*yen*).

There is another reference to this system in poem 120, which begins:

This is what poor scribe,
Who repeatedly comes to be tested at Southern Court?

Years? Possibly thirty or more;
Already passed through four or five selections.

Han-shan might not be talking about himself here, so we cannot safely conclude much from this about his own case. But the "selections" (*hsüan*) mentioned in the fourth line once again seem to point to someone who by scholastic achievement was *eligible* for appointment to office but did not make it in. (Also arguing in favor of seeing Han-shan as a talented, educated man who had studied for, and perhaps passed, the official examinations but then went "unused" is his adoption of the *Ch'u-tz'u tristia* theme in poems 10, 59, and 69).

At some point, Han-shan left his family and went to Han-shan, where he lived—we assume—for the rest of his life. In poem 300 he comments that he was born thirty years ago but "today" has come home to Han-shan, so we might be able to date his retreat to that age. But the number "thirty" seems throughout his poems to be a stock figure for "reaching adult age" or maybe as equal to one-third of one's life, so we must treat such figures with care. Remember that in poem 120, the unhappy scholar is already "thirty or more"; in addition, in poem 49, Han-shan speaks of returning home once he'd been gone for thirty years, only to find that more than half of his relatives and friends were already dead. I might add that in two later poems (294 and 196) he speaks of returning home again, having been gone now seventy years, and of his being, late in life, one hundred or more. Once again these numbers—seventy and one hundred—are common figures for a normal old age and may not represent his actual age. Moreover, these two poems—196 and 294—both belong to Han-shan II.

It is safe, I think, to call Han-shan a "Buddhist" recluse, but only with qualification. The symbolism he employs, the technical terms he uses, his general outlook on life (i.e., his belief in *karma* and reincarnation)—in all these ways he is a Buddhist, and specifically he favors Zen. Nonetheless, it seems unlikely that Han-shan ever took monastic vows and became ordained as a monk. In fact, one of his great delights is criticizing, making fun of, satirizing establishment clergy. There are two poems in the collection that might suggest that he actually *had* taken vows: these are poems 269 and 274. Poem 269 begins: "Ever since I 'left home,'" where "left home" *(ch'u-chia)* is the Buddhist term for entering monastic life, for being ordained. And in poem 274, Han-shan speaks of remembering when he had first "entered" *(kuei, "returned to")* Kuo-ch'ing Temple; again the term *kuei* implies official adoption of the faith. But both of these poems are by rhyme Han-shan II.

Finally, though we might safely call Han-shan a Buddhist recluse—or Zen Buddhist recluse—he was never a purist. That is to say, his "Buddhism" did not preclude reading Taoist books or doing "Taoist" things that might lead to long life (i.e., breathing exercises, calisthenics, eating long-life minerals and herbs). As the reader will see, Han-shan's attitude about the viability of all of these things is mixed: sometimes he approves, sometimes he expresses his doubts. It is certainly possible that this ambivalence on Taoist views is yet another sign of multiple authorship;[32] then again, ambivalent attitudes are often just part of life.

THE POETRY OF HAN-SHAN

Han-shan does not rank with the great poets of the T'ang, people
like Li Po (701–762), Tu Fu (712–770), Wang Wei (699–761), and Po
Chü-i (772–846). In fact his poetry, until modern times, has been
largely ignored by Chinese literary historians, the assumption being, I think, that there is little of literary value in his work. I hope
that my analysis of some of his poems will correct that impression.

In the *Ch'üan T'ang shih* and *Ssu-pu ts'ung-k'an* editions of the
poetry of Han-shan there are 311 poems.[33] Most of the poems have
eight lines and are written in five-word verse (five characters per
line). Of the 311 poems, 285 are in five-word verse, twenty in seven-
word verse, and six in three-word verse. (But note that in poem 270,
Han-shan [if it is Han-shan speaking] says that he wrote a total of
six hundred poems: five hundred in five-word verse, seventy-nine
in seven-word verse, and twenty-one in three-word verse.)

Han-shan is best known for what we might call his "Han-
shan" poems, poems in which he describes the place where he
lived and speaks of the difficulties of reaching the top of that mountain. Many of these are no more than description, and as such, they
are beautiful landscape poems; yet many of these poems are more
than that, for they symbolize the spiritual quest for enlightenment
and the difficulties and obstacles one encounters along the way.

But Han-shan wrote all kinds of poems, and one of the virtues
of having a complete translation of the poems is that Han-shan's
varied themes can in this way be known and appreciated. There are
many poems on standard Chinese poetic themes; poems describing
lovely court ladies out for a stroll; poems noting loneliness when
apart from family and friends; poems despairing over the shortness
of life and the longness of death. (In Appendix III, I attempt a
breakdown of the poems by theme.)

But all in all, Han-shan is a very odd poet. First of all, as is
well known, on occasion he uses colloquial expressions and phrases
in his poems, which would rarely be done in "good" verse.
(Though, in my opinion, too much has been made of his use of the
colloquial: many—I would say most—of his poems are written in
good, classical Chinese.)

Moreover, in some cases his "poems" are not poems at all.
Rather, they are simply sayings, parables, or aphorisms—many of
them quite clever—that happen to be written in metric, rhymed
lines. For an example we might look at "poem" 45:

Now all things have their use
And in using them, each has what is fit.

If in using something, you use what is out of place,
It will be totally lacking, and what's more, completely deficient.

A round chisel with a square handle;
How sad! In vain it was made.

To use Hua-liu to catch mice
Can't compare with using a lame cat!

This seems to make the good Taoist point that values are relative. We would all value the prized steed over the lame cat, but the true value of something depends upon the situation. In any event, we would hardly think of this as a poem in normal terms. (Explanatory notes to this poem can be found in the Translations below.)

More important in terms of Han-shan's uniqueness as a poet is the fact that he often employs fresh, striking, and dramatic images, which really stand out in a tradition of poetry that uses stock symbols in set situations (e.g., if you are seeing a friend off to a new government post, your "lapels" must always be stained with your tears).

For example, at the end of poem 113—and these dramatic images are normally found at the end of a poem where they make the strongest impression—Han-shan decides that even though success in the examinations is really a matter of fate, he will try one more time this year, because:

After all, with a blind boy shooting at the eye of a sparrow
A chance hit is also not hard!

A poignant way to say the chances are slim.

There is another good illustration of this technique at the end of poem 13, a poem which is well written in terms of poetic technique. That poem goes:

At the hall of jade hangs a curtain of pearls;
Inside is a beautiful maid.

In appearance surpassing immortals and gods,
Complexion glowing like the peach or the pear.

At the Eastern inn spring mists collect;
At Western lodge fall winds arise.

And when the seasons have changed thirty years,
She too will look like pressed sugar cane!

The poet could have said she will be "wrinkled," but the image of "pressed sugar cane" makes that point very well. Note how this poem develops. The first line, speaking as it does of jade and pearls, introduces the idea of something beautiful that is also eternal and pure; jade and pearls have those associations in Chinese symbolism—they are incorruptible. The second line then ties those ideas of eternal beauty to the woman by association; she is not only beautiful but has a beauty that will not fade. That this association is intended is confirmed by line 3—"In appearance surpassing immortals and gods"—so she is like, or superior to, the gods and the immortals. The poem continues: "Complexion glowing like the peach or the pear." Peaches are the fruit of immortality to the Chinese; peaches are eaten by the immortals and the gods. But while this line continues the theme of immortality and beauty, it also introduces the possibility of change, since peaches and pears, though they might be the fruit of the gods, are living and changing, seasonal things. The next couplet accordingly moves into the realm of plant life and change: "At the Eastern inn spring mists collect; At Western lodge fall winds arise." Plants come to life in the spring and die again in the fall, and Chinese count their years in terms of springs and falls. Thus the penultimate line now talks in terms of the years: "And when the seasons have changed thirty years"—yes, what? the reader asks—"She too will look like pressed sugar cane!"[34]

For yet another illustration of the graphic images Han-shan used, we might look at poem 70, which also introduces one of Han-shan's common themes. As the reader will see, Han-shan is morally indignant about a number of things that people in the world commonly do. He dislikes the greed of the rich; he has no time for old men who marry young women and for those who do the reverse; he continually berates corrupt clergy; and he speaks out strongly against those who eat fish and meat. In poem 70 his disgust at this practice is clear:

Pigs eat the flesh of dead men,
And men eat the guts of dead pigs.

Pigs don't seem to mind human stench,
And men—to the contrary—say pig meat smells sweet!

When pigs die, throw them into the water;
When men die, dig them a hole in the ground.

If they never ate one another,
Lotus blossoms would sprout in water that bubbles and boils.

It perhaps helps to understand line 4 if we note that the Chinese word for sausage is *hsiang-ch'ang*—literally, "fragrant bowels." (I think the point at the end is that it will never happen.)

Poems against the greed of the rich are identified in Appendix III. One of the best of the lot is 104, where the niggardliness of the rich is clearly shown. That poem reads:

The young rich meet in high halls;
Colored lanterns, how dazzling and bright.

Now arrives one who owns not a candle,
Hoping to sit off to one side.

He'd not expected to be forced to leave,
To return to the dark, to stay there and dwell.

Helping others—is your brightness decreased?
Hard to believe! That you'd begrudge surplus light.

Finally, by way of illustrating Han-shan's moral indignation, he condemns the practice of old men marrying young girls in what is again, poetically, a well-structured verse. The poem is 115, and it reads like this:

"Young" Mr. Liu—he's eighty-two;
"Old" Mrs. Lan—she's all of eighteen!

Man and wife together for one hundred years;
Mutual affection—their feelings chaotic and unrestrained.

Playing with jade, he's nicknamed "the tiger";
Tossing down tiles, she's called "chubby cheeks."

One frequently sees, with the shoots put out by withering poplars;
They meet with death [at the hands of] Blue Maid!

In lines 5 and 6, "the tiger" means a new baby boy, and
"chubby cheeks" is a term of endearment for a baby girl. But we
only understand the significance of the last two lines if we know
that the *liu* of Mr. Liu means "willow" or "poplar" and that the *lan*
in Mrs. Lan is a word that means "blue." "Blue Maid" *(ch'ing-nü)* in
the last line is, on the one hand, the Goddess of Frost that kills
young new shoots in the fall and at the same time "Mrs. Lan," who
will, by implication, do the same to Mr. Liu and his "shoots."

At the end of Burton Watson's introduction to his translation of one
hundred poems by Han-shan, he notes that one of the striking
things about Han-shan's poems is that, contrary to what we might
expect, Han-shan the Buddhist in search of enlightenment is not
always blissfully content: at times he expresses frustration and despair. In Watson's words: "Commentators have been forced to resort
to some drastic wrenching in their interpretations of the poems by
the fact that Han-shan, though at times speaking from a pinnacle of
calm and enlightenment, just as often seems to be profoundly in-
volved in the misgivings and anxieties that enlightenment is supposed to dispel."[35]
    In what is perhaps the most painful poem in the collection,
Han-shan reflects on the fact that his sorrows are always with him.
This is poem 33:

I've heard it said that sorrows are hard to dispel;
These words, I've said, are not true.

Yet yesterday morn I drove them away,
And today I'm encumbered again.

The month comes to an end, but my sorrow doesn't end;
The year starts afresh, but my sorrows are also renewed.

Who is to know that under this cap of cane
There is fundamentally a man who's been sad a very long time.

    Let me stay with the theme of sorrow and frustration, even as I
begin to look at some of the "Han-shan" poems, poems that de-

scribe Han-shan's life as a recluse on a desolate mountain while saying something at the same time about the spiritual quest in the symbolism employed.

Throughout Han-shan's poems, the top of the mountain—being "up there," up above (or sitting with) the white clouds, up where we can see the clear sky, the sun, or the full moon—represents in some ways salvation, the realization of truth and the experience of purity, tranquility, and transcendence that comes with it. When we are "down" in the valleys, underneath the clouds (of ignorance), we wander around lost, looking for a way to the peak, slipping and falling and encountering obstacles in our way. If for Han-shan to *see* the bright sun or the full moon or the clear sky is to realize the truth, then failing to see those things—try as he might to glimpse a view—is equivalent to disappointment and despair. For example, look at poem 67, paying special attention to the last couplet.

> Here in the mountains—so very cold;
> It's been this way from of old; it's not just this year.
>
> Peak piled upon peak—constantly clotted with snow;
> Dark, secluded woods—every day spewing forth mist.
>
> Here things start to grow only after "Grain is in Beard,"
> And the leaves are coming down, even before the "Beginning
> of Fall."
>
> And here—here is a traveller hopelessly lost,
> Who looks and looks but can't see the sky.

Poem 31, which ends much the same way, is very interesting in that Han-shan starts each line with a reduplicated, descriptive binome (e.g., *yao-yao, lo-lo, chiu-chiu*; the complete romanization for the poem is given in the Translations). I try to indicate this in my translation by setting those first phrases off from the rest. The poem reads in this way:

> Dark and obscure—the way to Han-shan;
> Far apart—the shores of the cold mountain stream.
>
> Chirp, chirp—constantly there are the birds;
> Silent and still—in addition there are no men.

Whisper, whisper—the wind blows in my face;
Whirling and swirling—the snow piles up all around.

Day after day—I don't see the sun,
And year after year—I've known no spring.

Throughout his poems, as he does here, Han-shan claims that
the "way" to Han-shan is lost or obscure, making the Zen point
that there is no set "way" to realize enlightenment; one cannot be
sure, whether one reads the scriptures or practices meditation or
studies with a master, that that will necessarily lead him to the enlightened state of mind. That the shores of the cold mountain
stream are "far apart," in this poem, emphasizes the Buddhist understanding of life, that the shores of "ordinary existence" (saṁsāra)
and "enlightened existence" (nirvāṇa) are separated by a large river
or sea. Here Han-shan claims not only that day after day he does
not see the sun but that year after year he has known no spring. I
would also understand "spring" here in a symbolic way—he has
yet to feel that new surge of life, the fullness of life, that enlightenment brings.

The contrast between "valleys" and "peaks" in the spiritual
quest comes out clearly in poem 28, where once again the point is
made that there is no set path or road that will lead to the top of
Han-shan—or rather here, that such paths "never end"—i.e., do
not lead to the goal Buddhists seek. At the end of the poem, Han-
shan has somehow reached the top by simply "transcending the
cares of the world" and sits there with his only companions the
white clouds.

Climb up! Ascend! The way to Han-shan;
But on Han-shan the roads never end.

The valleys are long, with boulders in heaps and piles;
The streams are wide, with grasses both wet and damp.

The moss is slippery—it has nothing to do with the rain;
The pines sigh and moan, but they don't rely on the wind.

Who can transcend the cares of the world
And sit with me in the white clouds?

Much is made of the fact that Han-shan sometimes ignores—
perhaps intentionally breaks (see poem 286 below)—the rules of

"regulated verse" *(lü-shih)* that were so important during the T'ang. It is worth noting, therefore, that this poem *is* in regulated verse form: note that the two inner couplets—lines 3 and 4 and then 5 and 6—are strictly parallel, and the tonal sequence of the characters in every line is as it should be (see the comment on poem 28 in the Translations).

The key doctrine in Zen is that we already possess the enlightened mind that we seek: all beings possess Buddha-nature, and thus the only way to become enlightened is to realize one's true nature inside. That the state of one's mind is the key thing, not the path that one takes, is made clear in poem 9:

People ask the way to Han-shan,
But there are no roads that get through.

In the summer, the ice not yet melted,
And though the sun comes up, the fog is still thick and dense.

How has someone like me arrived?
My mind and yours are not the same.

If your mind, sir, were like mine,
You too could come right to the center!

Although most of Han-shan's "Zen" poems are easily understood in terms of general Zen themes (that there is no set "way," that the Buddha is on the inside not on the outside, and so forth), there are a few that require a bit more explanation. Let me close with one of those poems, poem 277.

In front of a cliff, all alone I silently sit;
The round moon brightly beams in the sky.

The ten thousand forms, as vague shadows appear in its midst,
But that one wheel—fundamentally, there is nothing on which
     it shines.

Free, empty, unbounded—my soul in itself it is pure;
Embracing the Void, I penetrate the mysterious and profound.

By using a finger we see the moon;
The moon is the hinge of the mind.

Behind this poem—and indeed behind a number of Han-shan's poems—is a metaphysical understanding of things shared by the T'ien-t'ai and early Zen schools (during the seventh and eighth centuries). That is, that in reality there is only one thing, the one mind. That one mind is in its true nature pure, undifferentiated, eternal, unchanging, forever enlightened—it is the true mind, it is Buddha-nature. But although in itself it is devoid of differentiation, it contains within itself all possible differentiation—all things that are seen, heard, sensed as existing outside of the subject, but also all feelings and perceptions experienced within (i.e., the ten thousand forms). But it contains them as a mirror contains all things it reflects—in its true nature, in its true substance (the glass), it is untouched by these things.[36]

Here seeing the moon—in itself, pure, complete, unchanging, undifferentiated, but something that seems to contain things in some shadowy way—this experience occasions "reflections" (if the reader will pardon the pun) on the nature of the true mind—his soul—for Han-shan. (Note how the fourth line moves Han-shan from the outside to the inside.) "Using a finger to see the moon" is a set phrase in Zen Buddhism meaning that *sutras* and the teachings of masters should point the way to the experience of enlightenment: but we must *use* the finger to see the *moon*, without making the finger the final goal. Here Han-shan uses the moon as a "finger" to point to the mind. "The moon is the hinge (or pivot—*shu*) of the mind." It is the door that opens into the experience of the really real.

TRANSLATOR'S NOTE

This translation is based on the *Ch'üan T'ang shih* edition of the poems (using the CTS published in Taiwan by Ming-lun in 1971): with the exception of a few variant characters, this is essentially the same as the *Han-shan-tzu shih-chi* in the collection *Ssu-pu ts'ung-k'an (ch'u-pien)*, which prints a Sung dynasty text from the collection of a Mr. Chou of Chien-te. I have also used the *Tse-shih-chü ts'ung-shu ch'u-chi* (Chang Chün-heng, comp. 1926) edition of the *Han-shan shih-chi*, which prints a copy of another Sung text stored at the Keifukuin (in Japan). The *Tse-shih-chü ts'ung-shu* text appears to be identical with the *Kunaichō* (Imperial Library) text in Japan. The *Tse-shih-chü/Kunaichō* text is the earliest extant version of the Han-shan poems,[37] and it serves as the base text for two recent annotated editions of the poems—Iriya Yoshitaka's *Kanzan* (Vol. 5 in *Chūgoku shi-*

jin senshū [Tokyo: Iwanami Shoten, 1958]), and Iritani Sensuke and Matsumura Takashi's *Kanzanshi* (Vol. 13 in the series *Zen no goroku* [Tokyo: Chikuma Shoten, 1970]).[38]

For help with annotation, I have mainly relied on the excellent notes in Iritani and Matsumura's *Kanzanshi*. In addition, I have found useful comments and notes in the following works: (1) Hakuin's *Kanzanshi sendai kibun* (Vol. 4 in *Hakuin oshō zenshū*),[39] (2) Ch'en Hui-chien's *Han-shan-tzu yen-chiu* (Taipei: Tung-ta t'u-shu, 1984); and (3) Tseng P'u-hsin's *Han-shan shih-chieh* (Hua-lien: Tung-ching Temple, 1971).

For documentation, I have used concordanced editions wherever possible. Page numbers for the following texts refer to the Harvard-Yenching Index Series editions: *Chou-i (I ching); Chuang-tzu; Ch'un-ch'iu ching-chuan (Tso chuan); Hsiao ching; Lun-yü;* and *Mao-shih (Shih ching)*. For the *Ch'u-tz'u*, page numbers refer to the Taiwan verson of Takeji Sadao's *Soji Sakuin*, which is published with the SPPY text *(Ch'u-tz'u so-yin: Ch'u-tz'u pu-chu* [Taipei: Chung-wen, 1979]). Page numbers for the *Wen-hsüan* refer to the text that matches the *Wen-hsüan so-yin* (Taipei: Cheng-chung, 1985).

All references to the dynastic histories *(Shih-chi, Han shu, Hou Han shu, San-kuo chih, Chin shu,* and *Hsin T'ang shu)* are to the Chung-hua shu-chü punctuated editions done in Peking. For the *Yüeh-fu shih-chi*, I have used the recent Chung-hua shu-chü edition (Peking, 1979). For Six Dynasties poets and poems, I have used the standard Ting Fu-pao edition, *Ch'üan Han san-kuo Chin nan-pei-ch'ao shih* (Taipei: Shih-chieh, 1969). All references to Buddhist scriptures are to volumes and pages in the *Taishō shinshū daizōkyō* (Tokyo: 1924–29) herein abbreviated as T.

Finally, note that the symbols following poem numbers (i.e. *, †, **, and §) indicate the following:

*Classed by Pulleyblank as Han-shan II.
†Missing from the *Tse-shih-chü ts'ung-shu* and *Kunaichō* Library editions.
**Written in seven-character lines.
§Written in three-character lines.

NOTES

1. Unless Wu Chi-yu is right with his identification: see below in the text.

2. Tu Kuang-t'ing's (850–933) *Hsien-chuan shih-i,* cited in *T'ai-p'ing kuang-chi,* chapter 55, says that Han-shan "retired to live on Kingfisher-green Screen Mountain in the T'ien-t'ai range. This mountain is deep and far away: even in summer there is snow. It is also named Cold Cliffs. As a result, he called himself Master Cold Mountain" (see Vol. 1, p. 338 in *T'ai-p'ing kuang-chi* [Taipei: Wen-shih-che, 1981]). The *Ching-te ch'uan-teng lu* (compiled in 1004), chapter 27, has "Seventy li west of Shih-feng county there are two cliffs, one called Cold and the other called Bright. Since he lived on Cold Cliff, it is from this that he took his name." Finally, Chih-nan, in his postscript of 1189, says that "Cold lived and dwelt on a cold cliff, 70 li to the west of T'ang-hsing county, and from this he took his name."

3. See the end of his biography of Shih-te, Vol. 3, p. 521, in the edition *Kao-seng chuan san-chi* (Taipei: Yin-ching ch'u, 1961). Tu Kuang-t'ing, however, does not seem to know of this preface and records that a preface had been written by the Taoist Hsü Ling-fu (c. 760–c. 841), who had made the first collection of the poems. Tu says, "Hsü Ling-fu collected them [Han-shan's poems] and wrote a preface, the whole being divided into 3 *chüan.* It circulated about among men. But after ten or so years, it was suddenly no longer seen."

4. The text of the Lü-ch'iu Yin Preface stands at the head of the *Ssu-pu ts'ung-k'an* edition of the poems (pp. la–2a in SPTK, *ch'u-pien*). For a translation, see, for example, Wu Chi-yu, "A Study of Han-shan," *T'oung Pao,* XLV (1957), pp. 411–414.

5. For the Chih-nan postscript, see pp. 58–64 in *Han-shan shih-chi* (Taipei: Han-sheng, 1976). This is also found at the end of the text in the *Tse-shih-chü ts'ung-shu* edition.

6. See Ch'en Hui-chien, *Han-shan-tzu yen-chiu* (Taipei: Tung-ta t'u-shu, 1984), pp. 10–11.

7. See Wu Chi-yu, "A Study of Han-shan," pp. 392–403. The biography of Chih-yen is the source for this information: that biography is found in Tao-hsüan's *Hsü Kao-seng chuan,* Ch. 25, pp. 718–719 in *Kao-seng chuan erh-chi* (Taipei: Yin-ching ch'u, 1970).

8. Wu Chi-yu ("A Study of Han-shan," p. 406, note 4) says that Li-chou was only a Prefecture from 621–625, and that it was located in southern Chekiang.

9. See Hu Shih, *Pai-hua wen-hsüeh shih* (Taipei: Wen-kuang, 1983), pp. 173–178. Hu Shih also feels that Han-shan comes after, and imitates, the poet Wang Fan-chih, whom he dates to mid-T'ang.

10. On this point, see, for example, Wu Chi-yu, "A Study of Han-shan," p. 397, and Roberta Stahlberg, "The Poems of the Han-shan

Collection" (unpublished Ph.D. dissertation, Ohio State University, 1977), pp. 12–13.

11. Tsan-ning *(Sung Kao-seng chuan,* chapter 19, p. 519) says of Han-shan, "He retired to the T'ien-t'ai mountains, 70 li west of Shih-feng where there are two cliffs called Cold and Dark." The *Ching-te ch'uan-teng lu* (chapter 27, p. 159), again, has: "Seventy li west of Shih-feng county there are two cliffs, one called Cold and the other called Bright. Since he lived on Cold Cliff, it is from this that he took his name."

12. *T'ai-p'ing kuang-chi,* chapter 55, Vol. 1, p. 338.

13. *Sung Kao-seng chuan,* chapter 19, Vol. 3, p. 521.

14. Hu Shih, *Pai-hua wen-hsüeh shih,* p. 175. See also Huang Po-jen, *Han-shan chi ch'i shih* (Taipei: Hsin wen-feng, 1980), p. 4.

15. For V. T. Yang's review, see the *Journal of Oriental Studies* 6, no. 1–2 (1961–64): 253–274. On p. 261 Yang notes that Han-shan "could not have lived before the middle of the T'ang dynasty when Ch'an Buddhism became popular."

16. For Buddhist terms used in the poems, see Appendix IV, part A. The phrase *chien tzu-hsing* ("see your own nature") does occur in poem 238, but that poem appears to be late. Also, *wu-hsin* ("without mind" or "absence of mind"), which probably means much the same as *wu-nien,* occurs in poem 226.

17. See, for example, John McRae's *The Northern School and the Formation of Early Ch'an Buddhism* (Honolulu: University of Hawaii Press, 1986) and the articles in Whalen Lai and Lewis R. Lancaster, ed., *Early Ch'an in China and Tibet* (Berkeley: Berkeley Buddhist Studies Series, 1983).

18. Ibid., p. 264. But note that Patrick Carré *(Le Mangeur de brumes: l'oeuvre de Han-shan* [Paris: Phébus, 1985], p. 37 and then p. 75) feels that Han-shan's preoccupation with "regulated verse" rules of prosody reflect the concerns of late Sui.

19. See Iritani Sensuke and Matsumura Takashi, *Kanzanshi* (Tokyo: Chikuma Shoten, 1958), pp. 489–490.

20. See Iriya Yoshitaka, *Kanzan* (Tokyo: Iwanami Shoten, 1958), pp. 15–17.

21. Ibid, p. 11.

22. In Ronald C. Miao, ed., *Studies in Chinese Poetry and Politics,* Vol. 1 (San Francisco: CMC, Inc., 1978), pp. 163–185.

23. Ibid, p. 164.

24. Ibid, p. 174.

25. Ibid, p. 173. It is worth noting that Pulleyblank has also looked at the rhymed passage that occurs at the end of the Lü-ch'iu Yin Preface and concludes that it is "clearly of late T'ang vintage" (p. 174).

26. For the collected "legends" about Han-shan and his two companions Shih-te and Feng-kan, the reader should consult the following: (1) the biographies of the three (Shih-te and Han-shan are subsumed under Feng-kan) in Tsan-ning's *Sung Kao-seng chuan* 19 (pp. 517–521 in *Kao-seng chuan san-chi*); (2) the *Ching-te ch'uan-teng lu*, chapter 27 (Feng-kan, p. 158; Han-shan-tzu, p. 159; Shih-te, pp. 159–160); (3) P'u-chi's (Sung) *Wu-teng hui-yüan* (using the Taipei, Hsin wen-feng, 1983 edition) 2:50a for Feng-kan, 2:50ab for Han-shan, and 2:50b for Shih-te; and (4) Chü Ju-chi's (Ch'ing) *Chih-yüeh lu* (using the Taipei: Hsin wen-feng, 1983 edition), 2:29b–30b for Feng-kan, 2:30b–31b for Han-shan, and 2:31b–32a for Shih-te. In the *Wu-teng hui-yüan* and the *Chih-yüeh lu*, the biographies of the three are listed in the category "Incarnate Sages and Worthies" *(ying-hua sheng-hsien)*.

27. The translation here is by Wu Chi-yu, "A Study of Han-shan," p. 420. All of the stories concerning Han-shan that survive in various sources are translated into English in one form or another by Wu Chi-yu (pp. 411–422). In addition to the sweeping story cited here and the story of Lü-ch'iu Yin's visit, there are tales in which: (1) In 871 Han-shan, dressed like a beggar, visits Li Ho and is sent away, but when he returns a week later dressed as a rich man, he is hospitably received; (2) Ling-yu (771–853) meets Han-shan, who correctly predicts that Ling-yu will become a Buddhist and take orders at Kuo-ch'ing; (3) Han-shan asks Feng-kan how an old mirror will shine if it isn't polished and receives an enigmatic reply; (4) Feng-kan asks Han-shan (and sometimes Shih-te as well) to go to Wu-t'ai shan with him to see Mañjuśrī, but he refuses to go; (5) Han-shan takes a slice of eggplant that a monk is roasting and hits the monk on the back with it, asking him, "What is this?"; and (6) Han-shan and Shih-te are visited by the Zen master Chao-chou (778–897), and they exchange clever banter in which the Five Hundred Arhats are identified as five hundred water buffaloes.

28. There are a number of allusions to T'ao Ch'ien's poems in Han-shan's poems, and a few that reflect T'ao Ch'ien's style and themes. All this is documented below.

29. Pulleyblank, "Linguistic Evidence," p. 165.

30. See poems 32, 47, 60, and 124. The "Streets of Lo-yang" was a *yüeh-fu* theme: see the notes to poem 47.

31. See poems 39 and 134.

32. See Iritani and Matsumura, *Kanzanshi*, p. 117, for their comment on poem 79.

33. For the number and sequence of the poems in other extant editions, see the "Translator's Note" below.

34. For allusions in the poem, see the discussion of the poem in the translations. "Pressed sugar cane" is one of a number of images that Hanshan borrows from Buddhist texts, specifically from the *Nirvāṇa-sūtra*.

35. Burton Watson, *Cold Mountain: 100 Poems by the T'ang Poet Hanshan* (New York: Columbia University Press, 1970), p. 14.

36. For more on the basics of T'ien-t'ai philosophy, see, for example, Fung Yu-lan, *A History of Chinese Philosophy*, Vol. II, translated by Derk Bodde (Princeton: Princeton University Press, 1953), pp. 360–384. The one mind (or true nature) that contains all possible things remains key in *The Platform Sutra of the Sixth Patriarch* (attributed to Hui-neng, d. 713). See especially sections 23–25 of that text, pp. 147–147 in Philip B. Yampolsky, translator, *The Platform Sutra of the Sixth Patriarch* (New York: Columbia University Press, 1967).

37. The earliest printed edition of the poems was the Chih-nan text published in 1189 by Kuo-ch'ing Temple. Chih-nan's postscript to this text survives; the text itself does not. It would appear that before this, two other editions had been in circulation. Tu Kuang-t'ing tells us that the Taoist Hsü Ling-fu collected the poems and wrote a preface but that this text disappeared after ten or so years (see note 3 to the "Introduction"). Also, Tsan-ning, in his biography of Pen-chi of Ts'ao-shan *(Sung kao-seng chuan*, chapter 13, p. 327), one of the founders of the Ts'ao-Tung school of Zen, says that Pen-chi (840–901) "wrote a commentary called 'In Response to the Poems of Master Han-shan'" *(Tui Han-shan-tzu shih)*. This too is no longer extant. Tsan-ning again mentions Pen-chi's commentary in his biography of Han-shan (chapter 19, p. 519), where he says that "the poems he [Han-shan] wrote down on the house walls of country folk came to over 200 *shou.*" The number is intriguing. But the Chinese here is virtually the same as we find at the end of the "Lü-ch'iu Yin Preface," where it says over *300 shou:* I suspect that the "two *(erh)* in 200 is just a mistake for "three" *(san).*

38. The *Tse-shih-chü/Kunaichō* text differs in a number of ways from the CTS/SPTK text of the poems. There are quite a few variant characters, and poems 91, 164, 198, 211, 237, and 263 are omitted. Moreover, the inner couplets in 192 are omitted; what is poem 196 in CTS is two poems (195 and 186) in TSC; poems 233 and 234 in CTS are combined in TSC (in that count, poem 231); and the last ten lines of poem 159 are omitted. Finally, the sequence of the 305 poems in the *Tse-shih-chü/Kunaichō* edition is different than that of CTS/SPTK. Using the numbers of the following translation—

i.e., the sequence of the poems in the *Ch'üan T'ang shih)*—the order of the poems in the *Tse-shih-chü/Kunaichō* text is as follows: 2, 1, 3, 20, 51, 67, 14, 21, 295, 277, 4–13, 15–19, 163, 22–25, 27–50, 52–66, 68–76, 78–90, 92–115, 117–120, 116, 122–129, 272, 299–300, 167, 130–158, 160–162, 165–166, 168–185, 195, 196 (lines 5–8), 197, 186–188, 194, 192 (lines 1–2, 7–8), 193, 199, 196 (lines 1–4), 189–191, 200, 206–208, 201–205, 209–210, 212–236, 238–243, 159 (omits last ten lines), 26, 244–262, 264–271, 273–276, 278–294, 296–298, 77, 121, 301–311.

39. In Hakuin's text, the five-, seven-, and three-word poems are grouped together, and a number of poems are shifted around. The order of the poems in that edition is as follows: (five-word poems) 1–37, 39–83, 85–88, 90–122, 124–132, 165–168, 133–159a, 297, 160–164, 169–180, 182–191, 206–210, 212–269, 271–296, 159b, 298–303, 270; (seven-word poems) 38, 84, 89, 123, 181, 192–193, 195–205, 194, 211; (and three-word poems) 304–311. Poem 275 is here two poems, and the last eight lines of poem 159 are also treated as a separate poem that occurs between poems 296 and 298.

TRANSLATIONS

Preface to the Ch'üan T'ang Shih Edition of Han-shan's Poems

As for Master Han-shan, we don't know where he came from. He lived on Cold Cliffs in the T'ien-t'ai mountains in the county of T'ang-hsing. From time to time he would go back and forth between his retreat and Kuo-ch'ing Temple, wearing birchbark as his hat, dressed in a cotton-fur robe and worn-out shoes. Sometimes he would chant and recite in the long corridors; sometimes he'd whistle and sing through country homes. No one really understood him.

When Lü-ch'iu Yin was appointed to serve in Tan-ch'iu, as he was about to leave he ran into Master Feng-kan, who said he had come from T'ien-t'ai. Lü-ch'iu asked him what worthies fit to be taken as one's teacher this place had, and the Master replied, "There's Han-shan [who's an incarnation of] Mañjuśrī and Shih-te [who's an incarnation of] Samantabhadra. They tend the fires in the granary kitchen at Kuo-ch'ing Temple."

Three days after Lü-ch'iu arrived at his official post he went in person to the temple, where he saw the two men, and accordingly politely bowed down. The two men had a good laugh, saying, "Feng-kan's a blabbermouth, a blabbermouth! If you don't know Amitābha, what good does it do bowing to us?!" Then they left the temple and went back to Cold Cliffs, where Master Han-shan entered a cave and was gone, the cave closing up on its own.

He used to write down poems on bamboo trees and stone walls. Altogether, the poems he wrote on house walls in country homes come to over three hundred *shou*. I have edited them together in one volume.

No. 1

Whoever reads my poems
Must protect the purity in his mind.

Stinginess and greed must change into honesty day after day;
Flattery and deceit must *right now* become the upright!

Expel and banish, wipe out your bad karma;
Return to rely on,[1] accept your true nature.

Today! You must attain the Buddha-body;[2]
Quickly! Quickly! Treat this just like it's imperial law![3]

1. I here break up *kuei* and *i*, but as a compound *kuei-i* means to take Buddhist vows, to take up the faith.

2. *Fo-shen* (*buddha-kāya*, or *buddhatva*) is a term often used to mean the same thing as *fo-hsing*, Buddha-nature. See the article by Andrew Rawlinson, "The Ambiguity of the Buddha-nature Concept in India and China," in Lancaster and Lai, ed., *Early Ch'an in China and Tibet* (Berkeley, CA: Buddhist Studies Series, 1983), pp. 259–279.

3. *Chi-chi ju lü-ling* is a stock phrase of Taoist incantation said at the end of a chant addressed to spirits and/or demons. The phrase was first used at the end of official documents in the Han. A *lü-ling* was an order or command (from the emperor) that was written down as a law. A number of Taoist incantations that end in this way are translated into English by Michael Saso in his *The Teachings of Taoist Master Chuang* (New Haven: Yale University Press, 1978), pp. 141 ff. On the assumption of the imperial role and some of its trappings by Taoist clergy, see Anna Seidel's excellent article, "Imperial Treasures and Taoist Sacraments: Taoist Roots in the Apocrypha," in Michel Strickmann, ed., *Tantric and Taoist Studies in Honour of R. A. Stein, Mélanges Chinois et Bouddhiques*, Vol. XXI (1983), pp. 291–371.

No. 2

'Midst layers of cliffs—the place I divined to live;[1]
Up on bird's trails,[2] cut off from the tracks of men.

What is there by the side of my court?
White clouds wrapped 'round dark rocks.[3]

I've lived here a number of years;
Repeatedly seeing the change from winter to spring.

I send this message to the families of wealth;[4]
An empty name will do you no good.[5]

1. "Pu-chü" (Divining Where to Live) is the title of one of the pieces
in the *Ch'u-tz'u* (*Ch'u-tz'u pu-chu*, 6: 1a–3b, pp. 73–74). For a translation, see
David Hawkes, translator, *The Songs of the South* (London: Penguin Books,
1985), pp. 203–206. Han-shan clearly identifies with the author of this little
piece (attributed to Ch'ü Yüan) in choosing to live away from a corrupt and
compromising society.
2. *Niao-tao* are paths that are high and dangerous, so narrow that
only birds could get through.
3. Iritani and Matsumura (*Kanzanshi*, p. 10) here note two lines in a
poem by T'ao Hung-ching (456–536) that he supposedly addressed to Kao-ti
of Southern Ch'i (r. 479–482). In response to the emperor's question of
what there was in the mountains, T'ao replied: "In the mountains what is
there? On top of the peaks the white clouds are many" (see Ting Fu-pao,
ed., *Ch'üan Han san-kuo Chin nan-pei-ch'ao shih*, Vol. 3, p. 1234.) The line
"White clouds wrapped 'round dark rocks" is a line first used by Hsieh
Ling-yün (385–433) in his poem "Passing by my Estate in Shih-ning" (*Wen-
hsüan* 26: 25a, p. 366). Hsieh wrote this in 422 when he visited his estate in
Shih-ning (50 li west of the modern Shang-yü in Chekiang—not far at all
from the T'ien-t'ai range) on his way to Yung-chia. He later retired to Shih-

ning. For a translation of Hsieh's poem, see J. D. Frodsham, *The Murmuring Stream: The Life and Works of the Chinese Nature Poet Hsieh Ling-yün (385–433), Duke of K'ang-Lo* (Kuala Lumpur: University of Malaya Press, 1967), Vol. 1, p. 118. The circumstances surrounding the poem's composition are discussed in Chapter 2 (pp. 26–41).

4. Literally "families with bells and tripods of bronze" *(chung-ting chia)*.

5. Iritani and Matsumura *(Kanzanshi,* p. 10) note the similar last line in poem 7 of the "Nineteen Old Poems" of the Han ("Ku-shih, shih-chiu shou" *Wen-hsüan* 29: 4ab, p. 398). Watson translates: "What good are empty names?" (Burton Watson, *Chinese Lyricism: Shih Poetry from the Second to the Twelfth Century* [New York: Columbia University Press, 1971], p. 26). That Han-shan has this poem in mind is possible but uncertain—the poem is addressed to an old friend who has risen high in society and forgotten his former friend. In any event, as the reader will see, the "Nineteen Old Poems" is a set of poems from which Han-shan draws repeatedly for his themes.

No. 3

Delightful! The road to Han-shan;
Yet one finds no trace of horses or carts.[1]

One valley tied to another—hard to keep track of the twists and
    the turns;
Peak piled upon peak—nobody knows how many layers there are.

The dew sheds its tears on thousands of kinds of plants,
While the wind sighs and moans through pines that are all
    the same.

At times like these, if you lose track of the path,
Your form must ask your shadow which way to go.[2]

---

1. One is reminded here of T'ao Ch'ien's (365–427) "Drinking Wine"
poems. No. 5 in that series of 20 opens with the lines, "I built my hut
beside a traveled road, yet hear no noise of passing carts and horses"
(James Robert Hightower, translator, *The Poetry of T'ao Ch'ien* [Oxford: Clarendon Press, 1970], p. 130). For the Chinese text, see Yang Yung, *T'ao Yüanming chi chiao-chien* (Hong Kong: Wu-hsing chi, 1971), p. 144.

2. Again, what could be an oblique allusion to the kindred poems of
T'ao Ch'ien, here to his "Substance, Shadow, and Spirit" *(Hsing, ying, shen)*, though the words simply indicate in a strong way that the poet is
alone. (For a translation of "Substance, Shadow, and Spirit," see Hightower, *The Poetry of T'ao Ch'ien*, pp. 42–47.)

No. 4

For my home I delight in the hidden and concealed;
The place where I live is cut off from the noise and the dust.

The grasses I trample become my three paths;[1]
The clouds I behold, make up my neighbors on four sides
all around.

In helping me sing—for music, there are the birds;
I'd ask about the Dharma,[2] but to talk with there's no one at all.

Today I'm like the stinking cedar;
Several years are just like one spring.[3]

---

1. On the "three paths" (*san-ching*) as code for the retirement home of a recluse, see Iritani and Matsumura, *Kanzanshi*, p. 24. T'ao Ch'ien mentions his "three paths" in his rhapsody "The Return" (*Kuei-ch'ü lai; Wen-hsüan* 45: 19a–20b, p. 628), and Li Shan cites the *San-fu chüeh-lu*, which explains that the retired statesman of the Former Han, Chiang Hsü, opened up three paths on his farm.
2. *Fa*, the teaching of the Buddha.
3. The *p'o-so-lo* (our text has *so-p'o*) tree is the same as the *ch'un* or the *shu*, for which Bernard Read (*Chinese Medicinal Plants*, p. 100 [Taipei: Southern Materials Center, 1977], item 341) has *Ailanthus glandulosa*—"stinking cedar." Thus the allusion here is to *Chuang-tzu*, Chapter 1 (*Chuang-tzu yin-te*, p. 1, line 12), which Watson translates: "Long, long ago there was a great rose of Sharon [*ch'un*] that counted eight thousand years as one spring and eight thousand years as one autumn" (Burton Watson, *The Complete Works of Chuang Tzu* [New York: Columbia University Press, 1968], p. 30).

No. 5

Lute and books must be right by your side,
Of what use are wealth and rank?

In turning down the king's carriage, I followed the words
    of my virtuous wife;[1]
For my officer "Lord of the Cart," I have my filial son.[2]

The wind blows, drying my fields of wheat;
The water overflows, keeping full my fish pond.

I always remember those little wrens,
Who rest content with one twig.[3]

1. Alluding to the story of the wife of Yü-ling Tzu-chung of Ch'u, recorded in the *Lieh-nü chuan* (2: 10ab). When Tzu-chung was offered the post of prime minister by the king of Ch'u, he first consulted with his wife. He urged her to consider the great wealth and honor he would enjoy if he accepted the offer. But she reminded him that there was also great joy in his books and his lute (note the relevance to the present poem's first line) and that his new post would mean many worries and dangers. He turned the job down. For a translation of the story, see Albert Richard O'Hara, *The Position of Woman in Early China: According to the Lieh Nü Chuan "The Biographies of Eminent Chinese Women"* (Washington, DC: The Catholic University of America Press, 1945), pp. 73–74.
2. For *chin-ch'e*, "Lord of the Cart," Hucker (*A Dictionary of Official Titles in Imperial China* [Stanford: Stanford University Press, 1985], p. 165 (item 1118) has "Master of the Royal Chariots." The title goes back to the Chou, when those holding this office were "responsible for the maintenance, allocation, and decoration of all chariots used by the royal entourage."

3. Alluding to *Chuang-tzu*, Chapter 1 (p. 2, line 25), Watson *(The Complete Works*, p. 32) translates: "When the tailorbird builds her nest in the deep wood, she uses no more than one branch. When the mole drinks at the river, he takes no more than a bellyfull." These are the words of the recluse Hsü Yu, stressing his contentment with what he has, as he declines the offer of Yao to give him control of the world.

No. 6

Brothers young and old, "together" in five commanderies;
Fathers and sons, fundamentally one, though scattered now
in three regions.[1]

If you want to verify the union of the flying wild ducks,[2]
You must attest to the rambling of the White Hare.[3]

The sacred melon was received in a dream;[4]
The divine oranges he stored in his seat.[5]

My native country—how distant and far!
With the fish, I entrust these thoughts to the flow
of the stream.[6]

1. Han-shan seems to write this in response to two lines from Yü Hsin's (513–581) "Rhapsody on Broken Hearts" *(Shang-hsin fu)*, the latter written to describe the chaotic times at the end of the Liang. The two lines are "As for brothers young and old, into five commanderies they are separated and spread out; as for fathers and sons, scattered apart into three regions" (see *I-wen lei-chü* 34, p. 606). Note that for Han-shan the brothers are "together" *(t'ung)* even though they live apart, and fathers and sons are "fundamentally one" *(pen)*, even though living in separate domains.

2. The line might allude to the story in *Hou Han shu* 82A (Vol. 10, p. 2712) of Wang Ch'iao (some at the time said he was the immortal of antiquity Wang-tzu Ch'iao), who somehow arrived at court to meet with the Emperor without riding on a carriage. When a minister was sent to spy on him, the minister saw a pair of wild ducks flying in from the southeast. But when he went to capture the pair with a net, all he caught in it was a single magpie. (Read—*Chinese Materia Medica: Avian Drugs* [Taipei: Southern Materials Center, 1977], item 257, p. 18—says the *fu* is specifically the mallard.)

3. Reading the variant of *cheng* ("attest" or "verify") for *ching* ("manifest" or "display"), though obviously either character will work. A Master White Hare is mentioned in Ko Hung's *Pao-p'u-tzu* ("Nei-p'ien," chapter 13 ["Chi-yen"], 13: 3a) as one of the disciples of the long-lived P'eng-tsu back in the Yin dynasty. (For a translation of the relevant passage, see James R. Ware, *Alchemy, Medicine and Religion in the China of A.D. 320: The Nei P'ien of Ko Hung* [New York: Dover Publications, Inc., 1966], p. 218.) Thus these two lines mean—I think—that the only way one can "magically" fly off to distant places (in the present context, in order to be reunited with family or friends) is to be adept at the practices of Taoist immortals. Presumably the author's implied meaning is that he is not adept at such things. Ch'en Hui-chien *(Han-shan-tzu,* pp. 172–173) points out that "white hare" is another name for the moon and thinks that white hare here stands for gathering together or "reunion" (under the moon). The two lines make good sense without the literary allusions; one might also translate: "If you wish to experience the union of the flying wild ducks" (meaning simply to be united with family and friends), "then you must attest to the rambling of the White Hare" (i.e., you must be together with them under the moon).

4. In a story of filial devotion (see *Wei shu* 33 [Vol. 3, pp. 774–775]) we learn that when Sung Ch'iung's mother took ill, she had a craving for melons, but it was the end of the fall. But Ch'iung "saw some in a dream, and seeking them he accordingly received." The narrator adds that "people of that time all saw this as strange." Ch'en Hui-chien *(Han-shan-tzu,* p. 173), on the other hand, notes a number of literary associations of "sacred melons" *(ling-kua)* with Taoist immortals and immortality. Thus, the poet's point could simply be that—such things being received only in dreams—he has no such melons by means of which he can live long; he is simply a mortal.

5. Apparently alluding to an anecdote concerning Lu Chi (see *San-kuo chih* 57 [Vol. 5, p. 1328]). When he was six years old, he went to visit Yüan Shu, who at their meeting offered Lu Chi some oranges. Lu Chi proceeded to stick three inside his robe, which fell to the ground when he took his leave. Yüan Shu thought this a bit unbecoming of a guest, but Lu Chi explained that he intended to give these to his mother. Why Han-shan here calls these "divine" *(shen)* oranges is not entirely clear, unless this is simply used to balance the "sacred" *(ling)* melons of the previous line. Both of these lines seem to be ways of saying that the present author also thinks longingly of his mother now in this way.

6. I.e., his hope is that somehow his feelings for family and kin will get back to them, carried by the fish in the stream.

No. 7

I first was a student of books and swords,
And secondly met with a wise sagely lord.

In the East I protected, but my service received no reward;
In the West I attacked, but my strength got me no honor.

I studied literature and I studied war;
I studied war and I studied literature.

Today I'm already old;
What's left of my life isn't worthy of note.

Comment: Iritani and Matsumura *(Kanzanshi,* pp. 29–30)—following
the lead of Hakuin *(Kanzanshi sendai kibun,* 1: 12–13)—connect this piece
with a story about Han Wu-ti (r. 140–87 B. C.). In the *Han Wu ku-shih* (see
Lu Hsün ch'üan-chi [Shanghai: Jen-min wen-hsüeh, 1973], Vol. 8, p. 458) we
read that Wu-ti once ran into a court attendant *(lang),* an old man, and
discovering that the man had become an attendant under Emperor Wen (r.
179–157 B. C.), Emperor Wu asked why he had become old without meeting with further success. The attendant replied, "Emperor Wen delighted
in literature, and I delighted in maritial strength; Emperor Ching [r. 156–
141] liked the old, and I was still young; now you, sir, delight in the young,
and I'm already old. Thus, for three generations I have not met [with further reward]." Emperor Wu was so moved by his words that he promoted
him to Commander in Chief of Kuei-chi.
   Iritani and Matsumura also note that there is a variant of "three" for
"two" at the start of line 2, so the line could equally read: "And three times
met with a wise sagely lord." Still, the connection—tantalizing though it
might be—is not exact. The old attendant never claims to have studied both
literature and war *(wen* and *wu).* And the author of our poem claims to have
"protected" *(shou)* in the East—which sounds like he actually served for a
while in the civil domain—and he "attacked" *(cheng)* on the West. (It is not

clear whether East and West here mean geographical parts of the realm or simply refer to the civil and military branches of service, since civil officials lined up on the east side of the court at the capital and military officials on the west.) Finally, the author of our poem shows no sign of receiving reward in the end.

Hakuin also notes as relevant the following comments from the biography of Hsiang Yü in *Shih-chi* 7 (Vol. 1, pp. 295–296): "When Hsiang Yü was a boy, he studied the art of writing. Failing to master this, he abandoned it and took up swordsmanship. When he failed at this also, his uncle, Hsiang Liang, grew angry with him, but Hsiang Yü declared, 'Writing is good only for keeping records of people's names. Swordsmanship is useful only for attacking a single enemy and is likewise not worth studying. What I want to learn is the art of attacking ten thousand enemies!' With this, Hsiang Liang began to teach his nephew the art of warfare, which pleased Yü greatly. On the whole, Yü understood the essentials for the art, but here again he was unwilling to pursue the study in detail" (translated by Burton Watson, in *Records of the Historian: Chapters from the Shih Chi of Ssu-ma Ch'ien* [New York: Columbia University Press, 1958], p. 68).

No. 8

When Chuang-tzu spoke of his funeral affairs,
[He said,] "Heaven and Earth will be my coffins."[1]

My return[2]—this has its set time,
And all you'll need is one bamboo screen.

When I'm dead I'll feed the bluebottle flies;[3]
For mourning—no need to trouble white cranes.[4]

Starving to death on Mt. Shou-yang;
If your life has been incorrupt, then death is also a joy.[5]

1. See *Chuang-tzu*, Chapter 32 (p. 90, line 48). Watson (*The Complete Works*, p. 361) translates: "When Chuang Tzu was about to die, his disciples expressed a desire to give him a sumptuous burial. Chuang Tzu said, 'I will have heaven and earth for my coffin and coffin shell, the sun and moon for my pair of jade discs. . . . The furnishings for my funeral are already prepared—what is there to add?'"
2. i.e., his death.
3. To his disciples' concern that if they left his body alone, it would be eaten by crows and kites, Chuang-tzu responded: "Above ground I'll be eaten by crows and kites, below ground I'll be eaten by mole crickets and ants. Wouldn't it be rather bigoted to deprive one group in order to supply the other?" (Watson, *The Complete Works*, p. 361). Han-shan will feed the "bluebottle flies," reflecting Chuang-tzu's words, on the one hand, but also the words of Yü Fan, on the other, who despaired that he would have nothing but bluebottle flies for mourners (note the connection with the following line). In the *Yü Fan pieh-chuan*, cited by P'ei Sung-chih in his notes to Yü Fan's biography in *San-kuo chih* 57 (Vol. 5, p. 1323), Yü Fan, having been

exiled to the South by Sun Ch'üan, laments: "I must forever be sunk in this corner of the sea. Alive I'll have no one to talk to; and when I die, for mourners I'll have bluebottle flies." Note the relevance of these lines to poem 37 as well.

4. That is to say, he has no hopes of being carried off by the symbols of Taoist immortality.

5. Alluding to Po I and Shu Ch'i, men of virtue living in bad times— back at the beginning of the Chou dynasty (traditional dates 1122–255 B. C.)—who chose to starve to death on Mt. Shou-yang rather than serve King Wu, whom they regarded as a usurper. For an English translation of their biography (*Shih-chi* 61), see Burton Watson, *Records of the Historian: Chapters from the Shih Chi of Ssu-ma Ch'ien* (New York: Columbia University Press, 1969), pp. 11–15.

No. 9

People ask the way to Han-shan,
But there are no roads that get through.

In the summer, the ice not yet melted,
And though the sun comes up, the fog is still thick and dense.

How has someone like *me* arrived?
My mind and yours are not the same.

If your mind, sir, were like mine,[1]
You too could come right to the center.[2]

1. Han-shan cleverly uses the same *ssu-wo* ("like mine") here that he used first in line 5 ("someone like me"—*ssu-wo).
2. The center of the mountains, but more importantly the "center" of the self, to the experience of Buddha-nature inside.

No. 10

When Heaven produces one-hundred-foot trees,
They can be cut into long and strong boards.

How sad that this "material for pillars and beams"[1]
Is abandoned in some hidden vale.[2]

Its years may be numerous, but its heart is still strong;
So many its days—its bark gradually getting bare.

But if one who knows worth comes and takes it,
It can still be used for some stable "post."[3]

1. *Tung-liang chih ts'ai* (though the phrase here is *tung-liang ts'un*) is a stock phrase for a man of worth, the kind of stuff from which great statesmen are made.
2. "Abandoned" is *p'ao* and could possibly mean "sent into exile."
3. Note the double meaning of post—i.e., it is at one and the same time the wooden pole to be used in a barn and, symbolically, a government post that an old, but good, man might hold.

No. 11

I press my horse on to pass by the deserted city;[1]
Deserted cities move the feelings of the traveller.

High and low, the old battlements;
Large and small, ancient tombs.

Shaking on its own—the shadow of the lonely tumbleweed;[2]
Forever congealed—the songs sung at big trees.[3]

What I lament—these are all common bones;
What's more, you won't find their names in the histories of
the immortals.

1. While Han-shan here begins by "pressing his horse" (ch'ü-ma), the author of poem 13 of the "Nineteen Old Poems" begins by "driving his carriage" (ch'ü-ch'e) in a poem that is likewise concerned with thoughts of graves and death (see Wen-hsüan 29: 6ab, p. 399; translated by Watson in Chinese Lyricism [New York: Columbia University Press, 1971], p. 29).

2. Ku-p'eng is a stock image of the rootless, solitary traveller. The "battlements" of line 2 and the first four characters of the present line (tzu-chen ku-p'eng), are also mentioned by Pao Chao (414–466) in his "Rhapsody on a Deserted City" (Wu-ch'eng fu, Wen-hsüan 11: 10a–13a). For a translation, see Burton Watson, Chinese Rhyme-Prose: Poems in the Fu Form from the Han and Six Dynasties Periods (New York: Columbia University Press, 1971), pp. 92–95.

3. That is, at graves. "Big trees"—literally, kung-mu, trees that it takes both arms to go 'round—are trees that are planted by graves. The locus classicus for this association is the Tso chuan, Duke Hsi, year 32, p. 140.

No. 12

The parrot's home is the Western land,
But with forester's snare[1] it can be caught and brought here.

The beautiful women will play with it night and day;
In and out it will go, amid their rooms' screens.

As a gift, a gold cage to store it away;[2]
Locked in! It will lose its feathered clothes.[3]

Much better to be a goose or a crane,
Soaring and drifting up in the clouds.

---

1. Ch'en Hui-chien (*Han-shan-tzu yen-chiu*, p. 252) suggests that in addition to "forester's snare," *yü-lo* might be read as *yü-lo*, "amusement net."
2. Although there seems to be no direct allusion in Han-shan's poem to Mi Heng's (173–198) famous "Rhapsody on the Parrot" (Ying-wu fu; *Wen-hsüan* 13: 20a–23b, pp. 184–186), that parrots come from western lands and are kept in gold cages are themes also found there.
3. *Yü-i* ("feathered clothes") are things the immortals wear. It comes to mean the robes of a Taoist priest.

Comment: Parrots (*ying-wu*) were favorite playthings of wealthy ladies during the T'ang: note poem 14 below, and see Edward Schafer, *The Golden Peaches of Samarkand: A Study of T'ang Exotics* (Berkeley, CA: University of California Press, 1963), pp. 99–102. The point of the last two lines is that though parrots might be beautiful, many-colored, and talented—can speak and understand words—the goose and the crane, plain-colored and untalented, still live in nature and are free.

No. 13

At the hall of jade hangs a curtain of pearls;
Inside is a beautiful maid.

In appearance surpassing immortals and gods,
Complexion glowing like the peach or the pear.[1]

At the Eastern inn spring mists collect;
At Western lodge fall winds arise.

And when the seasons have changed thirty years,
She too will look like pressed sugar cane.[2]

1. Ts'ao Chih, in poem 4 of the series "Tsa-shih, liu-shou" (six miscellaneous poems; *Wen-hsüan* 29: 16a, p. 404), uses this same line (but he uses it to describe himself) in a poem lamenting not being used while the end of his years draws near. His last line is, "Glory and luster cannot be relied on for long."

2. The metaphor of pressed sugar cane is used in the *Nirvāṇa-sūtra* (*chüan* 12, Chapter 7:2, "Sheng-hsing p'in"; T. 374, Vol. 12, p. 436 middle), where the resultant flavorless dregs are compared to the effects of old age on the flourishing looks of a good man in his prime years. "Squeezed" by old age, he will lack the "three flavors" (*san-wei*)—"leaving home" (*ch'u-chia*), "reading and reciting [the sutras]" (*tu-sung*), and "sitting in meditation" (*tso-ch'an*).

Comment: The poetic structure of this poem is discussed in the Introduction.

No. 14

In the city, a maiden of beautiful brow;
Pearls at her waist—how they tinkle and ring.

She plays with her parrot in front of the flowers,[1]
Strums her p'i-p'a beneath the moon.

Her long song resounds for three months;[2]
Her short dance—ten thousand people will see.[3]

It won't necessarily be always like this;
Hibiscus can't withstand the cold.[3]

1. Parrots were a favorite plaything of rich women in the T'ang. See the comment to poem 12.
2. In the *Lieh-tzu*, Chapter 5 ("T'ang wen"), there is a story of a singing girl named Erh. A. C. Graham (*The Book of Lieh-tzu* [London: John Murray, 1960], p. 109) translates: "Once a woman named Erh of Han ran out of provisions while travelling East to Ch'i. She entered the capital through the Concord Gate and traded her songs for a meal. When she left, the lingering notes curled round the beams of the gate and did not die away for three days; the bystanders thought that she was still there. She passed an inn, where the landlord insulted her. She therefore wailed mournfully in long drawn-out notes, and all the people in the quarter, old and young, looked at each other sadly with the tears dripping down their faces and could not eat for three days. They hurried after her and brought her back, and again she sang them a long ballad in drawn-out notes. The people of the whole quarter, old and young, could not help skipping with joy and dancing to handclaps, forgetting that they had been sad just before. Afterwards they sent her away with rich presents." In the present poem, the sound of the

woman's song resounds for three *months,* not just three *days,* indicating, no doubt, that her song, or its effect, is that much more powerful than that of Erh. That her song is "long" probably means not only that it resounds a long time, but also that it is "long" in beauty and special sound.

3. Iritani and Matsumura (*Kanzanshi,* p. 18) feel that "short dance" also alludes to some story, but they are unable to document the source. It seems likely that Han-shan uses "short" here to serve as a complement to the "long" of the preceding line. No dictionaries gloss "short dance," and there is nothing on it in the *P'ei-wen yün-fu.*

4. That is to say, rich, talented, beautiful young women also grow old and die. Hibiscus (*fu-jung*) is a flower that blooms in early fall.

No. 15

Father and mother left[1] me plenty of books,
Fields and gardens—I long now for nothing more.

My wife works the shuttle—her loom goes creak! creak!
Our son is at play—his mouth babbles wa! wa!

Clapping my hands, I urge the flowers to dance;
Propping my chin, I listen to the birds sing.

Who can come and admire [this scene]?
The woodcutters always pass by.[2]

1. Reading *hsü* in the sense of bequeath. Ch'en Hui-chien (*Han-shan-tzu*, p. 180) suggests emending this to *tu*, "read," which would give, "Father and mother read lots of books."

2. "Woodcutters" are commonly associated with natural simplicity and purity in Chinese poems and with the life of the recluse. Along with fishermen and shepherds, they also commonly adopt and raise young heroes in legends and myths. On the latter, see, for example, Henricks, "The Hero Pattern and the Life of Confucius" (*Journal of Chinese Studies* 1: 3 (October 1984): 241–260). For some interesting observations on the woodcutter and the fisherman as central figures in the Chinese pastoral idyll, see J. I. Crump, *Songs From Xanadu: Studies in Mongol-Dynasty Song-Poetry (San-ch'ü)* (Ann Arbor, MI: Center for Chinese Studies, 1983), Chapter 4, "Tales by Woodsman for the Fisher's Ear," pp. 81–103.

No. 16

My house is placed beneath verdant cliffs;
The weeds in my courtyard I don't cut anymore.

Fresh wistaria hangs down twisting in loops,
Ancient boulders rise up lofty and steep.

Mountain fruits—the monkeys pick;
Fish in the pond—the egrets hold in their bills.

And I with my immortality books[1], one or two scrolls,
Sit 'neath a tree and read—mumble mumble.

1. I.e., books on alchemical potions and the like.

No. 17

The four seasons move on without stop or rest;
When one year is gone, again a new year arrives.

The ten thousand things have new life succeeding the old;
The nine heavens are without destruction and decay.[1]

When there's light in the East, there's also dark in the West;
And when petals fall, again the flowers will bloom.

It's only the traveller in the Yellow Springs;
Who goes into dark gloom and doesn't return.

1. One of the earliest and most common Chinese views of the cosmos is one in which there are nine heavens, one in the center of the sky and one in each of the eight directions surrounding the center.

Comment: Alternation and succession, described openly in the first couplet and denied for man in the last, are reinforced in the first three couplets by the words used in the third—i.e., the pivotal—position in each line. In the first two couplets we have *wu* (without) and *yu* (again, or another), followed by *yu* (have) and *wu* (have not). Since *yu* and *wu* are also translated by being and non-being, we also have the transition from non-being to being and being to non-being. Again, key words occur in the third position in the third couplet—*yu* (my "also" in the translation) and *fu* (repeat, reoccur).

In the realm of nature, plants and flowers die but come back to life; in the heavens life is eternal—there is no destruction or decay. In time, night is succeeded by day. It is only man who dies and does not return to life.

No. 18

Last year is gone, and I trade in a year full of sorrow;
But spring has come, and the colors of things are all fresh and
    new.

Mountain blossoms giggle at sparkling streams,
While trees[1] on the cliff sway in mists of green.

Butterflies and bees [with their fluttering and buzzing]
    in their own way speak of their joy;
Even more delightful the fish and the birds!

Rambling with friends, my emotion's not yet spent,
And 'til dawn I can't get to sleep.

1. Reading the variant of *shu* (tree) for *hsiu* (cave, peak).

No. 19

Your handwriting might be *too* dramatic and flowing;[1]
And in stature—you might be extremely large and tall.[2]

Still alive, you'll be a person with limitations,
And dead, you'll be a ghost with no name.

From of old, like this there've been many;
For you to fight it now, what good would that do?

But you can come join me in the white clouds,
Where I'll teach you the 'purple fungus' song.[3]

---

1. Literally, "too vertical and horizontal" *(t'ai tsung-heng)*. Here this is apparently a compliment; his handwriting is dramatically expressive with large, broad strokes.

2. Iritani and Matsumura *(Kanzanshi,* p. 45) think it is relevant here that the four things considered when hiring officials in the T'ang were appearance, handwriting, speaking ability, and judgment. For more on these four traits, see poem 113 and its notes.

3. *Tzu-chih,* "purple fungus," is one of the drugs of long life. It is identified as *Ganoderman japonicum* in Shiu-ying Hu, *An Enumeration of Chinese Materia Medica* (Hong Kong: Chinese University Press, 1980), p. 151. About it, the *Shen Nung pen-ts'ao ching* (1.23a) (Ssu-pu pei-yao edition) says: "It protects the body, benefits essence and breath, strengthens muscles and bones, and improves your complexion. If you eat it for a long time, your body becomes light, you do not age, and it lengthens your years."

No. 20

If you wish to find a place where you can rest,
Han-shan for long can keep you secure.

A slight breeze blows through secluded pines;
The closer you get the better it sounds.

Underneath is a man with graying hair;
Mumble mumble—he reads Huang and Lao.[1]

Ten years he's been unable to return;
He's forgotten the road he used when he came.

1. The books of Huang-ti (the Yellow Emperor) and Lao-tzu—i.e.,
texts dealing with Taoist practices of long life.

No. 21

Dashing, heroic the lad on the horse;
Waving his whip he points to the green willow.[1]

He says he will never die;
To the end not take a hazardous trip.[2]

Through the seasons the flowers delight in themselves,
Yet one morning they wither and fade.

Clarified butter and crystalline sugar;[3]
These 'til death he'll be unable to taste.

1. The "willows" *can* mean the red-light district of town—where the prostitutes live. That would fit in with this theme. On young men on horses with whips in their hands as a common *yüeh-fu* theme, see the comment to poem 47.

2. Literally, not "scale or sail" *(t'i-hang)*, a stock expression for making a distant and dangerous journey over mountain and sea.

3. On "clarified butter" as a metaphor for Buddha-nature, see the *Nirvāṇa-sūtra, chüan* 14 (Chapter 7:4, "Sheng-hsing p'in"; T. 374, Vol. 12, p. 449 top). It is the essence of milk, and Buddha-nature is the essence of Buddha's teachings. "Crystalline sugar," literally "stone honey" *(shih-mi)* is likewise the essence of sugar juice, arrived at by boiling it down. In *chüan* 8 of the *Nirvāṇa-sūtra* (T. 375, Vol. 12, p. 650 top), the Mahāyāna scriptures are compared to *shih-mi*, which, when swallowed, is either medicine or poison depending on whether or not it is digested. For the stupid who do not know about Buddha-nature, the Vaipulya scriptures are poison when ingested. For *shih-mi*, Read *(Chinese Medicinal Plants*, p. 251 [item 756B]) has "refined sugar." Also see Schafer, *The Golden Peaches of Samarkand*, (Berkeley, CA: University of California Press, 1963), pp. 152–154, who explains that *shih-mi* were lumps of sugar formed in various shapes and eaten as candy in the T'ang.

No. 22

There is a master who eats the pink clouds;[1]
His abode shuns the haunts of the common.

As for the seasons—truly crisp and cool;
In summer it's just like the fall.

Secluded brooks—a constant gurgle and splash;
Through tall pines the wind sighs and moans.

In here if you sit half a day,
You'll forget the cares of one hundred years.[2]

1. No doubt this is a self-styled name Han-shan gives himself. The pink clouds of morning are filled with Yang. Taoists often did their breathing exercises at dawn because the air at that time was charged with life.
2. Iritani and Matsumura (Kanzanshi, p. 48) see a possible allusion in this last line to poem no. 15 in the "Nineteen Old Poems." That poem opens with the lines "Man's years fall short of a hundred; a thousand years of worry crowd his heart" (translated by Burton Watson, Chinese Lyricism, p. 29; Wen-hsüan 29: 7a, p. 400.) These lines are more directly related to poem 135.

No. 23

It's in Han-tan that I live,[1]
And the sound of my song, melodically rises and falls.

Since I securely live in this place,
These songs I've known quite well from of old.

When you get drunk, never say "going home";[2]
Linger and tarry—the sun's not yet down.

In my house there's a place you can sleep for the night;
Embroidered quilts fill my silver bed.

1. Han-tan was the capital of the state of Chao in ancient times and famous for its taverns and beautiful sing-song girls. Obviously, one of those girls is singing *this* song.

2. In song 298 of the *Shih* (p. 79), the officers drinking at court *do* go home when they are drunk. Bernhard Karlgren (*The Book of Poetry*, p. 254) translates the relevant line: "Well-fed, well-fed, well-fed, are the teams of stallions; morning and evening they are in the palace; in the palace they drink wine; . . . when drunk they will go home; they go to rejoice together."

Note: Iritani and Matsumura (*Kanzanshi*, p. 49) note the resemblance of this poem to a number of *yüeh-fu* ballads—e.g., Shen Yüeh's (441–513) "The Sun Comes up in the Southeast" (*Yüeh-fu shih-chi*, Ch. 28, p. 420). There is also a striking resemblance to poem 5 in Juan Chi's (210–263) "Yung-huai shih."

No. 24

You may quickly paddle your three-winged boat;[1]
Be good at riding your thousand-li horse.[2]

But you'll never be able get to my home;
Which is to say, where I live is most
    wild and remote.[3]

A cave on a cliff, in the midst of a deep range of peaks;
Clouds and thunder, descending all day long.

If you're not a Master K'ung Ch'iu;[4]
You don't have the talent for saving others![5]

1. A "three-winged boat" (san-i chou) is a boat used in battle, noted for being light but strong.
2. That is, a horse that can travel a thousand li (1 li = ⅓ mile) in one day.
3. Iritani and Matsumura (Kanzanshi, p. 51) have a long note on yu-yeh, "remote and wild," drawing attention to the fact that yeh is a term that Confucius often contrasts with "culture" or "cultivated" (wen) (see, for example, Lun-yü 6: 18, p. 10). At first glance, this seems overdone, but there is another possible "Confucian" allusion in the next couplet—in I ching, Hexagram 3 (p. 4), under the image, we read "clouds and thunder collect; the gentleman in this way establishes his principles and policies to govern." Wilhelm (The I Ching, p. 17) translates: "Clouds and Thunder: The image of difficulties at the beginning. Thus the superior man brings order out of confusion." All of this seems relevant when we read the last couplet where Han-shan contrasts himself with Confucius.
4. I.e., Confucius.
5. And so I live here and not in the world—i.e., I am not a Confucius.

No. 25

As for the wise, you reject me;
As for the stupid, I reject you!

But since I'm neither stupid nor wise,[1]
From this moment on, let's hear no more from
    one another.

With the night, I sing at the bright moon;
With dawn, I dance on white clouds.

How can I fold my hands and keep my mouth shut,
And stiffly sit still, with my temple hair tumbling down?[2]

1. That is to say, I fall into neither of these groups.
2. I.e., he is too overcome with joy.
    Note: The relationship between the first four lines and the second four lines seems to be that Han-shan prefers to get out of society where distinctions like "wise" and "stupid" are made and enjoy himself in the realm of nature.

No. 26[†]

There is a bird striped with the five shades;
She perches in the Kolanut tree and eats the fruit of bamboo.[1]

Gracefully she moves, in accord with the proper and right;
Harmoniously she sings, with exact pitch and tone.

Yesterday she came—why has she arrived?
It's for me[2] she has for the moment appeared.

If you hear the sound of string and voice,
You should dance and delight in today.[3]

[†]Missing from the *Tse-shih-chü ts'ung-shu* and *Kunaichō* Library editions.

1. For *t'ung* (paulownia), see Bernard Read, *Chinese Medicinal Plants*, p. 26 (item 103). But Ch'en Hui-chien *(Han-shan-tzu*, p. 261) understands our bird to be the phoenix *(feng)* and the tree the *wu-t'ung*, which would make it the Kolanut, according to Read *(Chinese Medicinal Plants*, p. 78, item 272).

2. There is a variant of *chün* for *wu*, which would change the meaning to "It's for *you*."

3. *Analects* 17:3 (p. 35) records an anecdote in which Confucius seems to think that Tzu-yu is wasting his time instructing the inhabitants of Wu-ch'eng in music. The anecdote (D. C. Lau, translator, *Confucius: The Analects* [New York: Penguin, 1979] p. 143 [as 17:4]) reads: "The Master went to Wu Ch'eng. There he heard the sound of stringed instruments and singing. The Master broke into a smile and said, 'Surely you don't need to use an ox-knife to kill a chicken.' Tzu-yu answered, 'Some time ago I heard it from you, Master, that the gentleman instructed in the Way loves his fellow men and that the small man instructed in the Way is easy to command.' the Master said, 'My friends, what Yen says is right. My remark a moment ago was only made in jest.'"

Comment: Iritani and Matsumura *(Kanzanshi,* p. 334), like Ch'en Hui-
chien, feel that the bird referred to in the opening lines is the Phoenix,
harbinger of an age of great peace. They see in Han-shan's poem, however,
a Buddhist use of this theme: the phoenix here signals a time and place
where one can become enlightened, can become a Buddha.

No. 27

A thatched hut, the place where a rustic lives;
In front of his gate, horses and carts are few.[1]

The woods are secluded and dark—'specially suited for birds
    to collect;
The valley streams, wide and broad—from the beginning
    meant to hold fish.

Mountain fruits, hand in hand my son and I pick;
Marshy fields, together with my wife I plow.

And in our house what do you find?
Nothing more than a bed full of books.[2]

1. See note 1 to poem 3 above.
2. Iritani and Matsumura (Kanzanshi, p. 54) note the association of "a
bed full of books" (i-ch'uang shu) with retired scholars in a poem by Yü Hsin
(513–581) as well. But this is not necessarily an allusion.

No. 28

Climb up! Ascend! The way to Han-shan;
But on Han-shan the roads never end.

The valleys are long, with boulders in heaps and piles;
The streams are wide, with grasses both wet and damp.

The moss is slippery—it has nothing to do with the rain;
The pines sigh and moan, but they don't rely on the wind.

Who can transcend the cares of the world,
And sit with me in the white clouds?

Comment: On normal mountains the roads eventually end; but Han-shan is climbing the spiritual mountain. In the Zen sense, if you follow a set "way" (reading sutras, meditating, worshipping images), you'll never get to the "top." But if, in a flash, you "transcend the cares of the world," then, like Han-shan in the last line, you'll be on top, surrounded by the white clouds. This is a "regulated verse" poem: note how the inner couplets are strictly parallel. The tonal sequence is as follows: (P = level tone; T = deflected): (1) PTPPT, (2) PPTTP, (3) PPTTT, (4) TTTPP, (5) PTPPT, (6) PPTTP, (7) PPPTT, (8) TTTPP.

No. 29

The six extremities[1] constantly hem them in;
The nine rules [of conduct][2]—in vain do they discuss
   them 'mongst themselves.

Those with talent are discarded in the grasses and swamps,[3]
While those who are artless are locked in by their bramble
   doors.[4]

Though the sun rises, their cliffs are still dark;
Though the fog lifts, their valleys remain in a haze.

In their midst, the sons of great, wealthy men
Are, each one, completely without any pants.[5]

    1. The "six extremities" are illness, anxiety, poverty, evil, weakness, and to die young through misfortune.
    2. On the "nine rules" (or nine principles—*chiu-wei*), Ch'en Hui-chien *(Han-shan-tzu*, p. 181) understands these to be the "nine virtues," of which there are various lists (things such as loyalty, sincerity, respect, gentleness, pleasantness). Iritani and Matsumura *(Kanzanshi*, pp. 56–57), on the other hand, feel the nine *wei* are connected to the nine divisions of the "Great Plan" *(hung-fan)* as they are described in the *Shu* (Book of Documents). They are described in the "Hung-fan" of the *Shu* as follows (translated by Bernhard Karlgren, *The Book of Documents* [Stockholm: Museum of Far Eastern Antiquities, Bulletin 22, 1950], p. 30): "Heaven then gave Yü the Great Plan in nine sections, whereby the constant norms get their proper order. The first is called the five elements; the second is called to bring forth and use the five conducts; the third is called energetically to use the eight rules of government; the fourth is called to harmonize and use the

five regulators; the fifth is called to establish and use the august correctness; the sixth is called to regulate and use the three virtues; the seventh is called elucidatingly to use the determinators of doubt; the eighth is called thoughtfully to use all the verifications; the ninth is called enjoyingly to use the five felicities and with due awe to accept the six extremities."

3. I.e., they are not used at court and possibly exiled.

4. "Bramble door" *(p'eng-men)* is code for the life of the poor scholar.

5. In Chapter 4 of the *Lotus-sūtra* ("Hsin-chieh p'in"; T. 262, Vol. 9, p. 16, middle, 17 bottom) the Buddha is compared to a great man (or simply elder—*chang-che)* who turns over all his wealth to his prodigal son, a man who had lived a destitute life, having left his father at a young age. Thus, great treasures await all believers who return to the Buddha and recognize him as their true kin. For a translation of the story in question, see Leon Hurvitz, translator, *Scripture of the Lotus Blossom of the Fine Dharma (The Lotus Sutra)* (New York: Columbia University Press, 1976), pp. 84–100.

Comment: Given the nature of the allusion in the last couplet, it seems clear that Han-shan's point throughout is the poor lot, in the end, of those who fail to embrace the Buddhist faith. They remain in the dark, even though the sun (of wisdom) has already risen.

No. 30

White clouds soar high over jagged peaks;
The green water rolls back and forth in deep waves.

In this place I hear an old fisherman;[1]
Time after time he beats out his boat-songs.

Note after note—I can't bear to listen;
It makes me have many sad thoughts.

"Who says the sparrow has no beak;
How else could it bore through my walls?"[2]

1. An allusion to "The Fisherman" *(Yü-fu)* in the *Ch'u Tz'u* (Hawkes, *The Songs of the South*, pp. 206–207), where an old fisherman chides Ch'ü Yüan for his inability to change with the times and serve or not serve accordingly.

2. A direct quote from the *Shih*, No. 17. The full verse reads: "Who says that the sparrow has no beak? By aid of what else could it break through into my house? Who says that you have no family? By aid of what else could you urge on me a lawsuit? But though you urge on me a lawsuit, your family will not suffice" (Bernhard Karlgren, translator, *The Book of Odes*, [Stockholm: Museum of Far Eastern Antiquities, 1950], p. 10). Karlgren takes the singer to be a young lady being forced to wed, and the sparrow stands for the man's influential family. Arthur Waley *(The Book of Songs*, [New York: Grove, 1937] pp. 63–65), on the other hand, feels our singer is a young man being sued by a girl who represents herself as having no family.

Comment: Han-shan's point might be that although the fisherman's songs should not cause these emotions, they do (this seems to be Watson's interpretation). However, Ch'en Hui-chien's (Han-shan-tzu, p. 175) interpretation is that the allusion to the Shih simply stands for thinking of home. The sparrow does have a beak, and thus it can build its nest for its family in my wall. But Han-shan has gone into retirement alone—cut off from family and friends. Perhaps the fisherman's songs make him sad because he too (like Ch'ü Yüan) has not followed the old fisherman's advice; could he adjust to the times, he might still be at home.

No. 31

Dark and obscure—the way to Han-shan;
Far apart—the shores of the cold mountain stream.

Chirp, chirp—constantly there are the birds;
Silent and still—in addition there are no men.

Whisper, whisper—the wind blows in my face;
Whirling and swirling—the snow piles up all around.

Day after day—I don't see the sun;
And year after year—I've known no spring.

Comment: A very unique poem in that Han-shan begins every line with a descriptive binome. The only thing similar in earlier works is poem 2 in the "Nineteen Old Poems" of the Han, where six of ten lines begin in this way. In a later poem (No. 147), Han-shan *ends* every line with a descriptive binome. I append romanization (Wade-Giles system) of the poem for the reader to see, highlighting the descriptive binomes.

Yao-yao Han-shan tao;
Lo-lo leng-chien pin.

Chiu-chiu ch'ang yu niao;
Chi-chi keng wu jen.

Ch'i-ch'i feng ch'ui mien;
Fen-fen hsüeh chi shen.

Chao-chao pu-chien jih;
Sui-sui pu-chih ch'un.

No. 32

Those of young years—what do they worry about?
They worry about seeing their temple hair turn gray.

And when it turns gray, what then do they worry about?
They worry about seeing the days closing in.

And then they'll be moved to live facing Mount T'ai;[1]
Or exiled, to maintain their homes on Pei-mang.[2]

How can I bear to speak these words?
These words that bring pain to the old.

1. Mount T'ai—though our text uses the alternate name of Tai—in Shantung was the Eastern sacred peak in China. In popular belief it was the abode of the supreme ruler of all spirits in a terrestrial bureaucracy, who reported only to the Jade Emperor on high. He kept all records of birth and death. See, for example, Henri Maspero (translated from the French by Frank Kierman), *Taoism and Chinese Religion* (Amherst, MA: University of Massachusetts Press, 1981), pp. 102–104.

2. Pei-mang was the hill north of Lo-yang where royalty and nobility were buried. Mount T'ai and Pei-mang are parallel expressions in the Chinese—literally, the text says "Eastern Tai" and "Northern Mang."

No. 33

I've heard it said that sorrows are hard to dispel;
These words, I've said, are not true.

Yet yesterday morn I drove them away,[1]
And today I'm encumbered again.

The month comes to an end, but my sorrow doesn't end;
The year starts afresh, but my sorrows are also renewed.

Who is to know that under this cap of cane[2]
There is fundamentally a man who's been sad a very long time.

---

1. There is a variant of *shih*, "start," for *ts'eng*, indicator of past tense,
that would make the line read: "Yet yesterday morn I started to drive them
away."
2. A *hsi-mao* was a cap worn by commoners in the T'ang and Sung—
gentlemen who had not yet achieved any rank.

No. 34

Two tortoises riding a cart drawn by a young ox
Suddenly came out at the road-head to play.

A scorpion[1] came over from one side;
Weary to death, he wanted to ask them to give him a ride.

Not to carry him would go against human feelings,
But as soon as they took him on, they sank down under
 the weight.

In the snap of your fingers—indescribably short;
They extended their kindness and proceeded right then
 to get stung!

1. Reading the variant of *ch'an*, "scorpion," for *ku*, a wicked kind of poison.

Note: Ch'en Hui-chien (*Han-shan-tzu*, p. 275) feels that this story alludes to something in the Buddhist scriptures, but he cannot determine the source. Iritani and Matsumura offer no explanation. It might be that Han-shan's point is simply to draw attention to the fact that we often end up being harmed when, with the best intentions, we try to help others. However, Tseng P'u-hsin (*Han-shan shih-chieh*, p. 21) sees the poem as an allegory in which the two tortoises stand for wisdom and meditation, and the scorpion is *kleśa*. The point of the story, then, is that if one is not firm in carrying out one's vows, he can be brought to ruin from something outside (i.e., *kleśa*). As it turns out, Hakuin, in his commentary on this poem (*Kanzan shi sendai kibun*, 1: 34–35), also makes these associations, elaborating that the poem illustrates the problem of an early stage bodhisattva, indicated by the fact that the tortoises are riding a cart drawn by a *young* ox (*tu*), a bodhisattva whose "roots" are not yet developed and whose strength to carry out his vows is therefore weak.

No. 35

In the third month with silkworms still small,
Young girls come to gather the blooms.

By a bend in the wall they chase butterflies;
Approaching the stream, they toss stones at the frogs.

Their silken sleeves chocked full of plums;
With hairpins of gold[1], they dig out shoots of bamboo.

Noisily they debate the many spring colors and hues;
"This place is better than home!"[2]

1. A *chin p'i* is a hair ornament in the shape of a small knife. They were used by Indian doctors to scrape the eyes of people with eye disease.
2. There is a variant of *shih*, "is," for *sheng*, "superior to, better than"—i.e., "This place is truly our home."

No. 36

In the house to the east there lives an old broad
Who's been wealthy now four or five years.[1]

In former days she was poorer than me;
Now she laughs at my lack of coins.

She laughs at me for being behind;
While I laugh at her for being ahead.[2]

If we don't stop laughing at each other,
The east will again be the west.

1. The text literally says "three or five" years.
2. The "behind" (*hou*) and "ahead" (*ch'ien*) might also be read in a temporal sense—i.e., her laughing at me was done after [she became rich], while my laughing at her was done [even] before.

No. 37

Rich kids are stingy as can be[1];
Whatever might come their way, they find it difficult to
    accept with respect.

Their granary rice might be bright red,[2]
But they won't lend others a peck or a pint.

They turn over in their minds their twisted and devious
    schemes;
Before buying raw silk, they've already picked out brocades.

But when their end days draw near
For mourners they'll have bluebottle flies.[3]

    1. Ch'en Hui-chien (*Han-shan-tzu*, p. 233) understands *yang-chang* as *pu-jen*, "not benevolent." The expression literally means "haltered hands."
    2. i.e., it is rotting—rice changes color when it spoils.
    3. They will have no friends. See note 2 to poem 8 on bluebottle flies as mourners in the biography of Yü Fan.

No. 38**

I once observed a wise gentleman,
Broad in knowledge, noble in spirit—he was simply
without compare.

No sooner selected for office than his fine reputation spread
throughout the whole land;
His five-character poetic lines surpassed those of all other
men.[1]

As an official, he governed and transformed, excelling his
seniors in age;
His conduct, right and correct, could not be maintained by
the young coming on.

Yet all of a sudden, he coveted wealth and rank and
riches and women;
When the tiles are broken and the ice melted, you can't set
them out on display.[2]

**Seven-character lines.
 1. Iritani and Matsumura (*Kanzanshi*, p. 68) remind us that composition of five-character poems was part of the civil service examination system during the T'ang.
 2. *"Ping-hsiao wa-chieh"* (ice melted; tiles broken) is a well-known, four-character phrase indicating that something is totally ruined—in this case, the character of the scholar-official.

No. 39

A white crane with bitter peach in his bill
Went one thousand li, stopping to rest only once.

Wishing to go to P'eng-lai,
He took this along as his food.

Before he arrived, his feathers faded and fell;
Apart from the flock, his heart was anguished and sad.

He retreated, returned to the nest from whence he had come,
But his wife and his child no longer recognized him.[1]

1. For a similar theme, see poem 134.

Comment: This poem weaves together three different things: First, that the poem is essentially about the Taoist quest for immortality is indicated not only by the fact that this is a crane in flight, but also by the fact that his goal is a Taoist locus of immortals, the isle of P'eng-lai in the East, and for his food he takes along a peach, a fruit commonly associated with immortals and gods. That this is a "bitter peach" (k'u-t'ao) seems to indicate Han-shan's recognition of this quest as a difficult, perhaps *unpleasant* one. Second, the crane's quest seems to stand for Han-shan's own quest, and in poem 134 we read that Han-shan too became homesick for friends and kin, but going home found his wife no longer recognized him. Thus the poem seems to reflect Han-shan's own circumstances. Finally, elements of an old *yüeh-fu* song by the name of "Yen-ko ho-ch'ang-hsing," which has the alternate title of "Fei-hu hsing" (and in some texts the *hu* is a *ho*—a crane) also seem to find their way into this poem (for the "Yen-ko ho-ch'ang-hsing," see *Yüeh-fu shih-chi* 39: 14, pp. 576–577). The first part of that song describes a pair of swans flying from the northwest, but as they fly the female becomes ill. The male addresses her, saying, "I want to carry you in my bill, but my mouth is closed, and I can't get it open; I want to carry you on my back, but my feathers—how broken and in ruins are they." In the second part of the song, a woman addresses her husband, who is about to go on a distant journey (off to war), and points out that "on distant roads returning is difficult"; "I must [alone] maintain empty rooms."

No. 40

Accustomed to living in a secluded, retired spot,
Suddenly I head off to the heart of Kuo-ch'ing.[1]

On occasion I visit with Old Feng Kan,[2]
And as before come to see Master Shih.[3]

Alone I return and climb up Cold Cliffs,
Where there is no one to talk with about the unity of things.[4]

I seek out, explore the "sourceless stream";
The source might be exhausted but the stream is not.[5]

1. Kuo-ch'ing Temple was founded by Chih I in 598. It was located 10 li north of T'ien-t'ai county seat, on the south side of the southern peaks of the T'ien-t'ai range.
2. Preferring the variant *lao* to *tao* ("path") because of the parallel with the next line. But Ch'en Hui-chien (*Han-shan-tzu*, p. 192) glosses "Feng-kan tao," noting that to the north of T'ien-t'ai county seat, on the way to Kuo-ch'ing, there was a Ch'ih-ch'eng-shan (Mount Red City) which was frequented by Feng-kan.
3. Shih-te, that is.
4. Ch'en Hui-chien (*Han-shan-tzu*, p. 192) might be right in arguing that *ho-t'ung* is used in a technical Buddhist sense equivalent to *p'ing-teng* (*sama* or *samatā*), "unity" or "equality."
5. That is to say, one might discover the source—"exhaust" (*chin*) it in that way—but the truth that flows from that source will never be exhausted (also *chin*).

No. 41

If before this birth you were awfully stupid and dumb,
You won't be enlightened today.[1]

If today you are terribly poor,
It's all brought on by what you did in your previous life.[2]

If in this birth you again do not practice;[3]
In the next you'll still be as before.

Neither shore has a boat;[4]
Vast and wide—[the stream] is difficult to cross.

1. In the Zen sense—I think—of instantaneous enlightenment, "right this minute," but it can as well mean "this lifetime."
2. The causal relationship *(karma)* of this life and the one before seems to be conveyed literarily in the opening four lines by moving from *sheng-ch'ien,* "before this birth" to *ch'ien-sheng,* "previous life," and having two *chin-jih* "today" lines between.
3. Do not practice the Buddhist way—that is, *hsiu.*
4. The opposition of shores here made explicit,—*saṁsāra* and *nirvāṇa,* but also this life and the last, or next—seems to be prefigured in the opposition of the lines in the first three couplets: before/today, today/before, this birth/the next. The "boat" would be specific teachings or practices that would lead one to *nirvāṇa,* and in Zen there is no such thing. Han-shan might be developing the metaphor of the boat that carries sentient beings between the two shores, as it is described in *chüan* 9 of the *Nirvāṇa-sūtra* (T. 375, Vol. 12, p. 662 top).

No. 42

Dazzling and sparkling, the Lu family girl;
Right from the start she was named "Never Grieve."[1]

She loved to ride her flower-plucking horse;
Delighted in paddling her lotus—gathering boat.

Kneeling, she sat on a green-bear mat; [2]
On her shoulders wore blue-phoenix furs.[3]

How sad! That within one hundred years
She couldn't avoid returning to the mountains and hills.[4]

1. Iritani and Matsumura (*Kanzanshi*, p. 73) note two traditions concerning a Mo-ch'ou (never grieve). To begin with, there is a "Mo-ch'ou yüeh" in *Yüeh-fu shih-chi* 48:5 (p. 698), a song associated with a singing girl from Shih-ch'eng by the name of Mo-ch'ou. But the other tradition—and the one seemingly relevant here—concerns a girl from Lo-yang, who is celebrated in a poem attributed to Liang Wu-ti (r. 502–549). That poem is entitled "Ho-chung chih-shui" (The Water in the River) and goes like this (for the text, see Ting Fu-pao, ed., *Ch'üan Han, san-kuo . . . shih*, Vol. 2, p. 857):

> The water in the river flows to the East;
> The girl from Loyang was named Mo-ch'ou.
> When Mo-ch'ou was thirteen, she could weave finest silk;
> When fourteen, she gathered the mulberry at the head of the
>   Southern raised path.
> At fifteen she was married—the wife of Mr. Lu,
> At sixteen gave birth to a son called A-hou.

The Lu home had orchid rooms with cassia beams.
Inside the fragrances of wild tumeric and storax.
On her head golden hairpins in twelve strands.
On her feet silken slippers embroidered in the five shades.
Coral hangs from her mirror—so dazzling it produces a glare;
Servants even in height carry her slipper box.
When your life is filled with riches and rank—what more is
    there to hope for?
She only regrets she'd not been *earlier* married to the king of
    the East.

2. On the "green bear mat," see *Hsi-ching tsa-chi* 1: 5a (*Ku-chin i-shih*, Vol. 12). Emperor Ch'eng of the Han's beloved concubine, Chao Ho-te (younger sister of the notorious beauty Chao Fei-yen) had one with fur over two feet thick, and when she sat on it, her knees disappeared. The fragrance was such that if you sat on it, the smell lingered on for one hundred days.

3. Read (*Chinese Materia Medica: . . . Avian Drugs*, pp. 41–42, item 272) relates the "blue-phoenix" (*ch'ing-feng*) to the Manchurian Snow Pheasant. King Chao of the Chou (r. 1052–1000 B. C.) reportedly made two furs from the feathers of a blue phoenix. See *Shih-i chi* 2: 9a (*Ku-chin i-shih*, Vol. 5).

4. A nice way of saying she died.

No. 43

In Ti-yen[1] Master Tsou's wife;
In Han-tan the mother of one Mr. Tu.[2]

These two were the same in age,
And of the same kind their good looks.

Yet yesterday they met at a party,
[And the one with] ugly clothes was consigned to
the back of the hall.[3]

All because she wore a worn-out skirt;
She got to eat others' leftover biscuits and cakes!

1. Ti-yen would appear to be a place name, given the parallel with
the following line, but its location remains unknown. On this point, see
Ch'en Hui-chien, *Han-shan-tzu* p. 251, and Iritani and Matsumura, *Kanzan-shi, pp. 74–75.*
2. The two women in question are otherwise unknown.
3. What I translate "good looks" in Chinese is *hao mien-shou*, and a
mien-shou is what the Chinese call a "male concubine"—that is to say, a
catamite, a boy used for pederasty. But that the women "delighted" in male
concubines does not seem to go with the rest of the poem.

Comment: There is nothing in the Chinese ("ugly clothes—lined up at the back") of line 6 to indicate that a distinction is being made between the two women. But the emphasis of the previous couplet, stressing as it does that the two were the same in age and looks, makes good sense if a contrast is now being made. (I am indebted to Wen An-p'ing of the Stanford Center in Taipei for this suggestion.) But I may be wrong. And Hakuin (*Kanzanshi sendai kibun*, 1:41) does cite an intriguing anecdote from the *Ta-chih-tu lun* (Ch. 14, T. 1509, Vol. 25, p. 165 top) as something that may serve as background for what we find here. That we should love merit and not our "selves" and see that good things happen because of our merit, not what our "selves" are or do, is illustrated with the following example.

It's like the case of some Hinayana monks from Kashmir, practicing the *āraṇya* (forest dweller) *dharma* arriving at the Temple of the One King (or the temple of a king[?], *i-wang ssu*), where the temple is putting on a great feast. When the gatekeeper sees that their clothes are all dusty and worn, he will block the door and not let them advance. They might try this a number of times, but each time, because their clothes are all worn, they will be unable to advance. But then if, as an expedient means, they come back having borrowed good clothes, the doorman will see them and obey, and they can go forward without restraint. Having arrived at the feast, they will sit down and get many different kinds of good things to eat. But they will first give some food to their clothes. At which point the crowd of people will ask, "Why did you do that?" And they will reply, "We came a number of times, and each time we were unable to enter. Now it's because of our clothes that we are able to sit here and get these good things to eat. Truly, it is because of our clothes that we can get them. Therefore, we offer the food to our clothes."

No. 44

Alone I sleep at the foot of layers of cliffs;
The vapor and clouds through the day don't disperse.

Though my room is filled with dark and gloom,
In my mind I'm cut off from the clatter and noise.

In my dreams I go off to wander at the Golden Gates;[1]
As my soul returns, it crosses Stone Bridge.[2]

I have abandoned that which agitates me;
Clatter and clunk goes the gourd in the tree.[3]

1. Iritani and Matsumura (Kanzanshi, p. 76) identify the "Golden
Gates" (chin-ch'üeh) with the T'ien-t'ai peaks "Twin Gates" (shuang-ch'üeh)
mentioned by Sun Ch'o (c. 310–397) in his "Rhapsody on Roaming on
T'ien-t'ai" (Yu T'ien-t'ai fu, Wen-hsüan 11: 7b, p. 149). For a translation of
the relevant lines, see Burton Watson, Chinese Rhyme-Prose, p. 83 ("double
gates"). Also see Richard B. Mather, "The Mystical Ascent of the T'ient'ai
Mountains: Sun Ch'o's Yu-T'ien-T'ai-Shan Fu," Monumenta Serica 20 (1961):
241 text and note 91. The Golden Gates also mark the entrance to one of the
Taoist heavens—they lead into the palaces of Shang-ch'ing (Supreme Purity). And one of the names of the ruler expected to descend from the skies
in the apocalyptic hopes of the Shang-ch'ing sect of Taoism was "The Sage
Who is to Come of the Golden Gates of Shang-ch'ing." See Michel Strickmann, Le Taoïsme du Mao Chan (Paris: College de France, 1981), p. 209ff.
2. Richard Mather (above, p. 239, notes 71–74) translates Ku K'ai-
chih's comment on the "Stone Bridge" (shih-ch'iao): "On the Stone Bridge of
the T'ien-t'ai Mountains the path is not a full foot in width but several tens
of paces long; every step is extremely slippery, while below it looks down
on the Utter Darkness Stream" (for the text, see the notes to Sun Ch'o's fu
in Wen-hsüan 11: 6b, p. 148.)

3. For the story behind this, see the *I-shih chuan*. Hsü Yu, having retired, used his hands to drink until someone gave him a gourd, which,
when he had finished using, he hung on a tree. Whenever the wind blew,
it "clattered and clunked"; since it bothered him, he threw it away.

No. 45

Now all things have their use,
And in using them, each has what is fit.

If in using something, you use what is out of place,
It will be totally lacking, and what's more,
    completely deficient.

A round chisel with a square handle;
How sad! In vain it was made.[1]

To use Hua-liu to catch mice
Can't compare with using a lame cat![2]

---

1. The "round chisel with the square handle" was a known metaphor
in early China for things that do not fit. It is alluded to in a number of
texts. For example, in the Ch'u-tz'u ("Chiu-pien," 8: 7b–8a [p. 79] in SPPY
ed.), we find the lines: "If you take a square handle to use on a round
chisel, I am certain it will not fit, and you will not make it go in" (David
Hawkes, translator, The Songs of the South [London: Penguin], p. 212.) Also,
in the Chuang-tzu, Chapter 33 (p. 93, line 76), one of the paradoxical sayings
attributed to the sophist Hui-shih is: "Holes for chisel handles do not surround the handles" (Burton Watson, trans., The Complete Works of Chuang
Tzu [New York: Columbia University Press], pp. 75–76.)
    2. Hua-liu was one of eight prized steeds that belonged to King Mu
of the Chou (r. 1001–946 B. C.). Han-shan alludes to a line in Chuang-tzu,
Chapter 17 (p. 43, line 36). Watson (The Complete Works, p. 180) translates:
"Thoroughbreds like Ch'i-chi and Hua-liu could gallop a thousand li in one
day, but when it came to catching rats they were no match for the wildcat
or the weasel—this refers to a difference in skill."

Comment: The point of this observation seems to be the good Taoist point of the relativity of values. We have fixed ideas about what is good and bad: we all categorically prefer a prized horse to a lame cat. But good and bad depend on one's situation.

No. 46

Who is it that lives forever and doesn't die?
The business of death, from the beginning has treated us all
    the same.

No sooner do you start to remember your tall eight-foot man,
Than all of a sudden he turns into a pile of dust!

The Yellow Springs[1] has no sun of dawn,
But the green grasses have their seasonal spring.

When I walk to this place that grieves my heart,
With the wind in the pines, the sorrow is enough to kill me.

1. The underworld; the place where souls go at death.

No. 47

Riding a bay—coral whip in his hand—
He charges through the streets of Lo-yang.

Smug and assured this beautiful youth;
He puts no stock in old age.

But the gray hair will surely appear;
Can that ruddy glow be maintained for long?

Take a look at that hill of Pei-mang;[1]
This is your Isle of P'eng-lai![2]

1. The royal cemetery north of the capital at Lo-yang.
2. One of the isles of the immortals in the Eastern sea.
Comment: The final couplet is open to a number of interpretations, but I think the point is that though you might hope to live forever with the immortals on P'eng-lai, the *cemetery* is where you will "live" forever. Iritani and Matsumura *(Kanzanshi,* p. 80) point out the many *yüeh-fu* themes we find in this poem. "Tzu-liu ma" (Black bay steed), for example, is a *yüeh-fu* title, and there are fifteen poems on this theme in the *Yüeh-fu shih chi* (Chapter 24, pp. 352–355), including one by Emperor Yüan of Liang (r. 552–554), in which we find mention of the "coral whip" and the "beautiful youth." These expressions occur as well in a "Ch'ang-an shao-nien hsing" (A Song of the Youths of Ch'ang-an) by Ho Sun of the Liang in *Yüeh-fu shih-chi* 66 (p. 959). "Ch'ang-an shao-nien hsing" songs form a sub-category of "Shao-nien hsing" songs in the *Yüeh-fu shih-chi* (Chapter 66, pp. 953–961). "Lo-yang tao" (The Streets of Lo-yang) songs form still another category in the *Yüeh-fu shih-chi* (Chapter 23, 20 *shou,* pp. 339–343).

No. 48

All day long, it's always just like you're drunk;
Passing years—never for a moment do they stay.

Buried, you'll lie beneath daisy fields,
Where the morning sun[1]—Oh, how dim and how dark!

When your bones and your flesh are dissolved, scattered and
    vanished,
Your *hun* and your *p'o*[2] will then start to wither and fade.

Even if you had a mouth that could bite through steel,
You'd have no way to read the *Lao-ching*.[3]

1. Reading the variant of *jih* ("sun") for *yüeh* ("moon"). Similar sen-
timents and words in poem 46 seem to corroborate this.
    2. In modern folk belief the *hun* is the spiritual soul that transmi-
grates; the *p'o* is the physical soul that stays near the body in the grave,
eventually fading away.
    3. The *Lao-tzu*, the *Tao-te ching*.
    Note: Ch'en Hui-chien's *(Han-shan-tzu,* p. 199) reading of the last two
lines—"If you end up with a bit of steel in your mouth [i.e., are reborn as
a horse or a cow]; is it not because of your reading of the Huang-Lao
texts?"—is enticing but not convincing.

No. 49

Once I sat down facing Han-shan;[1]
And I've lingered and tarried here now thirty years.

Yesterday I came looking for relatives and friends,
But more than half have gone to the Yellow Springs.

Gradually it diminishes, like the remnant of wax,[2]
And the long flow of life seems like a fast-moving river.[3]

This morning—I confront my lonely shadow;
Before I know it, my tears flow down in two streams.

1. Sat down (tso) to meditate, that is. One is reminded that Bodhi-dharma, the First Patriarch of Zen in China, is reported to have sat in meditation facing a wall without moving for nine years.
2. The stub of the candle that gets smaller the longer the flame burns.
3. An allusion to the well-known words of Confucius in Analects 9: 17 (p. 16): "While standing by a river, the Master said, 'What passes away is, perhaps, like this. Day and night it never lets up'" (translation by D. C. Lau, Confucius: The Analects, p. 98.)

No. 50[+]

They call to one another as they gather hibiscus;[1]
How delightful! The pure water in the stream.

Rambling and playing, unaware of the setting sun,
Time and again, they see the strong winds arise.[2]

The waves gently cup the young Mandarins,
While breakers toss and bob Tufted ducks.[3]

At this time they take shelter with their boat and oars;
Surging, overwhelming, their feelings never end.[4]

[+]Missing from the *Tse-shih-chü ts'ung-shu* and *Kunaichō* Library editions.

1. Similar to the opening line of poem 6 of the "Nineteen Old Poems" *(Wen-hsüan* 29: 4a, p. 398)—"I cross the river to gather the hibiscus"—where husband and wife, separated by a great distance, think of one another.

2. Note that the sun sets while the winds "come up" *(ch'i)*, which starts the up and down motion of the waves found in the next couplet.

3. On *hsi-chih* as "Tufted Ducks," see Read, *Chinese Materia Medica . . . Avian Drugs*, p. 259, item 260.

4. *Hao-tang*, "overwhelming," describes the surging movement of waves, but here it also describes the lovers' feelings.

Note: Iritani and Matsumura *(Kanzanshi*, pp. 82–83) note a story about Hsüan-tsung of the T'ang (r. 712–756) with his lover Yang Kuei-fei on a summer outing to escape the heat, where the *nü-kuan* (female official in charge of concubines) sees Tufted Ducks bobbing on the water and compares them to the Mandarin ducks inside in bed. Mandarin ducks *(yüan-yang)* are stock symbols of conjugal bliss.

No. 51

My mind is like the autumn moon;
An emerald lake—pure, clean, and bright.

There is nothing with which it compares;
Tell me, how can I explain?

No. 52

Drooping willows, dark, like mist and fog;
Wind-swept petals, whirling about like sleet.[1]

The husband resides in "Apart from Wife" Region;
The wife lives in "Thinking of my Husband" County.

Each dwells at Heaven's opposite shore;[2]
When will they once again meet?

I send this message to the shining moon tower;
Never take in a pair of flying swallows.

---

1. *Hsien* is "sleet," though snow seems a more apt image.

2. A line that occurs as well in poem 1 of the "Nineteen Old Poems," a poem also about separation, and presumably separation of lovers. Watson (*Chinese Lyricism*, p. 20) translates the opening lines of that poem: "On and on, going on and on; away from you to live apart; ten thousand li and more between us; each at opposite ends of the sky. The road I travel is steep and long; who knows when we meet again?" (For the text, see *Wen-hsüan* 29: 1b–2a, p. 397.)

Comment: Ch'en Hui-chien (*Han-shan-tzu*, p. 102) and Tseng P'u-hsin (*Han-shan shih-chieh*, p. 31) both feel that the point of the final two lines is that the tower should not let mated swallows build a nest in it, since mated swallows would remind the poet of his/her missing mate. Iritani and Matsumura (*Kanzanshi*, p. 85) feel, however, that these words are intended to *admonish* the lonely wife not to take up with a new lover. Their interpretation is appealing. The tower is told not to *chu*, "store away or hoard" (secretly hide?) the flying swallows. Moreover, the tower (or pavilion—*lou*) on which the bright moon shines is specifically associated with a lonely wife at home in a poem by Ts'ao Chih (poem 1 of his series "Ch'i-ai," Seven Sorrows, in *Wen-hsüan* 23: 15a p. 316). That poem, where the wife grieves for her lord who's been away on travels for more than ten years, begins: "The bright moon shines on a high tower. . . Upstairs is a wife with sad thoughts."

No. 53

When we have wine, let's hail each other to drink;
When we have meat, let's call on each other to eat.

We are men who, sooner or later, will end up in the
    Yellow Springs,
So while young and strong, we must exert all our strength.

Jade girdles only glitter awhile;
Hairpins of gold—not ornaments that will last for long.

Old Mr. Chang and old lady Cheng;
Once they were gone, there was no more news.

Comment: The question is, in what way should we exert all our strength? Does Han-shan have in mind Buddhist or Taoist ways to immortality that will help us to avoid death? The answer seems to be the *carpe diem* answer that we should enjoy ourselves while we can. That this is so seems confirmed by the fact that line 4 seems to allude to the *yüeh-fu* tune of "Ch'ang-ko hsing" (*Yüeh-fu shih-chi* 30, p. 442). That song ends with the lines, "[The ten thousand things] always fear the arrival of fall; brown and yellow, the flowers and leaves decline. The one hundred rivers flow East to the sea; when will they return to the West? If when young and strong, you do not exert all your strength; when grown and old, in vain will you painfully pine."

No. 54

How delightful! That good man;
His build, awe-inspiring in the extreme!

In springs and autumns, not yet thirty,
But for talents and arts—one hundred kinds.

With bridle of gold, he chases 'round with the chivalrous
knights;[1]
With serving vessels of jade, he gathers together with
friends.

He has only one kind of fault;
He does not transmit the inexhaustible lamp![2]

1. Kuo Mao-ch'ien's *Yüeh-fu shih-chi* (63, pp. 914–915) contains a song
by Ts'ao Chih entitled "Pai-ma p'ien" (The White Horse), which also describes a young lad riding a horse with bridle of gold chasing around with
the knights *(hsia-k'o)*.
2. An allusion to the *Vimalakīrti-sūtra*, where in Chapter 4 ("P'u-sa
p'in," T. 475, Vol. 14, p. 543 middle), Vimalakīrti addresses a group of celestial maidens in the following way: "Vimalakīrti said, 'Sisters, there is a
dharma-theme named 'the inexhaustible lamp.' You should study it. The
inexhaustible lamp is just like one lamp which ignites a hundred thousand
lamps. The dark ones all become bright, and its brightness is never exhausted. Even so, sisters, one bodhisattva opens up and leads a hundred
thousand living beings, bringing them to put forth the thought of supreme,
perfect enlightenment, and his own thought of enlightenment is not
quenched or used up. Following the Dharma preached, he increases all his
own good dharmas. This is called 'the inexhaustible lamp'" (translated by
Richard H. Robinson, "The Sutra of Vimalakīrti's Preaching," unpublished
manuscript, p. 15).

No. 55

Peach blossoms want to live through the summer,
But the wind and the moon press on—they won't wait.

You may look for men of Han times;
Not a single one still remains![1]

Day by day blossoms alter and fall;
Year by year people transform and change.

Today where we kick up the dust
In olden times was the great sea.[2]

1. The phrase *neng-wu* can mean, "Can it be that there is not?!" But Han-shan seems to use the phrase as a very strong negation—"absolutely none." See also poem 140 and the accompanying note in Iritani and Matsumura *(Kanzanshi*, p. 200).

2. Han-shan seems to know of a story recorded in the *Shen-hsien chuan* (attributed to Ko Hung, 283–343) in the biography of Ma-ku (Chapter 7, pp. 27b–28a in *Li-tai chen-hsien shih-chuan* [Taipei: Tzu-yu, 1970]). There we read that the two immortals, Ma-ku and Wang Yüan, met during the Han dynasty at the home of Ts'ai Ching. Ma-ku said to Wang Yüan, "Since I last waited on you, I've seen the Eastern Sea three times turn into a mulberry field." To which Wang Yüan replied, "The sages all say in the ocean you can repeatedly kick up the dust."

No. 56*

I've seen the neighbor's girl on the East;[1]
In years—she's perhaps eighteen.

The homes to the West all compete in coming to ask
  for her hand;
They wish to marry, to live together as husband and wife.

They'll boil the lamb, stew up the rest of the meats;
All get together and carry out their obscene slaughter.

All grins and smiles—what a delight! Ha! Ha! Ha!
While bleating and wailing, the animals greet death.

*Pulleyblank: Han-shan II
1. The *locus classicus* for the "neighbor's girl on the East" (*tung-chia nü*) is Sung Yü's (fl. 280 B. C.) "Teng T'u-tzu hao-se fu" (*Wen-hsüan* 19: 9b–11b, pp. 254–255), where Sung Yü says: "As for the beautiful women in the world, none are like those of the state of Ch'u; and as for the beauties in Ch'u, none are like those of my village; and as for the beauties in my village, none is like the daughter of my eastern neighbor."

No. 57*

A farmhouse in the country with many mulberry groves;
Oxen and calves fill the cart tracks in the stables.[1]

But I'm willing to believe in cause and effect,[2]
And sooner or later his thick skull will crack.

When with his own eyes he sees [his wealth] bit by bit
    slip away.
He'll at last realize that each thing has a life of its own.[3]

With pants made of paper and drawers made of tile,[4]
In the end, you will die of starvation and cold.

*Pulleyblank: Han-shan II
1. All signs of wealth.
2. For *k'en-hsin*, "willing to believe," Tseng P'u-hsin (*Han-shan shih-chieh* p. 34) has *mao-hsin*, "opposed to belief in"—i.e., "He refuses to believe in . . . But sooner or later." The variant makes sense, but I can find no textual authority for this emendation, and Tseng offers none.
3. i.e., he has no control over his possessions. On "he'll at last realize"—the phrase is *tang-t'ou*; *tang-t'ou pang-ho* is a Zen phrase meaning something like "beating and yelling face to face." It is what Zen masters do to awaken disciples to the error of their ways.
4. i.e., things that are easily destroyed.

No. 58

I've seen tens of hundreds of dogs,
Each one with hair matted and dishevelled.

Those that are sleeping, sleep by themselves.
And those on the move, move about on their own.

But if you toss them a bone,
They'll fight over it, snapping and snarling at one another.

Truly it's because the bones are so few,
And if the dogs are many, there's no way to divide
    them in some equal way.

Note: Tseng (*Han-shan shih-chieh*, p. 35) is probably right in seeing this as an allegory directed against monks, who fight over rice, and common people, who fight over profit. Han-shan clearly knew—and had in mind— the following anecdote recorded in the *Chan-kuo ts'e* (5: 8b, "Ch'in-san"): "All the officers of the empire joined the Alliance and gathered in Chao to urge an attack on Ch'in. 'There is no need to worry over this, your majesty,' said Ch'in's minister, Marquis Ying, to the king of Ch'in. 'Allow me to get rid of them. Ch'in has no quarrel with the officers of the empire. They gather now to make plans for an attack against Ch'in simply because each seeks wealth and fame for himself. Look at your own hounds—some are sleeping, some are up, some walk about and others are simply standing where they are. In any case, they are not fighting. But throw a bone to them and they will all be on their feet in an instant, snapping at each other. Why? You have given them a reason to fight each other" (translated by J. I. Crump, *Chan-kuo Ts'e* [San Francisco: Chinese Materials Center, Inc., 1979], p. 113, item 101, "The dogs and the bone").

No. 59

I strain my eyes to see into the distance;
White clouds—all around like the boundless sea.

The sparrow hawk and the crow are so full they can just barely
    move;
While the *luan* and the *feng*[1], starving, anxiously pace.

Swift-footed steeds are banished to the gravel and rocks,
While lame, feeble donkeys can come to court.

Heaven's too high; we can't ask it why,
But the wrens and the cuckoos are on the Blue Waves.[2]

---

1. The *luan* and *feng* are two fabulous birds that appear in ages of
virtue and peace. *Feng* is often translated as "phoenix." The *feng* is said to
be red in color, the *luan* bluish-green.
    2. On the "Blue Waves" (*ts'ang-lang*), see below.

Note: Iritani and Matsumura (*Kanzanshi*, pp. 94–95) draw attention to the numerous phrases and words in this poem that are found in the *Ch'u-tz'u*, and as they say, it is not that any line in the poem has a direct allusion to a specific line/poem in the *Ch'u-tz'u*; it is rather that the whole is written in the same spirit. Like Ch'ü Yüan, Han-shan laments the lot of the virtuous man living in bad times (the *tristia* theme) who is passed over, when others, less talented and less virtuous, are chosen to serve. Iritani and Matsumura specifically comment on: (1) the phrase "strain my eyes" (*chi-mu*); (2) "see into the distance" (*ch'ang-wang*); (3) the *hsi* particle in the middle of the first line; (4) the phrase "like the boundless sea" (*mang-mang*); (5) the "sparrow hawk and crow" (*ch'ih-ya*) as evil birds (in the *Ch'u-tz'u* it is the sparrow hawk and the owl—*hsiao*); (6) the *luan* and the *feng* as symbols of virtuous men; (7) the phrase "anxiously pace" (*p'ang-huang*); (8) the phrase "feeble donkeys" (*ch'ien-lü*); and (9) mention of the river Ts'ang-lang. Iritani and Matsumura read *chiao-chia* in the last line as *chiao-liao* and see here an allusion to the *Chuang-tzu* (Chapter 1, p. 2), where we read: "When the tailor-bird builds her nest in the deep wood, she uses no more than one branch" (translated by Watson, *The Complete Works*, p. 32). The tailor-bird (or wren) here is like a recluse, and to say that the wren is on (or "in"— *tsai*) the Ts'ang-lang is to draw attention—they feel—to the fact that Ch'ü Yüan committed suicide by drowning. (There is perhaps a touch of irony in the fact that Ch'ü Yüan here would choose the Ts'ang-lang in which to drown, since it is the Ts'ang-lang that the "fisherman" uses as his example in chiding Ch'ü Yüan for not being able to dispassionately adjust to bad times ("When the Cang-lang's waters are clear, I can wash my hat-strings in them; when the Cang-lang's waters are muddy, I can wash my feet in them" [translated by Hawkes, *The Songs of the South*, p. 207]). My own feeling is that "the wrens on the Ts'ang-lang" is another sign of things being out of order: wrens and cuckoos (the *chia* is the *tu-chüan* [cuckoo]—Read, *Chinese Materia Medica: Avian Drugs*, item 306, p. 73) are not water birds— they should not be where they are.

No. 60

Lo-yang has lots of young girls,
Who on spring days flaunt their beauty and charm.

Together they snap off the flowers by the road,
Each putting some into her lofty chignon.

Chignons so lofty—with flowers encircling the knot;
When men see them they all glare and leer.

"Don't seek tender feelings from us;[1]
We're about to go home and see our husbands!" [2]

1. On *shan-shan lien*, line 7, I can find no gloss of *shan-shan; shan* by itself means "sour," "the taste of vinegar." Ch'en (*Han-shan-tzu*, p. 269) understands *shan-shan* in the sense of *lien-ai*, "tender love." Iritani and Matsumura (*Kanzanshi*, p. 96) read *shan-shan* as *ts'an-ts'an*, which normally means sad, but here they feel it means "deep love or affection." Tseng P'u-hsin (*Han-shan shih-chieh*, p. 36) seems to suggest that it's the kind of affection/desire that makes your mouth water (as with sour things).

2. The last two lines are open to a number of interpretations. For example, they might also say, "Purposely seeking warm, tender love; they wear them home to show to their husbands."

No. 61

Girls in the spring show off their good looks and style;
Together they head for the edge of the southern fields.

Looking at flowers, they lament the lateness of day;
They sit in the shade of a tree, fearing that the wind
    might blow.

A young man comes over from the side of the road
On a white horse with bridle of gold.[1]

"Why must you bother us so long?
Our husbands might find out!"

1. See note 1 to poem 54.

No. 62

A flock of maidens out to play in the evening sun;
A breeze comes up, filling the road with their fragrant
    perfume.

Sewn onto their skirts, butterflies of gold;
Tucked into their chignons, Mandarin ducks of jade.

Their young ladies-in-waiting wear kerchiefs[1] of red
    gauze;
Eunuchs, dressed in trousers of purple brocade.

They've come to observe one who has lost his way;
Temple hair turning white—his heart filled with concern.

1. Agreeing with Ch'en Hui-chien *(Han-shan-tzu* p. 249) that *chen,* which normally means "closely knit," must here be a noun. He suggests reading it as *chieh,* meaning "kerchief."

Comment: The last two lines are open to a number of interpretations. Tseng P'u-hsin *(Han-shan shih-chieh,* p. 37) would make them a question— "Did they give a look to someone who has lost his way, someone whose temple hair . . . ?" Watson follows this approach in his translation. But there is nothing in the Chinese to indicate interrogative mode. One might also read, "Having observed *them,* one who has lost his way; His temples turn white—his heart filled with concern."

No. 63

If you run into a demon or ghost,
The first thing is never be frightened or alarmed.[1]

Be calm and firm, never pay it any heed;
If you call out its name, it must certainly leave.[2]

To burn incense and ask for strength from the Buddha,
Or respectfully bow and seek aid from monks

Is like a mosquito biting a iron ox;
It has no place to sink in its teeth.[3]

1. Iritani and Matsumura (*Kanzanshi*, p. 99) note *ti-i mo* ("the first thing is never . . . ") as T'ang colloquial for a strong prohibition.

2. For Chinese belief that certain demons are harmless and disappear if you know and call out their true names, see, for example, Chapter 17 in the "Nei-p'ien" of Ko Hung's *Pao-p'u-tzu* (especially 17: 4a–5a). In James Ware's translation of this section of text, the relevant passage begins: "The mountain power in the form of a little boy hopping backward on one foot likes to come and harm people. If you hear a human voice at night in the mountains talking loud, its name is Ch'i. By knowing this name and shouting it, you will prevent it from harming you." And the passage concludes—after listing the names/titles of a variety of demons—with the words: "Only if you know the names of these creatures will they be unable to harm you" (translated by James R. Ware, *Alchemy, Medicine and Religion in the China of A. D. 320: The Nei P'ien of Ko Hung* [New York: Dover Publications Inc., 1981], pp. 287–289.)

3. i.e., such methods will have no effect. The example of the mosquito biting an iron ox might have been common within Zen schools. We find the phrase once again in the notes to "model 58" of the *Pi-yen lu* (Blue Cliff Record; originally compiled in 1128). For the text, see T.2003 (Vol. 48, p. 191 middle); the note is translated in Thomas and J. C. Cleary, translaters, *The Blue Cliff Record*, Volume II (Boulder, CO: Shambhala, 1977), p. 382.

No. 64

Vast, overwhelming, the waters of the Yellow River;
They flow to the East—on and on without end.[1]

Distant, distant, we do not see them clear,
[But for] person after person, life comes to an end.

If you wish to ride the white clouds,
What must you do to sprout wings?

At the time when your hair is still black,[2]
Whether moving or still, you must exert all your strength.[3]

1. In the *Tso chuan* (Duke Hsiang, year 8—566 B. C.; Vol. 1, p. 265) one Tzu-ssu begins his speech urging that Lu join forces with Ch'u in attacking Cheng with the words, "In the poetry of the Chou (*Chou-shih*) it says, 'If we wait for the [Yellow] River to clear—how long is man's life?'" That the Yellow River never clears was *clearly* well known for a long time in China. On this line, Hakuin (*Kanzanshi Sendai kibun*, 1: 57–58) also cites Wang tzu-nien's *Shih-i chi* (cited in the *Shih-wen lei-chü ch'ien-chi* 16), which says, "Cinnabar Mound burns once in a thousand years; the Yellow River clears once in a thousand years."

2. As a youth or young adult.

3. But does Han-shan mean do all you can to attain immortality— i.e., work at the Taoist techniques of long life—or does *nu-li*, "exert all your strength" here mean—as it seems to mean in poem 53—that we may as well enjoy ourselves while we can?

No. 65

Riding this rotten wood boat,[1]
We gather the fruit of the *nimba*.[2]

Moving, I go out into the sea,
Where the billowy waves roll on and on without end.[3]

We've just brought provisions for one night,
But to that other shore—it's still 3000 li.

From what is *kleśa* produced?
Sad indeed! The arising of causal-made pain.[4]

1. Han-shan's way of talking about the body, or perhaps the Self, the five *skandhas* in Buddhism, the five constituents of being: form, feeling, will, perception, and consciousness.

2. The *nimba* (*jen-p'o*; *Azadirachta indica*) is a tree with very bitter seeds and fruit. The nimba is specifically compared to *kleśa* at the start of Chapter 34 of the *Nirvāṇa-sūtra* ("Chia-yeh p'u-sa p'in," Pt. 4; T.375, Vol. 12, p. 831 top), where we read: "Of *kleśa* there are two kinds: one is cause and the other is effect. Because the cause is evil, the effect is therefore evil; because the effect is evil, therefore the seeds are evil. It's like the fruit of the *nimba*—since the seeds are bitter, the flowers, fruit, stem, and leaves are all bitter."

3. The "water and the waves" is a favorite metaphor in Chinese Buddhism. The water by itself—calm, clear, unmoved—stands for true reality, the undifferentiated one, the one mind of the T'ien-t'ai and Hua-yen. The waves in the analogy thus represent the differentiated world, perception of discrete, real things, the waves being caused by the winds of karma.

4. So it is karma that brings about pain. Note how this goes back to the first couplet; we gather the bitter (*k'u* "pain" in the last line) fruit of our actions.

No. 66

If you are silent and never speak,
What will the next generation transmit?[1]

If you live retired in thicket and woods
How will your bright wisdom ever appear?

Withered, decayed trees are not a strong defense;[2]
With wind and frost, they suffer early death and disease.

With a clay-ox plowing a field of rocks,
You'll never have a rice-harvest day.[3]

1. Alluding to the words of Tzu-kung, recorded in *Analects* 17: 17 (p. 36). D. C. Lau translates (*Confucius: The Analects*, p. 146 [17: 19]): "The Master said, 'I am thinking of giving up speech.' Tzu-kung said, 'If you did not speak, what would there be for us, your disciples, to transmit?' "

2. To protect or "defend" your life (*wei-sheng*) means to take care of your health—something a recluse might find it difficult to do.

3. The uselessness of rocky fields is pointed out by Wu Tzu-hsü in his words, "To realize our will against Ch'i is like obtaining a rocky field— there's no use in it" (*Tso chuan*, Duke Ai, year 11 [482 B. C.]; Vol. 1, p. 482). A "clay-ox" (*t'u-niu*) is presumably one intended for regular soil, but it could also be an ox *made* of clay.

No. 67

Here in the mountains—so very cold;
It's been this way from of old—it's not just this year.

Peak piled upon peak—constantly clotted with snow;
Dark, secluded woods—every day spewing forth mist.

Here things start to grow only after Grain is in Beard,[1]
And the leaves are coming down, even before the Beginning
of Fall.[2]

And here—here is a traveller hopelessly lost,
Who looks and looks but can't see the sky.[3]

1. *Mang-chung* is one of the twenty-four divisions of the Chinese ag-
ricultural year, a period of fifteen days in the middle of June (June 7–22).
2. "Beginning of Fall" (*li-ch'iu*) occurs in the middle of August, about
August 8–24.
3. In Buddhism the sky is sometimes a symbol of the enlightened
mind, especially in Mahāyāna Buddhism, where it is equated with *śūnyatā*,
emptiness. It is clear, undifferentiated, without obstacle; it is only the
clouds of ignorance that prevent us from seeing it. One wonders if—in a
Zen sense—it is not Han-shan's trying to see the sky that prevents him
from seeing it.

No. 68

A sojourner in the mountains—heart troubled and concerned;
Constantly lamenting the seasons passing by.

Bitterly I toil to gather mushrooms and thistles;[1]
Can all this sorting and choosing really make me immortal?

My courtyard opens up as the clouds start to roll away;
Woods are bright—the moon perfectly full.

Why have I not gone back home?
The cassia trees make me reluctant to leave.[2]

1. Mushrooms and thistles are staple fare for seekers of long life. My "thistles" translates *chu*, *Atractylis*, for which an alternate name is *shan-chi*, "mountain thistle." On "*Atractylis*," G. A. Stuart (*Chinese Materia Medica: Vegetable Kingdom* [Taipei: Southern Materials Center, Inc. 1979; originally published 1911], pp. 57–58), notes that the "drug is a warm, stomachic, stimulant, arthritic, tonic, and diuretic remedy used in fevers, catarrh, chronic dysentery, general dropsy, rheumatism, profuse sweating, and apoplexy. It enters into the composition of several of the most famous prescriptions in use among the native faculty. Among these may be mentioned the Ku-chen-tan, 'strengthening virility elixir'; the Pu-lao-tan, 'elixir of longevity'; and the Ling-chih-tan, 'elixir of felicity.' "
2. "Cassia trees" (*kuei*) are associated with recluses and immortals and immortality in the *Ch'u-tz'u* and elsewhere. The relevant evidence is compiled by Iritani and Matsumura (*Kanzanshi*, pp. 20–21) in their notes to poem 295 (their poem no. 9).
Note: The third couplet seems to describe—in Han-shan's way—an enlightenment experience; the clouds of delusion are gone, and the bright moon of wisdom is full and clear. The full moon is a stock Buddhist image of the enlightened mind.

No. 69

There's a man sitting[1] in a mountain pass;[2]
The clouds roll up around him! Rose-colored clouds hem him in.

He holds in his hand a fragrant flower! Which he hopes to
    transmit;[3]
But the road is long! Difficult to travel that far.

In his heart, disappointment and regret—also suspicion and
    doubt;
In years already old, having accomplished nothing at all.

The crowd ho-ho's this worn-out nag,[4]
But he stands alone! In being loyal and pure.

1. Reading the variant of *tso*, "sit," for the particle *hsi*. I here follow
the *Tse-shih chü* text (14a), which has five-character lines throughout (also
see Iritani and Matsumura [*Kanzanshi*, pp. 104–106] and Ch'en Hui-chien
[*Han-shan-tzu*, pp. 185–186]). In the CTS text, lines 4 and 5 are six-character
lines with the particle *hsi* in the middle. In the CTS text, the particle *hsi*
occurs in lines 1–5 and 8; in the *Tse-shih chü* text, it occurs in lines 2–4 and
8. I use ! to indicate *hsi*.
    2. Reading the variant of *hsing*, mountain pass, for *ying*, "pillar."
    3. One is reminded of the Zen *kōan*, "Buddha Twirls a Flower,"
where he "transmits" the truth of Zen to Kāśyapa in this way. See, for example, Paul Reps, translator, *Zen Flesh, Zen Bones* (New York: Anchor
Books), p. 95—*kōan* no. 6 in "The Gateless Gate." If this allusion is intended by Han-shan, his meaning in saying the "road goes on and on"
might be that the distance separating him from the world is too great for
him to make contact with people and transmit the beauty that he has
found. But the *Ch'u-tz'u* imagery and language (see below) make it more
likely that Han-shan identifies with Ch'ü Yüan—i.e., the "flower" represents his virtue and talent, which he hopes will be used.

4. The CTS mistakenly has *chien*, "cripple" or "worn-out horse," at the start of line 8. On the "feeble donkey," see poem 59 and accompanying notes.

Note: Iritani and Matsumura (*Kanzanshi*, pp. 104–106) again point out the obvious *Ch'u-tz'u* imagery in this poem. As *Ch'u-tz'u* phrases and terms—in addition to the particle *hsi*—they cite "the road is long" (*lu-man*); "disappointment and regret" (*ch'ou-ch'ang*); "suspicion and doubt" (*hu-i*); "no accomplishment" (*wu-ch'eng*); "ho-ho" (*wo-i*); "this nag" (*ssu-chien*); "I stand alone" (*tu-li*); and "loyal and pure" (*chung-chen*). They also note that the opening strongly resembles the opening of "Shan-kuei" (Mountain Spirit) in the "Nine Songs"; for the text, see *Ch'u-tz'u* 2: 19b–22a (pp. 33–35), translated by Hawkes in *The Songs of the South*, pp. 115–116.

No. 70

Pigs eat the flesh of dead men,
And men eat the guts of dead pigs.

Pigs don't seem to mind human stench,
And men—to the contrary—say pig meat smells sweet.[1]

When pigs die, throw them into the water;
When men die, dig them a hole in the ground.[2]

If they never ate one another,
Lotus blossoms would sprout in water that bubbles and boils.[3]

---

1. The Chinese word for sausage in *hsiang-ch'ang*, "fragrant" or "sweet-smelling" bowels.

2. I am reading this as imperative—this is really what we should do. But Han-shan could just be making a statement: "When pigs die, we throw them into the water," and so forth.

3. I assume this is Han-shan's way of saying this is never going to happen.

No. 71

What a delight! The body of chaos;[1]
We didn't eat—what's more we didn't piss!

But then it happened that someone drilled and bored;
Because of this we have the nine holes.[2]

Day after day, we make clothing and food;[3]
Year after year—fret over taxes and rent.[4]

A thousand people will fight for one coin;
Forming a crowd and shouting for all they're worth.

1. *Hun-tun*—chaos—is the condition that existed before differentiation occurred. Han-shan has in mind the story in *Chuang-tzu*, Chapter 7 (p. 21, lines 33–35), where the emperors of the Southern and Northern seas bore holes in Chaos so that he too can see, hear, and breathe. On the seventh day of boring (there are seven holes in chaos in the *Chuang-tzu* version), he died. For Watson's translation, see *The Complete Works*, p. 97. For a detailed study of the chaos theme in early Taoist thought, see Norman Girardot, *Myth and Meaning in Early Taoism* (Berkeley, CA: University of California Press, 1983).

2. Two eyes, two ears, and so on. The story in *Chuang-tzu* only mentions the seven holes in the head.

3. Or "we work for the sake of clothing and food."

4. *Tsu-tiao* (my "taxes and rent") was the T'ang system of taxation requiring fixed amounts of cloth and grain each year from each eligible male. See D. C. Twitchett, *Financial Administration under the T'ang Dynasty* (Cambridge: Cambridge University Press, 1970), especially Chapter II.

No. 72

Weeping and wailing—what is the cause?
Tears, like beads of pearls.

There must be some parting or separation,
Or worse than this—someone has met with disaster and
    death.[1]

If your lot is with the destitute and poor,
You'll never be able to understand cause and effect.

In the graveyard I look at corpses of the dead,
But the six paths don't concern me.[2]

1. I take Han-shan here to be answering the question raised in line 1—these are the causes. But the couplet could as well simply state the facts of life—of necessity, there will be separation and death, so why bother to weep? Such appears to be the interpretation of Iritani and Matsumura (*Kanzanshi*, p. 109).

2. The "six paths" (*liu-tao* six *gatis*) are the six possibilities for rebirth: (1) in hell, (2) as a hungry ghost, (3) as an animal, (4) as an asura (demon), (5) as a human, and (6) as a god (deva). Tseng (*Han-shan shih-chieh*, p. 43) understands the "me" of this line to be the true Self speaking, the Buddha-nature inside.

No. 73

Womenfolk idle when it comes to weaving the warp;
The menfolk too lazy to hoe in the fields.

Frivolously addicted to shooting at birds;[1]
Tapping time with their dancing slippers, they pluck
    and they strum on the strings.

If you're worried about freezing your bones, you must be
    anxious about making your clothes;
If you want to fill up your belly, growing the food
    is the first thing to do.

And now who will think about you,
As you bitterly cry out to the sky?

---

1. Literally, the text says they are addicted to "carrying crossbow pellets under their arms," *hsia-tan*.

No. 74

Not to practice the "true and orthodox way,"[1]
But follow perversions[2]—we call them "devout old hags."[3]

Their mouths rarely confess their shame to the gods
      and the Buddhas,
While their hearts are full of jealousy and hate.

Behind your back they're eating fish and meat,
While in front of others they chant Buddha's name.

If this is the way you cultivate yourself,
It will be difficult indeed to escape from the river of hell.[4]

---

1. *Chen-cheng tao*, a common phrase used for the Buddhist way.
2. *Hsieh*, probably short here for *hsieh-chien*, *mithyā-dṛṣṭi*, "per-verted views."
3. *Hsing-p'o* are old women believers.
4. Named *nai-ho*.

No. 75

In this world there's one class of fool,
Who's dazed and bewildered—just like a mule!

Oh, he still understands human speech,
But with his desire and lust, in form he's more like a pig.

The steep place [where he lives] is difficult to fathom;[1]
[It's where] true words, to the contrary, turn into the false.

Who is there that can talk to him?
To let him know he should never live here.[2]

1. *Hsien-hsi* means "steep and difficult to climb." I believe the point is that these people are so far removed from common, sensible people that one cannot even guess what is on their minds.
2. The "here" is ambiguous; it might mean here in this cut-off realm, or it might mean here in the world with the rest of us.

No. 76

There's a fellow whose surname is Haughty-and-Rude;
His name, Greed—his nickname Dishonest.

There's not a speck of understanding in him!
In all things, a person detested by others.

Death he hates like the bitter Gold Thread;[1]
Life he fondly regards, like the sweetness of crystalline
    honey.

He still hasn't stopped eating fish;
In eating meat, all the more, he never gets his fill.

1. On *huang-lien* as "Golden Thread," see Read, *Chinese Medicinal Plants*, p. 170, item 534. Stuart (*Chinese Materia Medica: Vegetable Kingdom*, p. 125) identifies *huang-lien* as "*Coptis teeta*" and notes that "the color of the main portion is a deep, rich yellow. The taste is intensely bitter, but aromatic. The more brittle the root is, the more highly its reputed virtues. It is regarded by Chinese doctors as a sort of panacea for a great many ills. It is supposed to clear inflamed eyes, to benefit the chest, to combat fever, and to act as an alternative or alexipharmic drug."

No. 77

Even if you live [in a house of] rhinoceros horn[1]
Or wrap yourself 'round[2] with belts of the eyeballs of
 tigers,[3]

Use branches of peach to rid yourself of pollution[4]
Or make necklaces of garlic buds,

Warm your stomach with dogwood wine[5]
Or empty your mind with Medlar broth,[6]

In the end you'll return—you'll not escape death;
A waste of yourself, the search for long life.

1. i.e., consume that much. For the marvelous medicinal properties of "rhinoceros horn" (*hsi-chüeh*), see Read, *Chinese Materia Medica: Animal Drugs* (Taipei: Southern Materials Center, 1976), item 355. Quoting in part, we read that it is used "to cure devil possession and keep away all evil spirits and miasmas . . . to remove hallucinations and bewitching nightmares. Continuous administration lightens the body and makes one very robust. For typhoid, headache, and feverish colds . . . to dispel fear and anxiety, to calm the liver and clear the vision."

2. Reading *jao*, "abundant," as *jao*, "to surround."

3. Again see Read, *Animal Drugs*, item 351. I quote: "The ball is macerated overnight in fresh sheep's blood, then separated and dried over a low flame and powdered. For epilepsy, malaria, fevers in children, and convulsions."

4. The apotropaic qualities of the peach in China are well known. See, for example, Bodde's discussion of the "Peachwood Gate Gods," during the "Great Exorcism" in the Han in *Festivals in Classical China* (Princeton: Princeton University Press, 1975), pp. 127–138.

5. "Dogwood" is a common dictionary gloss for *chu-yü*. Hu Shiu-yin (*An Enumeration of Chinese Materia Medica* [Hong Kong: The Chinese University Press, 1980], p. 21) says it is Evodia (*Evodia rutaecarpa*). Stuart (*Chinese Materia Medica: Vegetable Kingdom*, p. 479) lists a *chu-yü-chou*, which he identifies as *Congee of Boymia rutaecarpa* and notes that it is a "carminative and [is] recommended for pain in the bowels."

6. For "Medlar" (*kou-ch'i*), Hu (*An Enumeration*, p. 53) has "Chinese matrimony-vine" (*Lycium chinense*). Stuart (*Chinese Materia Medica: Vegetable Kingdom*, pp. 436 and 483) notes both a *kou-chi-chiu* ("Tincture of *Lycium chinense*") and a *kou-chi-chien* ("Decoction of *Lycium chinense*"). Of the former he says, "The seeds of the plant are boiled soft, the pulp expressed, and fermented with rice and leaven. . . . This is a tonic preparation and is useful especially in sexual debility." On the latter, "In the spring and summer the stalk and leaves are used, and in the autumn and winter the root and seeds. . . . It is prescribed as a tonic and antifebrile remedy. It is also said to abort cancerous swellings."

No. 78

By divining I chose a remote spot to live;
T'ien-t'ai—there's nothing further to say.

Gibbons wail—the valley mist, damp and cold;
The glow from the peak reaches to my straw door.

I break off some leaves to cover my home in the pines;
Build a pond, channelling water in from a spring.

Already content that bothersome matters are all put to rest,[1]
I pick bracken to live out the rest of my years.[2]

1. *Hsiu wan-shih* (or *wan-shih hsiu*), literally "put to rest the 10,000 affairs," is commonly used in Zen to indicate the state of mind of one sitting in meditation. See Appendix II, "Buddhist Terms," for other such occurrences in the poems of Han-shan.

2. Iritani and Matsumura (*Kanzanshi*, p. 115) indicate a possible allusion to the Po I/Shu Ch'i story (see note 4 to poem 8) in this last line with the reference to picking "bracken" (*chüeh*): Po I and Shu Ch'i ate ferns (*wei*) in retirement but eventually starved to death.

Note: The actions of picking and breaking off occur a number of places in the poem. Han-shan "picks by divination" (*pu-tse*) this remote place to live in line 1 and picks (*ts'ai*) bracken ferns at the end. He breaks off (*che*) leaves in line 5 and lives in a place broken off from the rest of the world.

No. 79

"To increase" means to increase one's essence;[1]
This can be called "the increased."[2]

"To change" means to change one's form;
To this we give the name "the changed."

If you can increase and what's more can change,
Then you can ascend to the registers of the immortals.

If you can neither increase nor change,
In the end you'll not avoid misfortune and death.

1. "Essence," *ching*, is one of three vital powers in the body, according to the Taoists, the other two being *shen*, "spirit," and *ch'i*, "breath." Essence is normally identified with semen in men and with a comparable fluid in women.

2. Or "beneficial." The word is *i*, which means both "to increase" and "to be beneficial."

Note: Iritani and Matsumura (*Kanzanshi*, p. 117) note that elsewhere Han-shan seems to speak out against Taoist long-life practices; they feel this poem shows that there was more than one author of the Han-shan poems. They also point out the remarkably similar lines to these found in Chapter 56 of the Sung, Taoist encyclopedia, *Yün-chi ch'i-ch'ien* (HY 1032, *Cheng-t'ung Tao-tsang*, Vol. 37, p. 29714 bottom): "Of the so-called 'Way of increase and change'—'to increase' means to increase one's essence; 'to change' means to change one's form. If you can increase and can change, your name will ascend to the registers of the immortals; If you neither increase nor change, you'll not depart from misfortune and death." Either the *Yün-chi ch'i-ch'ien* is using the words of Han-shan, or—what seems more likely—both texts follow some common Taoist source.

No. 80

In vain I labored to explain the Three Histories;[1]
Wasted my time, reading through the Five Classics.[2]

As old age comes on, I examine the Imperial Records;[3]
As before, I live as a common man.

Divining with milfoil, I meet with the hexagram
    "Obstruction;"[4]
In control of my life, the star "Emptiness and Danger."[5]

I'll not be so lucky as the tree by the stream,
Which year after year has its season of green.[6]

1. Normally understood to be the *Historical Records* (*Shih-chi*), the *History of Han* (*Han shu*), and the *History of Latter Han* (*Hou Han shu*).

2. The *Book of Songs* (*Shih*), the *Book of Documents* (*Shu*), the *Book of Changes* (*I*), the *Record of Rites* (*Li-chi*), and the *Spring and Autumn Annals* (*Ch'un-ch'iu*).

3. Following Iritani and Matsumura (*Kanzanshi*, p. 118) in understanding *huang-chi* to mean census reports. His position therefore is that of a lowly scribe. Ch'en Hui-chien (*Han-shan-tzu*, p. 200) and Tseng P'u-hsin (*Han-shan shih-chieh*, p. 47), however, both understand *huang-chi* to mean Taoist books on immortality. Their understanding of line 4 would thus be that so far this study has done him no good.

4. Hexagram 39, *chien*. "Obstruction" is Wilhelm's translation: see Richard Wilhelm, *The I Ching or Book of Changes* (Princeton, NJ: Princeton University Press, 1950), pp. 151–154.

5. The star *hsü-wei*. Chinese believe that one's fate is controlled by the star/constellation dominant in the skies at the moment of birth. *Hsü-wei* apparently refers to the "lunar lodging" (*hsiu*) *hsü*, a constellation of two stars that Edward Schafer (*Pacing the Void: T'ang Approaches to the Stars* [Berkeley, CA: University of California Press, 1977], p. 81) translates as "Barrens." This is the lodging of the moon in the last month of fall, and it controls length of life and wealth. There is a star close by *hsü* said to control danger (*ssu-wei*).

6. Perhaps an oblique allusion to the title of poem 2 of the "Nineteen Old Poems" of Han—"Green, green the grasses by the stream" (*ch'ing-ch'ing ho-p'an ts'ao*) (for the text, see *Wen-hsüan* 29: 2ab, p. 397; Watson has a translation in *Chinese Lyricism*, p. 23).

No. 81*

Emerald-green stream—water in the spring crystal clear;
Moon over Han-shan dazzling white.

Silently I know that my soul by itself is enlightened;
As I see into the truth of emptiness, the external spheres
become more and more still and serene.[1]

*Pulleyblank: Han-shan II.
1. "See into . . . " is *kuan-k'ung*, to see into or "contemplate" in meditation (*vipaśyanā*) the emptiness (*śūnyatā*) of all things. The "external
spheres" (*ching*) means the external world as perceived by the senses and
mind.

No. 82

At present I have but one coat;
It's not made of gauze, and it's not made of silk.

You may ask, "Of what shade is it made?"
Well, it's not red, but it's also not purple.[1]

In the summer I treat it as a shirt;
In the winter it gets used for a quilt.

Winter and summer, this way then that it gets used;
Throughout the whole year I've just got this one.

1. Red and purple (*hung-tzu*) appear in a later poem (No. 241—but there it is *chu-tzu*) as the colors of clothes worn by high-ranking officials and the rich. That all seems in line with the fact that this coat is also not made of "gauze" or "silk." Han-shan might also have in mind, however, a line from the *Analects* (*Lun-yü* 10: 5, p. 18). Arthur Waley (*The Analects of Confucius* [New York: Vintage, 1938], p. 147) translates: "A gentleman does not wear facings of purple or mauve, nor in undress does he use pink or roan." He explains in a note that his "roan" is usually translated as purple and that these colors were avoided by gentlemen because they were reserved for periods of fasting and mourning.

No. 83*

White duster with candana handle;[1]
Its fragrant odor can be smelled all day.

Supple and gentle, like rolling fog;
Waving and fluttering, similar to drifting clouds.

Respectfully presented to guests, it fittingly goes with the
    summer;
Lifted up high, it brushes off dust.

Time after time in the chambers of abbots,[2]
It's used to point out the way to those who are lost.[3]

*Pulleyblank: Han-shan II.
1. A variety of sandalwood grown in India.
2. "Chambers of abbots" can also be simply "abbots;" *fang-chang* means both the room and the one who occupies it.

3. The "duster" (*fu-tzu*) figures prominently in stories of Zen masters. Charles Luk—*Ch'an and Zen Teaching*, Series Two (London: Rider & Company, 1961), pp. 75–76—translates the following anecdote from the *Ching-te ch'uan-teng lu*: "Yang Shan replied, 'I had (some) experience of this; when I saw monks coming from all quarters, I raised my dust-whisk and asked them, "In your places, is this one expounded or not?" I again asked them, 'Apart from this one, what have the elder masters been doing in your places?' Ling Yu praised the master and said, 'From olden times this has always been the Sect's tooth and nail.' " Luk then notes (p. 76, note 1): "The act of raising the dust-whisk is the performance of great function to show that which raises it. Yang Shan meant, 'At your monasteries, do your masters directly point at the mind to teach you how to realize your self-nature and attain Buddhahood?' 'This one' in Ch'an indicates that which raises the dust-whisk but not the whisk itself. The second question, 'What have the old masters been doing?' means what have been their activities, or performance of function in accordance with the transmission of mind, to enlighten their disciples. Kuei Shan praised Yang Shan for his use of all the best devices of the Sect to receive and guide visiting monks, because his method was the direct pointing at the mind as taught by Bodhidharma."

No. 84**

Through covetousness and greed some people look for the happy
life;
They do not know that calamity awaits them in this body of
one hundred years.

But they only need see the dust in the glow[1] or the bubbles
that float in the foam;
Then they'll understand that impermanence ruins
and destroys all men.

The great man—when his spirit and will are straight and firm
like iron;
When he does not bend to corruption—the Way in his heart
being naturally true.

When his conduct is thorough, his integrity high—like
bamboo under the frost;[2]
Only then does he know not to vainly use soul and mind.

**Seven-character lines.
1. *Yang-yen* are the dust particles seen in rays of the sun.
2. The metaphor of the bamboo—the intention appearing to be that
the bamboo, or at least the best bamboo, is unaffected by the frost, not
wilting or bending—appears to carry through the entire line. The great
man's conduct is thorough (*mi*), just as the bamboo remains "dense" (also
mi), and his integrity (*chieh*) is high, just as the joints in the bamboo (also
chieh) remain high, since it refuses to bend.

No. 85*

So many different people,
With hundreds of plans for seeking profit and fame.

In their hearts they covet the search for glory and honor;
In managing their affairs, they think only of wealth and rank.

Before their minds know the briefest moment of rest,
Off they go in a rush, like mist and smoke.

Family members—truly one close-knit group;
One single call, and one hundred will, "Yes, Yes," appear.

But before seventy years have passed;
The ice will melt and the tiles will be broken, cast away.[1]

When you're dead, all things come to an end;
Who will go on as your heir?

When mud pellets are submerged in water,
Then you know they're neither intelligence nor smarts![2]

---

*Pulleyblank: Han-shan II.

1. Han-shan adds the character (*chih*), "throw away"(?) to this well-known four-character phrase—*ping-hsiao wa-chieh*, a way of saying that something totally falls apart—in this case, the family that seemed so united. See poem 38, note 2.

2. Because they dissolve into nothingness. The mud pellet—we assume—is a metaphor for the family mentioned before; there too the cohesion is only temporary. But it could as well be a general metaphor for life.

No. 86

Greedy people love piles of goods,
Just like the owl loves its young.

But when owls grow up, they eat their mothers;[1]
Lots of possessions also cause harm.

Get rid of them, and good luck is born;
Amass them—disasters arise.

Have no possessions, and you'll have no disasters;
Then you can flap your wings in the blue clouds.

1. For Chinese traditions on the owl (*hsiao*)—including the belief that the young eat their mothers when they grow up—see Read, *Chinese Materia Medica . . . Avian Drugs*, pp. 87–88, item 316.

No. 87

Away from home, ten thousand li,
You lift up your swords to strike the Hsiung-nu.

If you get the advantage, then they will die;
If you lose it, then it's your loss of life.

If it's their life; you show no compassion;
So if it's your life—once again, in that, what is the crime?

If I taught you "the technique that would not fail,"[1]
Not to covet would be the best plan.

1. Literally, a "one hundred victory" technique.

No. 88

Anger is the fire in the heart[1]
That can burn up a forest of merit.

If you wish to walk the bodhisattva's path,
With patience[2] protect the true mind.

1. Anger/hatred (*ch'en, dveṣa*) is one of the "three poisons" (*san-tu*) in Buddhism: the other two are greed (*t'an, rāga*) and ignorance or delusion (*ch'ih, moha*). See Appendix II for references to these terms in Han-shan's poems.
2. *Jen-ju, kṣānti.*

No. 89**

For the sake of burying your heads in stupidity, dizzy and dim,
You love the direction of ignorance—the demons' dark cave.[1]

Time and again I've urged you to start cultivation early;
But on this you've remained obstinately stupid, minds
        unconscious, confused!

Unwilling to believe and accept the words of Han-shan,
You turn and you turn, doubly increasing karma's waves.[2]

You'll just have to wait 'til they cut off your head and divide
        you in two,
Then you'll know that your own body is a thing that
        is both slave and thief!

**Seven-character lines.
    1. Literally, the cave of the *rākṣasas, lo-ch'a,* demons best known for
their habit of eating people.
    2. Remembering that waves, in the analogy of water and waves,
stand for deluded perception of a differentiated world—the waves being
caused by the winds of *karma.* The text does not literally say "increasing
waves"; rather, it has *ku-ku,* the sound made by lapping waves.

No. 90

The evil destinies[1]—so terribly boundless and vast;
Dim and dark, lacking the light of the sun.

Among men, eight hundred years[2]
Still can't compare in length to living in here half a night.

At this level, that whole lot of fools.
Just to discuss their situation can bring me great pain.

I urge you, sir, to seek release,[3]
To recognize and hold on to the Dharma-king.[4]

1. *O-ch'ü* the three evil destinies are: (1) to go to hell, (2) to become a hungry ghost, or (3) to be reborn as an animal.
    2. Probably an indirect allusion to P'eng-tsu, China's Methusaleh, who is said to have lived eight hundred years.
    3. *Ch'u-li*, release from attachments (*upādāna*).
    4. Literally, the text has the "king in the dharma" (*fa-chung wang*), and Iritani and Matsumura (*Kanzanshi*, pp. 129–130) feel that, on the basis of a similar line at the end of poem 162 (see below—"To recognize and hold on to the king and lord of the heart," *hsin wang-chu*), "dharma" here refers to the ten thousand things or the lord of the ten thousand things, the heart. Thus *fa-chung wang* would be "the king in the heart"—i.e., the Bud-dha. However we arrive, the point is the same—we should recognize and hold on to the Buddha inside.

No. 91[†]

The world has lots of "wise"men;
Stupid dolts! Who bitterly labor in vain.

They do not seek future good;
Only know to create the causes of evil.

The Five Perversions[1] and Ten Evils[2] are their kind,
The Three Poisons[3] they take as their kin.

The minute they die they go into hell;
There forever, like the silver kept at the mint.[4]

[†]Missing from the *Tse-shih-chü ts'ung-shu* and *Kunaichō* Library editions.

1. The *wu-ni* (*Pañcānantarya*), on which Soothill and Hodous have: "The five rebellious acts or deadly sins, parricide, matricide, killing an arhat, shedding the blood of a Buddha, destroying the harmony of the sangha, or fraternity" (*A Dictionary of Chinese Buddhist Terms*, p. 128).

2. *Shih-o* (*Daśākuśala*); Soothill and Hodous (*Dictionary*, p. 50) list them as: "killing, stealing, adultery, lying, double-tongue, coarse language, filthy language, covetousness, anger, perverted views."

3. Anger, greed, and ignorance—see poem 88, note 1.

4. i.e., silver that is never taken out.

No. 92

Heaven high, high—without limit;
Earth thick, thick—no extreme.

Living things lie in between;
Relying on their powers of creation.

Head-on they clash as they search for full bellies and warmth,
Making their plans to gobble each other up.

Cause and effect—neither examined with care;
Like a blind boy asking the color of milk.[1]

1. An allusion to the *Nirvāṇa-sūtra* (Ch. 14, "Sheng-hsing p'in"; T.374, Vol. 12, p. 446 bottom, 447 top), where the impossibility of heretics' (i.e., non-Buddhists—*wai-tao*, the *tīrthikas*) understanding the "four *pāramitā*" of knowledge and the four qualities of *nirvāṇa* (*ch'ang lo wo ching*—permanence, bliss, self, and purity) is compared to the impossibility of a blind man understanding the color of milk. The text reads: "It is like the case of a man born blind, who does not know the color of milk: he would then ask someone else what the color of milk is like. The other person would respond that the color is white like that of the cowry. The blind man would then further ask, 'Is the color of milk like the cowry in sound?' The other would reply, 'No.' So he would further ask, 'What is the color of a cowry like?' The other man would reply, 'It's like the tip of a rice stalk.' The blind man would then further ask, 'Is the color of milk soft and pliant like the tip of a rice stalk? What's more, what is the tip of a rice stalk like?' Someone would answer, 'It's like the snow that rains down.' The blind man would then continue, 'This tip of a rice stalk—is it cold like snow? Snow, furthermore, is like what?' Someone would reply, 'It's like a white crane.' So in this way, the man born blind, although he might hear these four metaphors, in the end would not be able to understand the color of milk."

No. 93

In this world there are several groups of people;
When we discuss it—as for beauty, there are various kinds.

If Old lady Chia was granted a husband;[1]
Huang-ti and Lao-tzu originally had no wives.[2]

The Wei clan's boy was so cute and charming;[3]
The Chung family's daughter was extremely ugly.[4]

If they go off to the West,
Then I'll walk on the East side.

1. "Old Lady Chia" (Chia-p'o) apparently refers to the beauty mentioned in the *Tso chuan* (Duke Chao, year 28; Vol. 1, p. 427), who was married to an official (*ta-fu*) from the state of Chia, who was so ugly that for three years she neither spoke nor smiled. Finally, after he returned from hunting, having shot a pheasant, she smiled. (The anecdote is also recorded in *Ch'u-hsüeh chi*, Ch. 19: 3, "Ugly People" [Ch'ou-jen]—see *Ch'u-hsüeh chi* [Taipei: Hsin-hsing, 1972], Vol. 2, p. 1026.) Tseng P'u-hsin (*Han-shan shih-chieh*, p. 53), by contrast, identifies Old Lady Chia as the Empress of Emperor Hui of the Chin (r. 290–306).

2. The legendary ruler (traditional reign dates 2697–2596 B. C.) and early philosopher (supposed contemporary of Confucius, c. 500 B. C.), whose names are linked as co-authors of a type of Taoist statecraft ("Huang-Lao" thought) popular in the early years of the Han (c. 200 B. C.).

3. *Wei-shih erh* presumably means Wei Chieh, grandson of Wei Kuan in the Chin, a young man known for his beauty who was sickly and weak and died at the age of twenty-seven. His biography is recorded in *Chin shu* 36 (Vol. 4, pp. 1067–1068), and he is cited as one of the "Beautiful Men" (*Mei chang-fu*) in Ch. 19: 1 of the *Ch'u-hsüeh chi* (Vol. 2, p. 1017). Tseng P'u-hsin (*Han-shan shih-chieh*, p. 53) identifies the "Wei-shih erh" as the daughter of Wei Ch'üan.

4. The "Chung family's daughter" (Chung-chia nü) is most likely Chung-li Ch'un, who was extremely ugly yet became Queen of Ch'i, consort of King Hsüan (r. in Ch'i from 342–324 B. C.), because of the sageness of her advice. Her story is recorded in *Lieh-nü chuan* 6: 8b–10a; for a translation, see Albert Richard O'Hara, *The Position of Woman in Early China* (Washington, DC: The Catholic University of Amenza Press), pp. 171–174.

Note: The examples given seem to indicate that a beautiful face—or bodily beauty—does not necessarily entail good fortune in life (examples 1 and 3, lines 3 and 5—one man and one woman) and that wisdom and physical beauty do not necessarily go hand in hand (examples 2 and 4, lines 4 and 6—again, male and female examples given). I take Han-shan's point in the last couplet to be that he would prefer to be ranked with Huang-ti and Lao-tzu and Chung-li Ch'un—to be known for his "beauty" of mind.

No. 94

Gentlemen of worth do not covet;
It's the fools who love smelting gold.

If their wheat fields encroach upon others',
They say, "The *bamboo* groves are all ours as well."

They flex their muscles, searching for riches and wealth;
Grind their teeth, driving on their old nags.

You must look beyond the suburban gate;
Pile after pile [of graves], at the foot of cypress and pine.[1]

1. A number of graveyard songs come to mind, including poem 13 of the "Nineteen Old Poems" of the Han. Watson (*Chinese Lyricism*, p. 29) translates the opening lines: "I drive my carriage from the Upper East Gate, scanning the graves far north of the wall [literally, the graves to the north of the suburbs]; silver poplars, how they whisper and sigh; pine and cypress flank the broad lane" (*Wen-hsüan* 29: 6a, p. 399).

No. 95

Midst the clamor and din,[1] you buy fish and meat,
Shoulder it home to feed wife and kids.

Why must you kill other things
And use them to give life to yourselves?

This is not the condition that leads you to Heaven;
It's purely the dregs of Hell.[2]

When you see Hsü the Sixth talking to a broken pestle,
You'll then start to know that it makes no sense.[3]

1. Iritani and Matsumura (*Kanzanshi*, p. 133) follow Irida in reading *hung-hung* as "power" or "authority" (*wei-shih*). I can make no sense of that reading. *Hung* by itself means "singing," and it seems clear to me that *hung-hung* represents the noise made at a Chinese market by buyers and sellers.

2. "Sediments" (*tzu*) here meant in the sense of the poor state that results at the end.

3. Meaning—I think—that eating fish and meat makes about as much sense as trying to converse with a broken pestle. But my interpretation is tentative.

No. 96

There are those who take the cedar
And call it white candana.

People studying the Way are as numerous as the sands;
Still, only a few will attain *nirvāṇa*.[1]

They throw away gold—to the contrary, shoulder off
    weeds;[2]
Deceive others—but also end up deceiving themselves.

It's like piling up sand in one place;
You'll still have trouble turning it into one unified lump.

1. Han-shan uses an early transliteration of *nirvāṇa, ni-wan*.
2. In Chapter 9 of the *Nirvāṇa-sūtra* ("Ju-lai-hsing p'in"; T. 374, Vol. 12, p. 421 bottom), the lazy and negligent are compared to stupid thieves who "throw away the true treasure and carry off weeds and chaff."
Note: The second couplet shows us what the first couplet was about: with people seeking *nirvāṇa*, false experiences (the cedar—*ch'un*) are sometimes taken for the true (the white, fragrant, candana—*pai chan-t'an*). The two woods are similar, but not the same; both are strong and fragrant and used to make things. But only candana is used to make Buddhist images. The final couplet seems to add that, no matter how many *close* experiences one has, those experiences will never, collectively, add up to the experience of *nirvāṇa*.

No. 97*

People steam sand planning to make rice,
And when they begin to get thirsty, only then do they
    start to dig out their wells.[1]

You may use all your strength polishing bricks,
But can you ever turn them into mirrors?[2]

The Buddha said we are all fundamentally the same;[3]
All have the nature that is True and Just So.[4]

You must simply, carefully think all things through;[5]
It's no use to idly quarrel and compete.

*Pulleyblank: Han-shan II.
1. One could also translate, "To steam sand hoping to make rice; *is like* . . . " *Cheng-sha ch'eng-fan* ("steam sand, make rice")—which is close to the words we have here—is a set phrase representing a useless endeavor. The *locus classicus* for the simile would appear to be Chapter 6 in the *Sūrangama-sūtra* (T.945, Vol. 19, p. 131 bottom), where we read: "For this reason Ananda, to cultivate meditation without having cut off licentiousness is like steaming sand and rocks, hoping they will turn into rice. At the end of a hundred or a thousand kalpas, you could only call this 'hot sand.' " On being thirsty and then digging a well—Ts'ao Chih (192–232), in his "Remonstrating against the Attack of Liao-tung" (*Chien fa Liao-tung piao*), points out that "to be thirsty and then dig one's well, or to be famished and only then plant one's seeds—[in this way] you can plan for things far away, but it will be difficult to respond [to the immediate situation] in the end" (for the text, see *I-wen lei-chü* 24 [Vol. I, p. 437].)

2. For the famous exchange between the Zen masters Huai-jang (677–744) and Ma-tsu (707–786) on polishing a tile in hopes of turning it into a mirror, see the biography of Huai-jang in the *Ching-te ch'uan-teng lu,* Ch. 5 (p. 92 in *Ching-te ch'uan-teng lu* [Taipei: Chen-shan-mei, 1967]). The anecdote is translated into English in Paul Peachey's translation of Heinrich Dumoulin's *A History of Zen Buddhism* (New York: McGraw-Hill, 1963), p. 98, as follows: "[Huai-jang asked Ma-tsu:] 'For what purpose are you sitting in meditation?' Ma-tsu answered, 'I wish to become a Buddha.' Thereupon the Master picked up a tile and started rubbing it on a stone. Ma-tsu asked, 'What are you doing, Master?' 'I am polishing this tile to make a mirror,' Huai-jang replied. 'How can you make a mirror by rubbing a tile?' exclaimed Ma-tsu. 'How can one become a Buddha by sitting in meditation?' countered the master."

3. *P'ing-teng, samatā.*

4. All have *chen-ju hsing*—i.e., we are all by nature *bhūtatathatā,* the name for the really real in much Mahāyāna thought.

5. To "carefully think things through" (*shen ssu-liang*) is clearly a good thing in the poems of Han-shan (for other references, see Appendix II, "Buddhist Terms"). Nonetheless, this kind of thinking (*ssu-liang*) is not *generally* approved of in Buddhism. *Ssu-liang,* intellection or reasoning, is the function of the seventh consciousness (*manas*) in the Consciousness-Only School of Buddhism, and in other schools of Chinese Buddhism as well. Fung Yu-lan (*A History of Chinese Philosophy,* Vol. II, translated by Derk Bodde [Princeton: Princeton University Press, 1953], p. 312) notes the following about this consciousness: "This seventh or *manas* consciousness 'perpetually thinks about the ego (*ātman*), to which it clings.' " Han-shan's use of *ssu-liang* as something that is good might indicate that he writes before Hsüan-tsang's translation of the treatises of this school into Chinese (Hsüan-tsang's dates are 596–664). Still, this is a poem that Pulleyblank classes as "Han-shan II" by the rhyme words used.

No. 98*

In investigating the affairs of this world,
Each small detail must be understood.

But understanding all things is never easy,
And everyone is partial to seeking what seems best for him.

When it's a matter of protecting ourselves, the bad points
    turn into good;
When it's a matter of defaming others, then what is right
    becomes wrong.

Thus we know the various types who talk in excess;[1]
Behind our backs, all go with what suits themselves.

Cold or hot we must judge for ourselves;
Never believe the lips of the servant.[2]

*Pulleyblank: Han-shan II.
1. Perhaps bragging about what they know or have done. The phrase is *lan-k'ou*, which literally means "run off at the mouth." It might also mean they are overly flattering in their praise—at least to your face.

2. That is to say—I think—never trust what others tell you about someone else; find out for yourself. In Zen, that one must experience enlightenment oneself and not rely on what others might tell you about it is a point that is also made in this way. In *kōan* 23 of the *Wu-men kuan* (T.2005, Vol 48, p. 296), a monk named Chien-ming, having been enlightened by some remarks of the sixth patriarch, says: "I was under the fifth patriarch many years but could not realize my true self until now. Through your teaching I find the source. A person drinks water and knows himself whether it is cold or warm. May I call you my teacher?" (Translated by Paul Reps, *Zen Flesh, Zen Bones* [Garden City, NY: Doubleday, 1957] pp. 108–109.)

No. 99

Dispirited, at a loss-the many impoverished scholars,
Starving and cold, taken to the extreme.

Living unemployed, they delight in writing their poems;
Plodding, plodding,[1] they use up the strength of
    their minds.

Lowly men's words—who will collect them?
But I urge you, put an end to your sighs.

Were they written on cheap flour biscuits,
Even begging dogs wouldn't give them a bite.

---

1. *Cha-cha* is the noise made by the shuttle on a loom.

No. 100

If you'd like to know a metaphor for life and death,
You can compare them to water and ice.

When water congeals it turns into ice,
And when the ice melts, it reverts to the condition of water.

Having died, you'll definitely be reborn;
Being born, you'll still return to the condition of death.

Water and ice do no harm to each other;
Life and death are also both good.

No. 101

As I reflect on the days of my youth;
For hunting, I'd head off to the high plains.

"State messenger"—this post was not my design.
"Immortal"—that isn't even worth mentioning!

On and on I'd race my white horse;
Shout out the hares, release the green hawks.

Unaware [of how it came to be]—my life now greatly
  a shambles, in ruins.
White-haired and old—who will take pity on me?

Note: Iritani and Matusmura (*Kanzanshi*, p. 142) note the connection between this poem and the "songs of youth" (*shao-nien hsing*) recorded in the *Yüeh-fu shih chi* (Vol. II, pp. 952–958). In those songs as well, riding and hunting are common themes.

No. 102

I stop and rest at the bottom of the deep woods;
From birth I've been a farmer.

In character—simple and honest;
Speech devoid of flattery and self-praise.

I preserve my Self—I don't inspect jade;[1]
If I believe in the Lord, then I have pearls.[2]

How can I float and drift together with them,
And look not beyond the wild ducks on the waves?[3]

1. Iritani and Matsumura (*Kanzanshi*, pp. 143–144) see two possible references to *Chuang-tzu* here. One is to an anecdote about Chuang-tzu preserved in *Han-shih wai-chuan* (though now found only by citation in *I-wen lei-chü*, Ch. 83 [Vol. II, p. 1422]) where King Hsiang of Ch'u sent a messenger with 1000 *chin* in gold and 100 pairs of *pi* (circular pieces of jade with holes in the middle) to get Chuang-tzu to serve as Prime Minister, but Chuang-tzu firmly refused. The second story is recorded in *Chuang-tzu*, Chapter 20 (p. 53, lines 38–41), where Confucius laments to Master Sang-hu that his friends and kin are all leaving him. Master Sang-hu then says (Watson, *The Complete Works*, p. 215): "Have you never heard about Lin Hui, the man who fled from Chia? He threw away his jade disc worth a thousand measures of gold, strapped his little baby on his back, and hurried off. Someone said to him, 'Did you think of it in terms of money? Surely a little baby isn't worth much money! Or were you thinking of the bother? But a little baby is a great deal of bother! Why then throw away a jade disc worth a thousand measures of gold and hurry off with a little baby on your back?' Lin Hui replied, 'The jade disc and I were joined by profit, but the child and I were brought together by Heaven. Things joined by profit, when

pressed by misfortune and danger, will cast each other aside, but things brought together by Heaven, when pressed by misfortune and danger, will cling to one another. To cling to each other and to cast each other aside are far apart indeed!' "

2. A difficult line: the text is *hsin chün fang te chu*. *Chün* elsewhere in the Han-shan poems almost always means "you," and the contrast here is with the *wo* "my self" of the previous line. Iritani and Matsumura (*Kanzan-shi*, pp. 143–144) thus seem to read the line as, "I will let you, my lord, go after the pearl"—i.e., you want money; I have greater treasures in mind (my true nature, my Self). But surely the force of the *fang* in the line is "then" or "only then." Tentatively, my interpretation is that Han-shan's belief in the Lord (Buddha) is equivalent to having the treasure of pearls; the "pearl" (*chu*), after all, is the stock symbol of Buddha-nature. So he has no need to chase after valuable jades. Iritani and Matsumura see another allusion here to the *Chuang-tzu*. In *Chuang-tzu*, Chapter 32 (p. 90, lines 43–46; Watson, *The Complete Works*, p. 360), the pearl of the Black Dragon is something someone risks his life to get; thus the pearl is a metaphor for something of great value for which you would risk your life.

3. An allusion to *Ch'u-tzu'u*, "Pu-chü" (Divining Where to Live); *Ch'u-tzu pu-chu*, 6: 2b, p. 73. Hawkes, *The Songs of the South*, p. 205, translates the relevant passage: "Is it better to have the aspiring spirit of a thousand *li* stallion, or to drift this way and that like a duck on water, saving oneself by rising and falling with the waves?" Clearly Han-shan sees himself as one whose concerns go beyond the mere acquisition of money.

No. 103*

No need to attack others' faults;[1]
What use in showing off one's good traits?[2]

When it's time to go forward, then you can advance;
When it's time to withdraw, then you can retire.[3]

When salary's substantial anxieties build up,
When words are deep, first consider if the friendship
   is shallow.[4]

Having heard this, if you think it through,
A *small child* ought to see it himself.

---

*Pulleyblank: Han-shan II.

1. Perhaps alluding to *Analects* 12: 21 (p. 24), where we read (here using the translation of Waley's *The Analects of Confucius* [New York: Vintage, 1938], pp. 68–169): "Once when Fan Ch'ih was taking a walk with the Master under the trees at the Rain Dance altars, he said, ''May I venture to ask about 'piling up moral force,' 'repairing shortcomings,' and 'deciding when in two minds'?'' The Master said, ''An excellent question. 'The work first; the reward afterwards'; is not that piling up moral force? 'Attack the evil that is within yourself; do not attack the evil that is in others.' Is not this 'repairing shortcomings'?''

2. Some versions of the text simply repeat the ''no need'' of line 1 at the start of this line. In *Analects* 5: 26 (p. 9) Yen Yüan, in response to Confucius' request that each of his disciples tell him what is on his mind, replies: ''I should like never to boast of my own goodness and never to impose onerous tasks upon others'' (translated by D. C. Lau, *Confucius: The Analects*, p. 80).

3. In *Analects* 7: 11 (p. 12), Confucius says to Yen Yüan: "Only you and I have the ability to go forward when employed and to stay out of sight when set aside" (translated by D. C. Lau, *Confucius: The Analects*, p. 87). Also relevant, in *Analects* 15: 7 (p. 31), Confucius says of Ch'ü Po-yü: "When the Way prevails in the state, he takes office, but when the Way falls into disuse in the state he allows himself to be furled and put away safely."

4. i.e., one does not discuss weighty matters with casual acquaintances. This appears to be an allusion to *Hou Han shu* 52 (Vol. 6, p. 1719), the biography of Ts'ui Yin, where Ts'ui Yin says, "I have heard that it is stupid to have deep words where the relationship is shallow."

Comment: One way of reading these lines is that Han-shan simply wishes to point out the "common-sense" nature of these essentially "Confucian," "wise" observations.

No. 104

The young rich meet in high halls;
Colored lanterns, how dazzling and bright.[1]

Now arrives one who owns not a candle,
Hoping to sit off to one side.

He'd not expected to be forced to leave,
To return to the dark, to stay there and dwell.

Helping others—is your brightness decreased?!
Hard to believe! That you'd begrudge surplus light.

---

1. Virtually the same words are used to describe the banquet halls of the rich lord in "Hsiang-feng hsing" (*Yüeh-fu shih-chi* 34, Vol. I, p. 508).

Note: Throughout the poem Han-shan clearly has in mind the story of Hsü-wu of Ch'i, recorded in the *Lieh-nü chuan* (6: 13ab). O'Hara (*The Position of Woman in Early China*, pp. 182–183) translates: "Hsü-wu, the woman of Ch'i, was a poor woman in Tung-hai-shang of Ch'i, and she was in association of Li-wu, a neighboring woman. They all brought candles to pursue their weaving at night together. Hsü-wu was extremely poor and did not bring enough candles. Li-wu spoke to her associates and said, 'Hsü-wu does not bring enough candles. Please do not share the light with her at night.' Hsü-wu said, 'What is it that you say? Because I am poor I did not bring enough candles. I ordinarily rise early and go to bed late; I sprinkle, sweep, and arrange the mats, sitting always in the lowest place, all because I am poor and have not enough candles. Now, when there is one candle in the middle of the room, if one more person is added to the room, the light will not decrease; if one person goes out of the room, the light will not increase.' "

No. 105

In this world there are many wise scholars,
Who bitterly toil, probing the sources of obscure remarks.[1]

In the Three Principles[2] they stand all alone;
At the Six Arts[3] surpass other men.

Style and spirit exceptionally rare;
Excellence, excelling the crowd.

But they don't know the mind that's inside;[4]
They just pursue the external realms—chaotic, in great
    disarray.

1. *Yu-wen*, literally "obscure passages" or perhaps "little-known writings."
2. The *san-tuan* are the penmanship of the scholar, the swordsmanship of the warrior, and the eloquence of the debater.
3. The *liu-i* are better known: ritual, music, archery, charioteering, writing, and mathematics.
4. *Ko-chung i* seems to have a special Buddhist sense here as "the mind that's inside" (see Tseng P'u-hsin [*Han-shan shih-chieh*, p. 60]; also the translation of Iritani and Matsumura [*Kanzanshi*, pp. 149 and 349]). On the surface, the expression means "the meaning in this." Note also poem 254.

No. 106*

Layer after layer of beautiful mountains and streams;
Fog and rose-colored clouds, locking in hillsides of green.

Brushed by mountain mist, my thin cotton headband gets wet;
Morning dew dampens my raincoat of straw.

On my feet are my "travelling" sandals,[1]
In my hand, an old branch of cane.

Again I gaze out beyond the dusty world;
A realm of dreams—why should I bother with that any more?

*Pulleyblank: Han-shan II.
1. Yu-fang means to ramble in all four directions: this is an expression
often used in relation to Buddhist and Taoist monks and nuns.

No. 107

A volume crammed with "talented genius" poems;
Jug overflowing with "The Sage" wine.[1]

Out walking, I delight in seeing oxen with their calves;
Sitting down, I keep them nearby, left and right.[2]

Frost and dew come through my thatched eaves;
Dazzling moonlight shines through my "jar hole."[3]

At such times as these I sip one or two cups
And chant poems, two or three *shou*.[4]

1. When Ts'ao Ts'ao (155–220) forbade the drinking of wine at the beginning of the Wei (220–265), nicknames were developed for various kinds of wine. "Clear" wine (the best) was called "The Sage" (*sheng-jen*), while "muddied" wine was called "The Worthy" (*hsien-jen*) (see *San-kuo chih* 27 [Vol. 3, p. 739]).

2. Presumably the poems and wine.

3. A *weng-yu* is a window formed by inlaying the mouth of a broken jar in a wall. It is a sign of poverty.

4. Preferring the variant of *liang-san* ("two or three") to *wu-pai* ("five hundred").

No. 108

The family Shih had two sons;
With their skills they sought service in Ch'i and Ch'u.

Learning and warfare—each prepared himself well;
Relying on what he knew, each got just the right job.

Master Meng asked about their techniques;
"My children will instruct you themselves."

But in Ch'in and Wei, both of them failed;
Miss the time, and things just don't come together.[1]

1. *Chü-yü* are teeth that are uneven and do not match up.
   Comment: The tale Han-shan assumes his reader knows is found in the *Lieh-tzu*, Chapter 8 (8/4ab: SPPY ed.). For a translation, see A. C. Graham, *The Book of Lieh-tzu* (London: John K. Murray, 1973), pp. 162–164. To summarize, a certain Mr. Shih of Lu had two sons, one skilled in learning, the other in arts of war. They got jobs respectively in Ch'i and Ch'u, where they fared well and became very rich. A Mr. Meng, who lived close by the Shihs, also had two sons, equally skilled, but they remained unemployed and poor. So Mr. Shih's sons told him what they had done to succeed. Meng's sons then traveled to Ch'in and Wei. But they did not fare well at all. The first son was castrated and banished by the ruler of Ch'in, who thought this was no time for learning to be used. The other son lost both legs in Wei, the ruler not wanting to use his skills at this time but afraid he might be employed by a neighboring state. In the end, Mr. Shih explains to Mr. Meng, "Your Way was the same as ours, yet you failed where we succeeded—not because you did the wrong things, but because you picked the wrong time to do them" (tr. Graham).

No. 109*

Stopping for the night, the Mandarin ducks;
One drake joined with one hen.

With blossoms in bills they feed one another;
Preening their feathers, they follow each other around.

Playing, they fly into the mist and the clouds;
By evening, return to the sand on the shore.

They delight in the place where they live;
They don't try to seize Phoenix Pond![1]

*Pulleyblank: Han-shan II.

1. *Feng-huang ch'ih* was the name given in Chin dynasty times (265–419) to the location of the Central Secretariat (*chung-shu sheng*). Like the ducks, the author delights in his life as it is; he has no imperial pretensions.

Comment: In his "Nineteen Poems"—some texts say eighteen—presented to his older brother, Hsi K'ang (223–262) uses the pair of mandarin ducks (*yüan-yang*) in a similar way to symbolize the freedom he and his brother once knew (before his brother entered government service). Poem 1 in that series reads: "A mandarin drake and his mate take off, flutter flutter beat their wings. Dawn traveling to the lofty plain, at dusk to lodge at the orchid islet. *Yung yung* their harmonious call, looking back on their mate. Gazing up and down, noble and disinterested, carefree they sport at leisure" (translated by Peter Rushton, "An Interpretation of Hsi K'ang's Eighteen Poems Presented to Hsi Hsi on His Entry Into the Army" *Journal of the American Oriental Society*, 99, no. 2 (April–June 1979): 177. For the text, see *Hsi Chung-san chi* 1: 1b–2a).

No. 110

On occasion there are people who boast of their deeds,
Claiming their talents and arts surpass those of Chou
   and K'ung.[1]

But once you've seen them—they're bewildered and confused
   in their heads;
And when you observe them—their bodies look like those of
   ignorant fools.

You can pull them with a rope, but they'll never be willing
   to walk;
You can stab them with an awl, but they still will not move.

They're just like Master Yang's crane;
How pitiable! Standing there shaking its feathers.[2]

---

1. The Duke of Chou and Confucius.
2. Preferring the reading of *t'ung-meng*, "hair dishevelled," to the variant *tung-meng*, "confused in mind." "Master Yang" is Yang Hu (A. D. 221–278), who held office under Emperor Wu of the Chin (r. 265–290). He once bragged to a guest about how well his crane could dance, but when he brought it out on display, it just stood there and shook its feathers. The story is recorded in *Shih-shuo hsin-yü* 25: 47. For a translation, see Richard Mather, translator, *Shih-shuo Hsin-yü: A New Account of Tales of the World* (Minneapolis: University of Minnesota Press, 1976), p. 419.

No. 111

When I was young, I'd take the classics along when I hoed;[1]
Originally I planned to live together with my older brother.

But because I met with criticism from the other generation,[2]
I was, even more, treated coldly by my own wife.[3]

I have abandoned, rejected the realm of red dust;
Constantly I roam about with the books I love to read.

Who can lend me a dipper of water
To revive and retrieve the fish that's caught in the rut?[4]

1. Something any budding scholar should do. Iritani and Matsumura (*Kanzanshi*, p. 157) note that the *Wei-lüeh*, cited in P'ei Sung-chih's notes to *San-kuo chih* 23 (Vol. 3, p. 659, biography of Ch'ang Lin), says this was done by the impoverished Ch'ang Lin. Watson (*Cold Mountain*, p. 50) notes the same thing is said of Ni K'uan (in *Han shu* 58, Vol. 9, p. 2628).

2. Does he mean his older brother? The phrase is *t'a-pei*.

3. Han-shan might be alluding here to the well-known story of Chu Mai-ch'en, the Han woodcutter who carried his classics with him when he went to cut wood. His wife grew tired of his lack of success and left him, but she wanted to be taken back when Mai-ch'en at last became an official. See *Han shu* 64 (Vol. 9, 2791–2794). For a fictionalized account of the story, see Cyril Birch, translator, *Stories From a Ming Collection* (New York: Grove Press, Inc. 1958), pp. 19–22.

4. In *Chuang-tzu*, Ch. 26 (p. 73), Chuang-tzu is infuriated by a feudal lord's offer of three hundred gold pieces when he goes to ask for some rice for his starving family. He says to the ruler (translation by Burton Watson, *The Complete Works*, p. 295): "As I was coming here yesterday, I heard someone calling me on the road. I turned around and saw that there was a perch in the carriage rut. I said to him, 'Come, perch—what are you doing here?' He replied, 'I am a Wave Official of the Eastern Sea. Couldn't you give me a dipperful of water so I can stay alive?' I said to him, 'Why, of course. I'm just about to start south to visit the kings of Wu and Yüeh. I'll change the course of the West River and send it in your direction. Will that be all right?' The perch flushed with anger and said, 'I've lost my element! I have nowhere to go! If you can get me a dipper of water, I'll be able to stay alive. But if you give me an answer like that, then you'd best look for me in the dried fish store!'" Han-shan's needs, like those of Chuang-tzu and the fish, are very few.

No. 112

Transformation and change—the calculations have no limit;
Life and death, to the end never cease.

If you live in the Three Paths,[1] you'll have a bird's body;
If in the Five Peaks, you'll be nothing more than a dragon
     fish.[2]

If the age is corrupt, you'll become a Mongolian goat;
But if times are pure, you'll be a Lu-erh.[3]

Last time around you were a rich kid;
This time you'll become some poor scribe.

1. That is, the three evil *gatis* (*san-t'u*), which are to suffer in hell,
become a hungry ghost, or be reborn in animal form.
2. The five sacred mountains in China are Mount Sung at the center,
Mount T'ai in the East, Mount Hua in the West, Mount Heng in the South,
and Mount Heng in the North. The *lung-yü* (dragon fish) is one of the fan-
tastic creatures described in the *Shan-hai ching* (Ch. 7, "Hai-wai hsi-ching,"
p. 224) as living in Western lands. The text says: "*Lung* (dragon) fish live
high up, to the north. They resemble the *li* (wildcat). Some say this is the
hsia (shrimp). The *shen sheng* (spirit divine) ride on them and travel the nine
wildernesses. Some say the *pieh* (turtle) fish. This is north of Yao Wilder-
ness. This kind of fish resembles the *li* (carp)" (translated by Hsiao-Chieh
Cheng, Hui-Chen Pai Cheng, and Kenneth Lawrence Thern, *Shan Hai
Ching: Legendary Geography and Wonders of Ancient China* [Taipei: The Committee for Compilation and Examination of the Series of Chinese Classics,
1985], p. 157.) Iritani and Matsumura (*Kanzanshi*, p. 158) point to a connection of the Five Peaks with Taoism, and in their translation take this line to
refer to those who practice Taoist arts—such might be their fate.

3. Lu-erh was one of eight great steeds belonging to King Mu of the Chou (r. 1001–946). See also poem 45, note 2.

Comment: Though the second couplet, with its mention of the "three paths," seems to imply that the author ascribes to Buddhist notions of *karma* and fate, couplet 3 seems to assume other, non-Buddhist Chinese notions of fate—*viz.*, that one's lot is intimately related to the nature of the times in which one is born. Note also poem 253.

No. 113

My writing and judgment were perfect—they were not
weak;
But they detested my looks, so I did not receive
an appointment.[1]

By the Examinations Board twisted and broken;
They "washed away the dirt and looked for the
scabs and scars."[2]

Certain it is that it's all related to fate;
Still this winter again I'll try and see.

After all, with a blind boy shooting at the eye of a sparrow,
A chance hit is also not hard.

1. Han-shan's reference appears to be to the "selection" examinations administered to holders of degrees (there were three degrees in early T'ang—the *hsiu-ts'ai, ming-ching,* and *chin-shih*)—to determine who in the pool would actually be appointed to office (on which see Denis Twitchett, ed., *The Cambridge History of China*: Volume 3, *Sui and T'ang China, 589–906,* Part I [Cambridge: Cambridge University Press, 1979], pp. 275–276; also Ch'en Hui-chien, *Han-shan-tzu,* pp. 25–26). Officials in the sixth grade and below were recruited in an annual examination held during the fifth lunar month (Han-shan says the "winter" [?]), and they were examined in four different ways: first their "writing and judgment"(*shu-p'an*) were tested and then their "appearance and speech"(*shen-yen*) (see Robert des Rotours, *Le Traité des Examens: Traduit de la Nouvelle Histoire des T'ang,* Ch. XLIV, XLV [Paris: Librairie Ernest Leroux, 1932], pp. 42–44 and 213–222; for the original text—the T'ang "Treatise on Selection of Officials"—see *Hsin T'ang shu* 45, Vol. 4, pp. 1171–1172).

    2. i.e., they were bound and determined to find something wrong.
The saying apparently goes back to a piece called "Tz'u-shih chi-hsien fu"
by Chao I, recorded in *Hou Han shu* 80 (Vol. 9, p. 2631), where, of those
who select others for office, he comments: "With those they like, they bore
a hole in the skin to let out the feathers and fur; with those they dislike,
they wash away the dirt and look for the scabs and scars."

No. 114

For a poor ass, one foot will be insufficient,
While for a rich dog, three inches will be
    more than he needs.[1]

If you divide things in two, it will not be fair to the poor,
But if the middle portion is again divided in half, the rich
    will also be in straits.[2]

If we begin to make the donkey full and content,
Then, to the contrary, we will make the dog hungry and
    distressed.

When I think it through carefully for you,
It makes me both sad and depressed.

1. More precisely in terms of the grammar, "The poor ass will consider one foot to be lacking; [While] the rich dog will find three inches to be a surplus." I think it is relevant that the ass is a bigger animal than the dog; thus "natural" needs differ.
2. Translation is tentative, but I think the point is to now give the ass three-quarters of the lot and the dog one-quarter.
Comment: Iritani and Matusmura (*Kanzanshi*, p. 161) understand the poem to be a criticism of "mechanistic egalitarianism," which would distribute material goods equally to all. But Han-shan's point seems to be that people's needs are not the same.

No. 115

"Young" Mr. Liu—he's eighty-two;
"Old" Mrs. Lan—she's all of eighteen!

Man and wife together for one hundred years;
Mutual affection—their feelings chaotic and unrestrained.

Playing with jade, he's nicknamed "the tiger";[1]
Tossing down tiles, she's called "chubby cheeks."[2]

One frequently sees, with the shoots put out by withering
    poplars,
They meet with death [at the hands of] Blue Maid.[3]

---

1. For *wu-t'u* as another name for the tiger, see Read, *Chinese Materia Medica: Animal Drugs*, item 351.

2. *Kuan-na* describes baby girls that are pretty and plump. On the objects of jade and tile played with by small children, see *Shih* 189. Karlgren (*The Book of Odes*, p. 131) translates: "And so he bears sons; they lay them on a bed, they dress them in skirts, they give them as toys (chang-jades:) jade insignia; they cry shrilly . . . And so he bears daughters; they lay them on the ground; they dress them in wrappers; they give them as toys spinning-whorls; they shall have nothing but simplicity." James Legge (*The Chinese Classics*, Vol. 4, *The She King*, p. 306) notes on the lines: "The boy is placed on a couch—to do him honour; the daughter on the ground, to show her meanness. *Ch'ang*, 'the lower garment,' must be taken for robes generally. The boy is to be arrayed in full dress, while a swaddling cloth will be sufficient for the girl. *Chang* is a piece of jade fashioned into the shape of a half-mace, used in worshipping Spirits and as a symbol of dignity. The boy gets one of these to play with, while the girl gets only a tile, the emblem of her future employment, when, on a tile upon her knee, she will have to twist the threads of hemp."

3. "Blue Maid"(*ch'ing-nü*) is the Goddess of Frost, and it is the frost in the fall that will kill off new shoots from the tree."

Note: In the symbolism of the poem, the "Blue Maid" is not only the Goddess of Frost, she is also "Old Mrs. Lan"(since *lan*, like *ch'ing*, means "blue"), and in killing off the shoots of the poplar, she is killing off "Young Mr. Liu's" new children (since "poplar" is *yang*, which alone can mean the aspen or poplar, but which in combination with *liu* [*yang-liu*] means the willow). The "poplar in fall sprouting shoots" as metaphor for an old man marrying a young bride is referred to in the *I ching* (Hexagram 28, "Ta-kuo," nine in the second place; p. 128). Wilhelm (*The I Ching or Book of Changes*, p. 113) translates: "Nine in the second place means: A dry poplar sprouts at the root. An older man takes a young wife. Everything furthers." For Han-shan's attitude toward this kind of marriage, see also poem 128.

No. 116

There are so many vagrants starving and cold
Who see their lives as different than those of
    fishes and beasts.

Yet forever they're found beneath the grindstones,[1]
Constantly crying in nooks by the side of the road.

Day after day vainly thinking of rice;
All winter long not knowing the warmth of a coat.

All they receive is a bundle of hay,
That and five pints of bran.[2]

1. Like animals; the variant of "beneath temple rocks"(*miao-shih*)
works as well.
2. i.e., they are little better off than the animals after all.

No. 117

Outstanding! This little jug store;
Their wine—so rich and so thick.

Quite charming! Their high-flying banners;
They squint their eyes [to make sure] their measures are fair.

What is the reason they have no sales?
In their house they have lots of fierce dogs.

If a lad wishes to come buy some wine,
The dogs bite him and then off he goes.

Comment: Behind all of this lies the following story recorded in the *Han-fei-tzu* ("Wai chu-shuo, yu-shang," *Han-fei-tzu chi-shih* 13, p. 737): "Once there was a Sung man selling wine. His measures were very fair. His reception of customers was very courteous. The wine he made was excellent. He hoisted his banner in an imposing manner. Yet he had no business and the wine would become sour. Wondering at the cause, he asked his acquaintance, an elder of the village, named Yang Ching. 'It is because your dog is fierce,' replied Ching. 'If my dog is fierce, why does my wine not sell well?'

'Because customers are afraid of it. When people send out children with money and pots or jars to buy wine from you, your dog would jump at them and sometimes bite them. This is the reason why your wine does not sell well and becomes sour.'" The narrator goes on to draw the moral of this story in political terms. "Indeed, the state has dogs too. Thus experts in statecraft, bearing the right tact in mind, want to enlighten the sovereign of ten thousand chariots, whereas ministers like the fierce dog of the wine merchant would jump at them and bite them. This is the reason why the lord of men is deluded and experts in statecraft are not taken into service" (translated by W. K. Liao, *The Complete Works of Han Fei Tzu* [London: Arthur Probsthain, 1959], Vol. 2, p. 105). Watson's suggestion (*Cold Mountain*, p. 95) that the butt of Han-shan's sarcasm is Buddhist clergy is very appealing. Note that the "lad" of line 7—*t'ung-tzu*—also means "neophyte" in Buddhism.

No. 118

Alas! This place of corruption and filth;[1]
Demons[2] mixed together with men of worth.

If you say these are all the same group,[3]
How would we know that the Tao has no favorites?[4]

The fox pretends to the lion's position;
The crafty and false, to the contrary, are called "rare."

But when lead ore is put into the stove,
Then you will know this "gold" is not really real.[5]

---

    1. "Corruption and filth"—which is a good translation for *cho-lan*—fails to pick up some subtle suggestions relevant later on. *Cho* is muddy water—i.e., things are confused and mixed up; neat distinctions cannot be made—and *lan* can mean something false and not true.

    2. Literally, *rākṣasas, lo-ch'a*.

    3. i.e., make no distinction between the two.

    4. Alluding to the last line of *Lao-tzu*, Ch. 79. Chan (*The Way of Lao Tzu*, p. 237) translates: "The Way of Heaven has no favorites. It is always with the good man."

    5. Fake gold made by using lead would melt more quickly than the real thing. Following the variant of *chen* ("real") for *chih* ("knowledge").

No. 119*

Farmers, to escape from the hot summer months,
A dipper of wine—with whom enjoy?

Scattered about, rows of fresh mountain fruit;
Here and there, surrounding them, goblets of wine.

Roots from rushes will serve for their seats,
Leaves of the plantain, moreover, fill in for plates.

Once drunk, they sit with chins propped on hands,
And Mount Sumeru seems as small as a crossbow pellet.[1]

---

*Pulleyblank: Han-shan II.

1. i.e., all distinctions between small and large, significant and unimportant, are blurred. In the writings of the T'ien-t'ai school, Mount Sumeru (*Hsü-mi*)—or Mount Meru—and a "mustard seed" are sometimes used as stock images for large and small. Since all things have their basis in thought and thought alone is their substance, Mount Sumeru and a mustard seed are exactly the same—that is, as thoughts being thought, they occupy the exact same space in the mind. See, for example, the passages quoted in Fung Yu-lan, *A History of Chinese Philosophy* (tr. Derk Bodde) (Princeton, NJ: Princeton University Press 1953), Vol. II, p. 372.

Note: The poet T'ao Ch'ien (360–427) has a poem that in many ways resembles this, and makes much the same point but in a Taoist way. It is poem 14 in his twenty "Drinking Wine" poems. J. R. Hightower's (*The Poetry of T'ao Ch'ien* [Oxford: Clarendon Press, 1970], pp. 144–145) translation follows:

Sympathetic friends who know my taste
Bring a wine jug when they come to visit.
Sitting on the ground beneath the pine trees
A few cups of wine makes us drunk.
Venerable elders gabbing all at once
And pouring from the bottle out of turn.
Aware no more that our own 'I' exists,
How are we to value other things?
So rapt we are not sure of where we are—
In wine there is a taste of profundity.

No. 120

This is what poor scribe
Who repeatedly comes to be tested at Southern Court?[1]

Years? Possibly thirty or more;
He's already passed through four or five selections.

Inside his bag, he has no "blue beetles";[2]
Inside his basket, no yellow scrolls.[3]

Were he to walk up to a food stand,
He'd not even dare turn his head for a brief moment!

1. According to Ch'en Hui-chien (*Han-shan-tzu*, pp. 25–26), the "Southern Court" (*nan-yüan*) is where the list of names of people selected for office was posted. However, this refers to the examinations administered to men who had attained a degree but as yet received no appointment (see note 1 to poem 113; also note Twitchett, ed., *The Cambridge History of China*, Vol. 3, p. 276, on the meaning of *hsüan*, "selections"). Hucker (*A Dictionary of Official Titles in Imperial China* [Stanford, CA: Stanford University Press, 1985] p. 342, item 4136) on *nan-yüan* notes: "Established in 734 in the Bureau of Appointments (*li-pu*) of the Ministry of Personnel (also *li-pu*); responsible for determining seniority and reputation as elements considered in the reappointment or dismissal of an official." Ch'en Hui-chien says the office was established either in 734 or 740.

2. i.e., no money. For the story of how water beetles (*ch'ing-fu*) came to mean coins, see Bernard Read, *Chinese Materia Medica: Insect Drugs . . .* (Taipei: Southern Materials Center, 1977), p. 69, item 24. Chinese tradition about the water beetle holds that "if the mother be killed and smeared on money and the eggs smeared on the strings of cash, after the money is spent, it will return of its own accord to the original owner."

3. No books.

No. 121*†

If you're someone who constantly has daily needs,
You must be sparing of covetous thoughts.

As you get old, you will not be free,
And you'll gradually be rejected by others.

Sent off to the top of some desolate hill,[1]
The hopes of a lifetime in vain thrown away.

If, when the sheep have escaped, you give up fixing the pen,
Your disappointments 'til the end will not cease.[2]

---

*Pulleyblank: Han-shan II.
†Missing from the *Tse-shih-chü ts'ung-shu* and *Kunaichō* Library editions.
1. i.e., to be buried.
2. i.e., it is never too late to reform. "Wang-yang pu-lao" ("lost sheep, fix pen") is a set expression with this meaning. As early as the *Chan-kuo ts'e*, we find Chuang Hsin saying to the king of Ch'u: "I have heard peasants say, 'it's not too late to hail the hound when the hare's started, nor to repair the pen when the sheep has bolted'" (translated by J. I. Crump, *Chan-kuo Ts'e* [San Francisco: Chinese Materials Center, 1979], p. 264).

No. 122

Wastefully they constructed their "reaching the clouds"
    pavilions;[1]
In vain ascended their towers of one hundred feet.

They nourished their lives, and *still* they died young;
Though they entice you to study—will you receive feudal
    rank?!

It's useless to follow the "yellow bills";
Why must you detest turning grey?[2]

You must never be straight like an arrow;
However, you must also never be bent like a hook.[3]

---

    1. Iritani and Matsumura (*Kanzanshi*, p. 170) point out that Emperor
Ming of the Wei (Ts'ao Jui; r. 227–239) constructed a tower by this name in
237, but that here this name might be generic.
    2. "Yellow bills" (*huang-k'ou*) are young sparrows, and Han-shan
clearly has in mind the following story recorded in Liu Hsiang's *Shuo-yüan*
(10: 10b): "Confucius saw a netter, and what he had caught was all young
birds. Confucius said, 'Why is it that the yellow bills were all caught while
the large sparrows alone were not?' The netter replied: 'Of the yellow
bills—those that follow the big sparrows are not caught; of the big sparrows—those that follow the yellow bills can be caught.' Confucius turned
and said to his disciples: 'The gentleman is careful about whom he follows:
if he is not someone good, then there is the danger of traps and nets!'"
Han-shan's allusion to this anecdote has double significance. On the one
hand, he feels the pursuit of youth (to be a "yellow bill") is in vain; on the
other, the story illustrates that pursuit of rank can be fraught with danger
(i.e., if one "follows" the wrong group).

3. This appears to be an allusion to a popular children's song at the time of Emperor Shun of the Han (r. 126–144) which went: "The upright get cut like bow strings and die; the crooked, to the contrary, get feudal rank" (see Iritani and Matsumura, *Kanzanshi*, p. 170; they cite the source as *Hou han shu* 103.) Han-shan's point seems to be that one should never be so good (upright) that he would end up getting rank and thus dying young, and never be so corrupt that he would bend his principles to accord with the situation.

No. 123**

Clouds on the mountain piled up in layers,
    touching Heaven's azure blue;
Pathways secluded, forests deep—
    no travellers rambling out here.

In the distance I gaze at the lonely toad,[1]
    shining so dazzling bright;
Nearby I hear a flock of birds,
    chirping away—tweet tweet.

An elderly man sits all alone,
    perched upon his green peak;
Here at Few Homes retired he lives,[2]
    letting his head turn gray.

How sad! That past years and now present days,
Unaware, have just like the rivers flowed east.

**Seven-character lines.
    1. The Chinese find a toad (*ch'an*) and hare (*t'u*) in the moon. For
some interesting observations on this, see Chapter 5 ("The Bird in the Sun
and the Hare in the Moon") in Michael Loewe's *Ways to Paradise: The Chinese
Quest for Immortality* (London: George Allen & Unwin, 1979), pp. 127–133.
    2. "Few Homes" (Shao-shih) is one of the peaks on Mount Sung in
Honan. The famous Shao-lin Monastery, where Bodhidharma reputedly sat
facing a wall meditating for nine years, is located here.

No. 124

In homes of the wealthy and ranked, even distant
    kin will collect;
Only because there's *lots* of money and rice.

While from homes of the humble and poor, even
    blood kin will depart,
And it has no relation to the fact that
    the number of brothers is few.[1]

Hurry! You must return![2]
They're calling for worthies[3]—but the council door's not yet
    been opened.

It's a waste to walk on Vermilion Bird Street[4]
Wearing out the soles of your leather shoes.

---

1. Iritani and Matsumura (*Kanzanshi*, p. 173) point out that the opening lines of Ts'ao Shu's (?–308) "Kan-chiu shih" (*Wen-hsüan* 29: 20b, p. 406) are very similar: "In the homes of the wealthy and ranked, strangers will gather; In homes of the humble and poor, even relatives will leave."

2. Appropriately using the words *kuei ch'ü-lai*, the title of T'ao Ch'ien's rhapsody on his own "return" from the life of the official to that of farming being "Kuei ch'ü-lai hsi tz'u."

3. *Chao-hsien* indicates an official government call for worthies to serve.

4. Iritani and Matsumura (*Kanzanshi*, p. 173) locate "Vermilion Bird Street" (*chu-ch'üeh chieh*) in the capital of Ch'ang-an: Edward Schafer (*The Vermilion Bird: T'ang Images of the South* [Berkeley, CA: University of California Press, 1967], p. 259) adds that the entrance to the " 'old' palace of early T'ang . . . was named 'Gate of the Vermilion Sparrow.'"

No. 125

I've seen one stupid man
Who still lives with two or three wives.

They've raised now eight or nine sons,
Always going along with whatever seems right at the time.

"Males and Households"—that's the new levy;[1]
Wealth and goods, not something he formerly had.

When you see the Yellow Bark serving as the ass's crupper,[2]
Then you start to know that bitterness comes at the end.

1. If we follow the variant of *hu* for *fang*—though more on this be-low—the line thus reads *ting-hu shih hsin ch'ai. Ting* ("taxable male, aged 21–59") and *hu* ("household") were the two common bases used for taxa-tion during the T'ang, with the emphasis, before 780 at least, on the former (see D. C. Twitchett, *Financial Administration Under the T'ang Dynasty* [Cam-bridge: Cambridge University Press, 1970], pp. 24–48). The "household levy" (*hu-shui*) varied in accord with the "grade" ranking of the household, the grade being determined by the size and property of the household. Be-fore 780, the "household levy" was part of a system known as "selective impositions" (*ch'ai-k'o*); with the tax reform system of 780, the household tax and the land tax became the two most important taxes, forming what is known as the "two tax system" (*liang-shui fa*). Iritani and Matsumura (*Kan-zanshi*, pp. 174–174) speculate that this line might reflect the reform of 780, though I fail to see why a household with nine or ten taxable males, but otherwise poor, would suffer under the new regime.

There is a second, quite different, way to read this line. If we go with the variant *fang* instead of *hu*, the line might then read, "'Male Defender'"—this is his new assignment," meaning that the father of the poem (or his sons?) has been conscripted to serve in the army, and his family is bound to suffer, since he has put no money aside. Ch'en Hui-chien (*Han-shan-tzu*, p. 222) would read the line in this way.

2. Read (*Chinese Medicinal Plants*, p. 106, item 354) identifies *huang-po* as "Yellow Bark" (*Phellodendron amurense*). Stuart (*Chinese Materia Medica: Vegetable Kingdom*, pp. 316–317) notes that Yellow Bark is a tree that "grows to the height of thirty or forty feet, having a whitish outer bark and an inner yellow one. The latter is used in dyeing silk yellow, as well as in medicine. The drug, as it appears in the market, is in square or rectangular pieces, from three to five inches long, rough on the outer surface, and smooth, or striated longitudinally, on the inner surface. The interior is of a deep yellow color, and the taste is very bitter." The "crupper" (*ch'iu*) is a loop tied to a horse's tail and then fastened to the saddle.

No. 126

The new grain is still not yet ripe;
The old grain is already gone.[1]

Off to borrow a peck or so,
I stand hesitant outside the gate.

The old man came out and told me to go ask his wife;
Then his wife came out and sent me to ask the old man.

Being sparing[2] won't save the poor;
The more goods people have, the more their stupidity piles up.

1. Very similar lines open the preface to a poem by T'ao Ch'ien which Hightower translated as "Inspired by Events" (*The Poetry of T'ao Ch'ien*, p. 165): "The old grain is gone, and the new is not yet harvested."
2. *Ch'ien-hsi*, "to be sparing, economical," which in other circumstances might be praiseworthy.

No. 127

There are a good many affairs that deserve a good laugh;
I'll just briefly present three or four.

Duke Chang with his wealth indulged in luxury,[1]
While Mencius with his poverty was disappointed and
    frustrated.[2]

He just chose the dwarfs to be full,
Not caring that Fang-shuo might starve.[3]

With Pa songs the singers are many,
But with "White Snow" nobody chimes in.[4]

1. The "Duke Chang" Han-shan has in mind is presumably the Mr. Chang, alluded to in *Shih-chi* 129 (Vol. 10, p. 3282), who became rich by selling broth (or paste?—*chiang*).

2. The well-known Confucian philosopher—fl. 320 B. C. Han-shan cleverly uses the name of Mencius—Meng K'o—in describing his frustration—*k'an-k'o*.

3. Alluding to a story in the biography of the Han statesman Tung-fang Shuo (*Han shu* 65, Vol. 9, p. 2843), where Tung is put out that he—a man of great talent and height—is paid the same as the dwarfs who work in the stable. He speaks out to the emperor (translated by Burton Watson, *Courtier and Commoner in Ancient China* [New York: Columbia University Press, 1974], p. 81): "The dwarfs are somewhat over three feet in height, and as a stipend they receive one sack of grain and 240 cash each. I am somewhat over nine feet in height, and as a stipend I too receive one sack of grain and 240 cash. The dwarfs are about to die of overeating; I am about to die of hunger. If my words are of any use, I hope I may be treated differently from them. If my words are of no use, then dismiss me. There's no point in merely keeping me around to eat up the rice of Ch'ang-an!"

4. In "Sung Yü tui Ch'u-wang wen" (Sung Yü Replies to the Question of the King of Ch'u, *Wen-hsüan* 45: 1b–2b, p. 619), King Hsiang of Ch'u asks Sung Yü if he is guilty of some misdeed such that he is not praised more by the common people. Sung Yü in his response notes that in Ying there are some singers who start off by singing the song "Hsia-li Pa-jen" (Bottom Village—People of Pa), a song which is so well known and popular that several thousands of people join in. But when they sing "White Snow in the Spring" (Yang-ch'un pai-hsüeh), "those in the state who gather together and sing along are not more than several tens of people." He concludes from this that "the higher [in quality] the tune, the fewer [in number] those who can sing along." Clearly Sung Yü's conduct is of such high caliber that the common people don't even know about it.

No. 128

When an old man takes a young bride,
She won't stand it when his hair turns gray.

When an old woman weds a young gent,
He won't love her with her sallow face.

When an old man takes an old woman,
On both sides there will be no rejection.

When a young woman weds a young gent,
Both have a manner of tender concern.

No. 129

Majestic and stately that beautiful youth;
Widely read in the histories and classics.

Everyone calls him "Teacher";
All praise him as "Scholar."

He's not yet been able to gain official employment,
But he doesn't understand how to hold the handle
    of a plow.

In the winter he'll wear a tattered old gown;
I'm afraid this is being misled by one's books!

No. 130

The birds chat and converse[1]—feelings I can't really bear;[2]
At times like these, I lie down in my straw hut.

Cherries, in reds that sparkle and glisten;
Willows so straight—branches like hair hanging down.

Morning sun—swallowed up by green peaks;
White, puffy clouds—washed clean in clear mountain lakes.

Who there knows to leave the dust and the vulgar,[3]
And drive up the South face of Han-shan?

1. There is a variant of "play"(*nung*) for "converse" (*yü*).
2. Birds in a flock talking to one another often painfully remind the recluse of family and friends far away. Here Han-shan's feelings seem rather to be those of joy.
3. Addressing people in the world.

No. 131*

Yesterday—so far away;
In that garden, so charming and sweet.

Above me, pathways through peaches and plums;
Below me, calamus isle.

In addition, a woman in very fine silks;
In her cottage—wearing kingfisher feathers and plumes.

When we met, I wished to call out,
But choked up, I just couldn't speak.[1]

---

*Pulleyblank: Han-shan II.

1. Using virtually the same words we find in the last line of poem 10 of the "Nineteen Old Poems" (see *Wen-hsüan* 29: 5a, p. 399), a poem describing the lovestruck separation of the two constellations Herd Boy and Weaving Girl. Watson (*Chinese Lyricism*, p. 28) translates the poem: "Far far away, the Herdboy Star; bright bright, the Lady of the River of Heaven; slim slim, she lifts a pale hand, clack clack, plying the shuttle of her loom, all day long—but the pattern's never finished; welling tears fall like rain. The River of Heaven is clear and shallow; what a little way lies between them! only the span of a single brimming stream—they gaze and gaze and cannot speak."

Comment: I think Iritani and Matsumura (*Kanzanshi*, p. 187) are right in reading the poem at face value: the poet describes a lovely garden or park (*ch'ang-t'ing-yüan*) and a lovely woman he encountered there. It is tempting to see something more underneath, since peaches and plums and calamus (for *lan-sun* as "calamus," see Bernard Read, *Chinese Medicinal Plants*, p. 228, item 703) are all Taoist foods of long life and thus could stand here for that goal (the *Shen Nung pen-ts'ao ching* [1. 10b] notes that calamus [*ch'ang-p'u*] "opens the holes in the heart," "repairs the five organs," "makes the ear hear clearly and the eyes see well"). Also, *ch'ang* can mean *tao-ch'ang*, which in Buddhism can mean "the place of enlightenment." Ch'en Hui-chien (*Han-shan-tzu*, pp. 175–176), by contrast, notes metaphorical associations of "older and younger brothers," and "students" and "beautiful virtue" with peaches and plums, and the "beautiful worthiness of sons and grandsons" with calamus, suggesting the *ch'ang* in line 2 has something to do with the "place" where examinations were held.

No. 132

A man should never stay poor;
If you're penniless you must manage and plan.

When you raise only one cow,
She will produce all of five calves.

The calves will also bear young,
And the numbers will add up, on and on without end.

I send this message to Master Chu of T'ao:
My wealth is the same as yours.[1]

---

1. For the story of Master Chu of T'ao—alias Fan Li—and the wealth he amassed over the years through smart real estate deals, cultivated and added to by his sons and grandsons, see *Shih-chi* 129, "Huo-chih," Vol. 10, p. 3257.

Note: Han-shan was of course concerned about the lot of the poor. But one wonders if the message here is not symbolic. If one builds up good deeds, beginning with only one, the reward in the end is substantial.

No. 133

This man[1]—how anxious and ill at ease;
In divining where to live, you must take care of yourself.

In the south, malaria and miasmas abound;
In the North lands, the winds and frost are severe.

In desolate corners one cannot live;
Poisoned streams—it's not good to drink;

My soul! [I call to you] to return;[2]
Eat the mulberries in my family's grove.

1. Using the archaic *Shih ching* formula *chih-tzu* (see *Shih* 6, 9, 12, 28, or 156), though the complete formula is *chih-tzu yü-kuei*, "this woman (or man) is going home." Thus right from the start, the poem carries with it the sense of "returning home."
2. Again the Chinese is *kuei ch'ü-lai*; see note 2 to poem 124.
Note: Iritani and Matsumura (*Kanzanshi*, p. 191) show how Han-shan's poem follows the stages and themes of "Chao-hun" in the *Ch'u-tz'u* (*Ch'u-tz'u pu-chu* 9: 1a–15b, pp. 83–90; translated by David Hawkes, *The Songs of the South*, pp. 219–231). There the soul is encouraged to come back home by alternatively being shown the horrors that await it in the various directions of space and the delights that await it back home (including the good things it can eat). The last line of "Chao hun" is, "O soul, come back! Alas for the Southern Land!" (translated by Hawkes, *The Songs of the South*, p. 230).

No. 134

Last night I dreamed I went back home
And saw my wife in the midst of weaving at her loom.

She halted the shuttle, as though she had just had a thought,
Then she lifted the shuttle; it was as though she had lost all
    her strength.

I called to her—she turned to look;
Her response a blank stare—she didn't recognize me.

It must be we've been apart now so many years
That my temple hair is not its old color.

Note: See poem 39.

No. 135

Man's life does not fill one hundred;
Yet he harbors the grief of one *thousand* years.[1]

Though for yourself, your illness might start to improve;
In addition, you must fret for your sons and grandsons as well.

Below—examine the bottoms of the roots of the grain;
Above—look to the tops of the mulberry trees.[2]

When the balance weight drops into the Eastern sea,[3]
You will finally *begin* to know you can rest.

1. Almost word for word the opening lines of poem 15 of the "Nineteen Old Poems" (*Wen-hsüan* 29:7a, p. 400). For a translation, see Burton Watson, *Chinese Lyricism*, pp. 29–30. See also poem 22.
2. i.e., in life one must worry about every single detail from start to finish.
3. i.e., when you die, the balance is used to weigh out the worth of one's deeds.

No. 136

In this world there is one kind of group,
Blank and vacant like some block of wood!

When they speak, they show they know nothing,
Yet they say, "We don't have a single concern."

If you ask them about the Way—the Way they don't understand;
If you ask them about the Buddha—the Buddha they do not seek.

If you explore the matter in great detail,
Boundless! You'll drown in an ocean of grief.

No. 137

Master Tung when he was young,
He'd come and go in the capital.[1]

His shirt made of soft gosling yellow;
Appearance and manner—like that you'd see in a print.

Always rode on a "treading snow" horse;[2]
In light puffs the red dust would be raised.

Observers filled the sides of the road,[3]
Asking, "This is the son of what clan?"[4]

1. Apparently meaning Tung Hsien, the intimate favorite of Emperor Ai of the Han (r. 6 B. C.–1 A. D.), who was forced to commit suicide after Ai died (see *Han shu* 93, Vol. II, pp. 3733–3741).

2. i.e., a horse whose hooves are all white.

3. The same words are found in the *yüeh-fu* "Chi-ming" (cock crow)—*Yüeh-fu shih-chi*, Vol. I, p. 406—a song that also describes the rise and fall of those whose rank depends on political ties.

4. The same question is asked in Ts'ao Chih's "Pai-ma p'ien." See poem 54, note 1.

No. 138

This is the son of what clan?
He is a man who is hated a lot.

Doltish mind—always indignant and angry;
Eyes of flesh—like he's drunk, everything in a haze.

He sees the Buddha and yet does not bow,
Runs into monks but does not give them alms.

All he knows is how to cut up large pieces of meat;
Beyond this he has not one skill.

No. 139

People take their bodies as basic,
And in what is basic, it's the mind that's in control.

When the "basic" exists, the mind must not be depraved;
If the mind is depraved you'll lose your "basic" life.[1]

If you cannot yet avoid this disaster,
Why speak of carelessly using a mirror?[2]

Not reading the *Diamond-sūtra*[3]
Would make even a bodhisattva get ill.[4]

1. *Pen-ming* means, at one and the same time, "the life that is basic or fundamental" and "one's *own* life."
2. Iritani and Matsumura (*Kanzanshi*, p. 199) cite a line from the *Nirvāṇa-sūtra* (Ch. 34) in which the *Nirvāṇa-sūtra* is compared to a mirror that all sentient beings should look into to see who they really are. But looking at oneself in a mirror (*chao-ching*) was forbidden to monks under normal circumstances, and I think the point here is that having a "correct mind" is more important than obeying nit-picking rules.
3. A favorite *sūtra* of the Chinese and a text closely connected with the life of Hui-neng, the Sixth Patriarch of Zen. For a translation, see Edward Conze, *Buddhism Wisdom Books: The Diamond Sutra and the Heart Sutra* (New York: Harper Torchbooks, 1972).
4. Though Tseng P'u-hsin's interpretation (*Han-shan shih-chieh*, p. 81) is that if all living things are ill—because they do not know the one mind—then a bodhisattva will also be ill.
Note: This poem is similar in style to a number of other poems (see, for example, 149) in which Han-shan uses the same words in different lines and positions to say different things. Here the words are *hsin* ("mind") and *pen* ("basic") in lines 1–4.

No. 140

North of the city lives old man Chung;
His family has lots of meat and wine.

When old man Chung's wife died,
The mourners filled the courtyards and rooms.

When old Chung himself passed away,
Not one single person cried.[1]

Those who ate and drank of his cups and his chops,
How could they be so cold inside?[2]

1. On *neng-wu* as a strong negative, see poem 55, note 1.
2. So cold in "stomach and heart" (*hsin-fu*). Han-shan may be playing
on the fact that wine and meat normally warm one's insides.

No. 141

When the lowly ignorant read my poems,[1]
They don't understand—moreover, they snidely chuckle and jeer.

When the average and common read my poems,
They think them over saying, "Very important."

When the highest worthies read my poems,
They hold them firmly in hand, grinning from ear to ear.

When Yang Hsiu saw the words "young wife,"
One look, and he knew that it was "sublime."[2]

1. "Stupid folks at the bottom" (*hsia-yü*), the *locus classicus* of the expression being Confucius' remark (in *Analects* 17: 2, p. 35) about the stupid folks at the bottom and the intelligent people at the top. D. C. Lau (*Confucius: The Analects* [New York: Penguin Books, 1979], p. 143) translates: "The Master said, 'It is only the most intelligent and the most stupid who are not susceptible to change.'" In the first three couplets Han-shan clearly mimics the opening of Ch. 41 of the *Lao-tzu*. Chan (*The Way of Lao Tzu* [Indianapolis: Bobbs-Merrill, 1963], p. 174) translates: "When the highest type of men hear Tao, They half believe in it. When the lowest type of men hear Tao, They laugh heartily at it. If they did not laugh at it, it would not be Tao."

2. He knew the word was *miao*, the character *miao* being composed of the elements *nü*, "woman," and *shao*, "young"; the clue was *yu-fu*, "young woman (or wife or bride)." Yang Hsiu was Superintendent of Records (*chu-pu*) under Ts'ao Ts'ao (A. D. 155–220). For the anecdote to which Han-shan alludes, in which Yang Hsiu immediately unravels the riddle written on the back of a stele for Ts'ao Ts'ao, see *Shih-shuo hsin-yü chiao-chien* 11, no. 3, 441. Mather (*Shih-shuo Hsin-yü: A New Account of Tales of the World* [Minneapolis, MN: University of Minnesota Press, 1976], p. 293) translates: "Ts'ao Ts'ao once passed beneath the memorial stele to the maid Ts'ao O (in K'uai-chi, Chekiang) while Yang Hsiu was accompanying him. On the back of the stele they saw an inscription in eight characters: '*Huang-chüan yu-fu wai-sun chi-chiu,*' literally, 'Yellow pongee, youthful wife, maternal grandson, ground in mortar.' Ts'ao Ts'ao asked Hsiu, 'Do you understand it?' He replied 'Yes.' Ts'ao Ts'ao said, 'Don't tell me; wait while I think about it.' After they had traveled on for thirty *li*, Ts'ao Ts'ao finally said, 'I've got it!' He then had Hsiu record separately what he had understood it to mean. Hsiu wrote, ' "Yellow pongee" is *colored silk* (*se-ssu*), which, combined in one character, is *chüeh*, "utterly." "Youthful wife" is *young woman* (*shao-nü*),which, combined in one character, is *miao*, "wonderful." "Maternal grandson" is a *daughter's son* (*nü-tzu*), which, combined in one character, is *hao*, "lovely." "Ground in a mortar"is to *suffer hardship* (*shou-hsin*), which, combined in one character, is *tz'u*, "words." Ts'ao Ts'ao had also recorded it in the same way that Hsiu had. Sighing, he said, 'My ability is thirty *li* slower than yours!'" The point here is that intelligent people will also recognize at a glance that Han-shan's poems are "sublime," "utterly wonderful, lovely words!"

No. 142

By nature there are those who are stingy and close,
But I'm not in the stingy-close group.

My clothes are simple—worn for the purpose of dance;
My wine is all gone—I sip because I sing.

I always take one bellyful,
Which never makes my two feet get tired.[1]

When the daisies worm their way into your skull,
On this day, sir, you'll repent!

1. i.e., he is like the mole in Chapter 1 of the *Chuang-tzu*, who only drinks until he is full, taking no more than he needs. Watson (*The Complete Works*, p. 32) translates: "When the mole drinks at the river, he takes no more than a bellyful" (*Chuang-tzu*, Ch. 1, p. 2, lines 25–26).

No. 143

Out walking, I pass through some old, ancient graves;
The tears now are all gone—but I sigh for the living
and the dead.

One tomb broken open, crushing the outer coffin;[1]
The inner coffin laid bare—disclosing all the white bones.

Slanting off to one side—earthenware bottles and urns;
Though I sort and pick through—here are no cap-clasps or
tablets of jade.[2]

The wind comes up, stirring up the insides;
Ashes and dust, scattered about in the air.

1. Literally, crush the *huang-ch'ang*, "yellow innards," the yellow innards being the heart-wood of the cypress (*po*), from which outer coffins
(*kuo*) were made.
2. *Ts'an-hu*, worn and held by high ranking officials during imperial
audience—i.e., this is the grave of someone poor.

No. 144

The evening sun sinks[1] beneath western hills;
Grasses and trees reflect its dazzling glow.

What's more, there are places here dim and dark,
Where pines and creepers meet up and join.

And here, so many crouching tigers;
When they see me—manes rapidly stand up on end.

In my hand—not so much as a single inch blade;
How could I not fearfully tremble and shake?

1. Reading the variant of *hsia*, "goes down," for *ho*, "shine."
   Note: I think the poem is symbolic, and the symbolism seems to say that late in life (setting sun), even though there are things about oneself that are clear and understood, perhaps even things of which one can be proud (i.e., that dazzle like the grasses and trees), there remain hidden pockets where feelings and passions lie in wait (crouching tigers). Against these attacks, Han-shan feels impotent and helpless. Not only do tigers lie in wait in places "dim and dark" (*meng-lung*), they wait where "pines and creepers" (*sung-lo*) meet. Since pine trees stand for long life, could the point here be that tangled feelings cut off and choke our chances for long life?

No. 145

Go into the world,[1] and you're bound to be troubled
    and disturbed.
The affairs of the world are not all alike.

I'm not yet able to leave common customs behind;
It is these that follow me around.

Yesterday we mourned the death of Hsü Number Five;
Today we escort Liu the Third to his grave.

All day long I've been unable to rest;[2]
Because of this, my heart is saddened and grieved.

---

    1. *Ch'u-shen* normally means to enter government service, but that does not seem directly relevant here. Iritani and Matsumura (*Kanzanshi*, pp. 206–207) take *ch'u-shen* to mean "leave one's body" and enter *nirvāṇa*, which to me makes no sense at all.
    2. There is a variant of "day after day" (*jih-jih*) for "all day long" (*chung-jih*).

No. 146

If you have music,[1] then you must enjoy;
"Now is the time! It cannot be missed."[2]

Though they say we have one hundred years;
Can you live the full thirty thousand days?[3]

Our stay in the world—but a brief moment;
When you talk about money, never make all that racket and
noise!

The last chapter of the *Classic of Filial Piety*
In great detail sets out the complete situation.[4]

1. Or "happiness"—*lo* or *yüeh*—but music seems more in keeping with the allusion in the last line.

2. These are the exact words spoken by King Wu of the Chou when he was about to attack the Shang. See "T'ai-shih" (The Great Declaration) in the *Shu* (*Shang-shu K'ung chuan* 6: 2b). Legge (modern edition by Clae Waltham, *Shu Ching: Book of History* [Chicago: Henry Regnery Company, 1971], p. 115) translates: "What the people desire, Heaven will effect. You must aid me, the One Man, to cleanse for ever all within the four seas. Now is the time! It should not be lost."

3. Iritani and Matsumura (*Kanzanshi*, p. 208) see in these four lines yet another allusion to poem 15 of the "Nineteen Old Poems" (see poems 22 and 135). Watson (*Chinese Lyricism*, p. 29) translates that poem: "Man's years fall short of a hundred; a thousand years of worry crowd his heart. If the day is short, and you hate the long night, why not take the torch and go wandering? Seek out happiness in season; who can wait the year to come? Fools who cling too fondly to gold earn no more than posterity's jeers. Prince Ch'iao, that immortal man—small hope we have of matching him!"

4. The last chapter of the *Hsiao-ching* being Chapter 18, "Sang-ch'in" (Mourning for Kin). This includes the injunction that at such times "Though one hears music, one is not happy" (*wen-yüeh pu-lo*).

No. 147

Alone I sit, constantly disappointed and sad;
My feelings and innermost thoughts—how troubled they are
    and forlorn.

The clouds at the waist of the mountain spread out
    thick and dense; .
The wind at the mouth of the valley—mournfully it
    sighs and moans.

Gibbons come—the trees shiver and shake;
Birds enter the woods—their singing echoes tweet, tweet.

Pressed now by the times, my temple hair dishevelled hangs
    down.
At the end of the year, I'm old, filled with pain and regret.

Note: See poem 31. Here Han-shan ends each line with a reduplicated
binome. The poem would be romanized as follows:

> Tu-tso ch'ang *hu-hu;*
> Ch'ing-huai ho *yu-yu.*
>
> Shan-yao yün *man-man;*
> Ku-k'ou feng *sou-sou.*
>
> Yüan lai shu *niu-niu;*
> Niao ju lin *chiu-chiu.*
>
> Shih ts'ui pin *sa-sa;*
> Sui-chin lao *ch'ou-ch'ou.*

No. 148

One man with good belly and head;
The Six Arts, he knows them all well.[1]

When seen in the South, he's chased back to the North;
When encountered[2] in the West, he's rushed off to the East.

Always drifting, like floating duckweed;[3]
Never resting, like blown-about bramble.[4]

You ask, this is what type or sort?
His surname is Poor, his name Impoverished.

1. The *liu-i* being the six classic teachings of Confucians: the *Book of Poetry* (*Shih*), the *Book of Documents* (*Shu*), the *Record of Rites* (*Li-chi*), the *Music* (*Yüeh*), the *Book of Changes* (*I ching*), and the *Spring and Autumn Annals* (*Ch'un-ch'iu*).

2. Some texts simply repeat the "seen" of the previous line.

3. "Duckweed" (*p'ing*) standing for things that are rootless. A set expression in Chinese, descriptive of homeless wanderers, is *p'ing-fan nan-pei*, "drifting north and south like duckweed."

4. The "bramble" (*p'eng*), like duckweed, being a stock symbol of someone on the go, having no steady home. See poem 11.

No. 149

"When others are worthy—those you, my lord, should accept;
The unworthy, you should never associate with."

"If you, sir, are worthy, you'll be abided by others;
And if you're not, they should also reject you!

Have praise for the good, commiserate with those not able;
Disciples of kindness[1] will then find their place."

I urge you to follow the speech of Tzu-chang;
Decline and retreat from the words of Pu-shang.

1. *Jen-t'u*, more precisely, "disciples of humanity" (or benevolence).
Comment: The poem is similar in style to 139 above: Han-shan repeatedly uses the same words in successive lines—here the words are *t'a*, "others," *chün*, "you, my lord," and *hsien*, "worthy." All of this alludes to a passage in the *Analects* (19: 3, p. 39). D. C. Lau (*Confucius: The Analects*, p. 153) translates: "Tzu-hsia's disciples asked Tzu-chang about friendship. Tzu-chang said, 'What does Tzu-hsia say?' Tzu-hsia says, "You should make friends with those who are adequate and spurn those who are inadequate."

"Tzu-chang said, 'That is different from what I have heard. I have heard that the gentleman honours his betters and is tolerant towards the multitude and that he is full of praise for the good while taking pity on the backward. If I am greatly superior, which among men need I be intolerant of? If I am inferior, then others will spurn me, how can there be any question of my spurning them?'"

Lines 1 and 2 reflect the words of Tzu-hsia; lines 3–5 reflect the words of Tzu-chang, and line 5 of Han-shan's poem quotes almost directly the words of Tzu-chang. Pu-shang is another name for Tzu-hsia.

No. 150

The common and contemptuous are truly *completely*
  contemptuous;[1]
People's hearts—they are not the same.

Old man Yin laughs at old Liu,
And old Liu laughs at old man Yin.

For what reason do they laugh at each other?
Both move about in the midst of the vile and mean.

Were they to load carts, they would compete in piling
  them high as a mountain;[2]
The carts would then overturn, and they'd both be
  defeated and beat![3]

1. Iritani and Matsumura (*Kanzanshi*, p. 214) note that *chen-ch'eng* was colloquial in the T'ang for "really" or "truly."

2. *Ti-nieh* means "high" or "high and dangerous."

3. Following Iritani and Matsumura's interpretation of these last two lines. Alternatively, they might read, "With a loaded cart—they would dispute on a steep dangerous peak; The cart would overturn—and they'd both be defeated and beat!" "Defeated and beat" (*lung-tung*) is normally glossed as "soaking wet," but that makes little sense here. Iritani and Matsumura (*Kanzanshi*, p. 214) compile an impressive list of phonetically similar compounds from a variety of texts to show that *lung-tung* here, as in those cases, describes a condition of total defeat—"defeated, destroyed, beaten, and scattered."

No. 151

In those days when I had money,
I always loaned some to you for the taking.

Now you at present are warm and full,
But when you see me, you won't share and hand out.

You must remember your desire for help,
Just like my present hope for support.

"Have and have not" is something that tends to take
    turns;
I urge you, think it over with care!

No. 152

Man's life is but one hundred years;
Buddha's teachings fall into twelve groups.[1]

Compassion is like a wild deer,[2]
But anger resembles the family dog.[3]

The family dog—though you chase it, it won't go away,
Whereas the wild deer is always ready to flee.

If you want to conquer the heart of the monkey,[4]
You must listen to the lion's roar.[5]

1. The Mahāyāna canon has twelve divisions (shih-erh pu). They are:
(1) sūtra, (2) geya, (3) gāthā, (4) nidāna, (5) itivṛttaka, (6) jātaka, (7) abhidharma,
(8) avadāna (9) upadeśa, (10) udāna, (11) vaipulya, and (12) vyākaraṇa.
    2. Specifically the sika deer (lu). Compassion (tz'u-pei, karuna) is one
of the supreme Buddhist virtues.
    3. And anger (here ch'en-fen) is one of the six kleśas (delusions, defile-
ments). The analogies between compassion and deer, and anger and dogs
are drawn in the Nirvāṇa-sūtra, Ch. 14 (T.375, Vol 12, p. 396 top). There we
read: "The family dog is not afraid of people; the wild deer of mountain
forests run away in fear when they see people. Anger is difficult to elimi-
nate; it's like holding on to the family dog: the compassionate heart is easily lost; it's like those wild deer."

4. Another allusion to the *Nirvāṇa-sūtra* (Ch. 29, T.374, Vol. 12, p. 536 bottom), where the heart and nature of all living things is compared to that of the monkey. The text says: "The heart and nature of sentient beings is like that of the monkey. The nature of the monkey is that he rejects one thing and holds on to another. The heart and nature of sentient beings is also like this. They hold on to and are attached to the *dharmas* of form, sound, smell, taste, and touch without any temporary stop."

5. *Shih-tzu hou* (*siṁhanāda*) stands for the powerful preaching of the Buddha, frightening and conquering non-believers, just as the lion's roar frightens and intimidates the other animals of the jungle.

No. 153

Let me teach you several kinds of things;
Think them over—you will then know I'm wise.

In extreme poverty, endure selling your house;
When you are wealthy, you must *then* buy fields.

When your stomach is empty, don't be running around,
But when you have a pillow you must never sleep.

These words, if we want the masses to see,
We must hang them up on the east side of the sun.

Note: Tseng P'u-hsin (*Han-shan shih-chieh*, p. 88) glosses "house" here as *hsin-wang* (heart-king) and "buying fields" as *ching-chin*, the Buddhist virtue of *vīrya*, "vigor," making the point that even in extreme poverty one should *not* sell one's house. One should always work hard, never loving sleep, even when one's stomach is empty. But the message seems rather to be that one should be willing to sell one's house when poor, making up for it when one is wealthy, and that one should care for one's health (not run around) when he is poor, but be active again (never sleep) when he is rich (has a pillow to sleep on).

No. 154

Han-shan has many hidden wonders;
Climbers are always struck with awe.

When the moon shines, the waters are clear and bright;
When the wind blows, grasses rustle and sigh.

Withered plums, the snow becomes their blossoms;
Branchless trees have clouds filling in for their leaves.

Touched by rain, it's transformed—all fresh and alive;
If it's not a clear day, you cannot ascend.

No. 155

There is a tree that was born before the forest;
Count its years—exceeding others by twice the age.[1]

Its roots have been twisted by valleys and hills;
Its leaves have been changed by the wind and the frost.

Everyone laughs at the outside, all withered and old;
They care not for the elegance that lies within.

When the bark is done falling away,
The only thing left is "what's really real."[2]

1. But I wonder—given the text that inspires this poem (see below)—
if *i-pei* ("one time," "double") might not mean *i-pai*, "one hundred." *Pei* can
mean "one hundred men."

2. *Chen shih-tsai* is not a technical Buddhist term, but it seems clear
that Han-shan means by it much the same thing as *shih-hsing*, "true
nature," or *chen-ju*, *bhūtatathatā*.

Note: The entire poem closely follows a passage in Chapter 39 of the
Nirvāṇa-sūtra (T.374, Vol. 12, p. 597 top), which reads: "It's just like the fact
that beyond the village, there is a grove of Śālavana trees. In [those trees]
there is one tree that was born before the rest of the forest. It is all of one
hundred years. The forest caretaker irrigates it with water, all the time caring for it and protecting it. This tree is old and decayed, its bark and leaves
have all fallen off. All that remains is what's really real. The Tathāgata is
also like this."

No. 156

On Han-shan there's this naked critter;[1]
His body is white and his head is black.

In his hand he holds two books;
One's on the Way, and one is on Virtue.[2]

At home, he sets up no kettle or stove;
For his walks, he carries no mantle.[3]

Ever grasping the sword of wisdom,
He plans to cut down the thief of delusion.[4]

1. A *lo-ch'ung* ("naked critter") is an animal without hair or feathers—i.e., man.
2. i.e., the *Lao-tzu*, the *Tao-te ching*.
3. Specifically, the robe worn by Buddhists—*i-chieh*.
4. In the *Vimalakīrti-sūtra* (Ch. 11, "P'u-sa hsing"; T.475, Vol. 14, p. 554 top and middle) the Buddha addresses a group of bodhisattvas who come from the world-realm "Many fragrances," advising them that "the proper bodhisattva does not destroy the conditioned and does not abide in the unconditioned" (translated by Richard Robinson, "The Sūtra of Vimlalakīrti's Preaching," p. 48, unpublished manuscript). In explaining what this means, one of the things he lists is "with the sword of wisdom to slay the bandit passions."

No. 157

There is a man who fears turning gray,
Who's unwilling to give up his red sash.[1]

Gathering herbs, in vain he seeks to become an immortal;
Roots and shoots—chaotically he digs out and sorts through.

For several years he's done this with no result—
Blind to all else, his frustration building inside.

If you're a hunter dressed in monk's robes,[2]
Fundamentally, this is not something you can use.

1. i.e., he's unwilling to give up his concern for wealth and rank.
Iritani and Matsumura (*Kanzanshi*, pp. 223–224) say that gold seals with red
sashes (*chu-fu*, a cord on which the seal was tied from the belt) were be-
stowed on censors in the T'ang.
    2. A stock image in Buddhism of a monk who breaks the command-
ments—he merely dresses the part. The *locus classicus* of the metaphor is
the *Nirvāṇa-sūtra*, Chapter 7 ("Ju-lai hsing" T. 374, Vol. 12, p. 402 bottom).

No. 158

In former days I was poor, with just enough to get by,
But now I've reached the limit of poverty and cold.

Nothing I do ever works out;
Every path I follow leads to distress and despair.

Walking about in the mud, feet constantly twisted and bent;
Sitting with village friends, stomach always painful and sore.

Since I lost the gray spotted cat,
The old rat hovers 'round the rice jar.

No. 159*

I've seen the people in this world;
Dignified and imposing, they put on their good, polite airs.

They don't repay parents' kindness;
Their hearts—what kind do they have?

In debt, they owe others money;
With hooves and rings—only then do they start to regret.[1]

Each one of them tenderly loves wife and son.
But mother and father they do not support.

Older and younger brother they treat as though from some
      enemy clan;
In their hearts, always unhappy and sad.

[Their parents] remember the old days when they were young,
When they prayed to the spirits, wishing for them to be grown.

Now they're unfilial sons;
In the world there are many of this kind.

They buy meat for their own families to gobble down,
Wipe their lips saying, "Ah, now I'm full and content!"

Showing off, in speech they babble and gab,
Claiming in wisdom they have no match.[2]

But when Oxhead angrily gives them his stare,[3]
They'll then start to know that their time is already gone.[4]

They choose a Buddha and burn good incense;
Select a monk and present him with nourishing gifts.

Beg for alms in front of an arhat's gate,
But chase away all practicing monks.[5]

They don't understand that the man in *nirvāṇa*,
From the beginning has no distinguishing marks.[6]

They write their letters inviting famous monks,
And then give them money—two or three different kinds![7]

Yün-kuang was a good Dharma-master,
Yet he wore horns on top of his head.[8]

If you have not the indiscriminate mind,[9]
Sages and worthies—neither one will descend.

All sages make no distinction;
I urge you to stop grasping marks.

My teaching is profound—difficult to comprehend;
Devas and *nāgas* all turn and face me.

And now prostrate I bow
To the supreme Dharma-king.[10]

Compassionate, he takes great joy in giving;
His name fills the ten directions of space.

All living things on him depend and rely;
The body of wisdom is of diamond.

With my head on the floor, there is nothing to which
    I'm attached.
My master is the great Dharma-king.

*Pulleyblank: Han-shan II.
1. Tseng P'u-hsin (*Han-shan shih-chieh*, p. 93) suggests that this alludes to the story of Lu Po-ta of the T'ang, who, having borrowed one
thousand cash, swore an oath in front of the lender that should he fail to

repay, he should be reborn as an ox in this benefactor's home. He did not repay the money. In one year he died; in two, his benefactor indeed led an ox around town with the name of Lu Po-ta in white hair on its forehead. For this story, see *T'ai-p'ing kuang-chi*, 434: 13 (Vol. 5, p. 3523). The "rings" are those placed in the noses of cattle. The text literally says "hooves and bores" (*t'i-ch'uan*).

2. See Iritani and Matsumura (*Kanzanshi*, p. 332) for *i-tang* as colloquial for *p'i-ti*, "match" or "equal."

3. Oxhead (*niu-t'ou, Gośīrsa*) and Horseface (*ma-mien, Aśvamukha*) are the two attendants in hell who greet newly dead souls. The role of Oxhead goes to someone who ate meat in life. See Henri Maspero, *Taoism and Chinese Religion* (Amherst, MA: University of Massachusetts Press, 1981). p. 183 ff.

4. Following the variant reading of *shih-chüeh shih i-hsiang*. The alternate reading of *ch'u-ch'ü shih shih-hsiang* makes much less sense.

5. Assuming that *hsien ho-shang* means much the same as *hsien tao-shih*, "a well-trained practitioner."

6. *Hsiang-chuang, hsiang* (*lakṣaṇa*) being distinguishing features in phenomena. Mahāyāna philosophy insists that such features are not real, not permanent features of reality.

7. i.e., they distinguish between them in terms of benefits received. "Write them letters" is *feng-shu*, which means, literally, a sealed memorial or a sealed request presented to a superior.

8. Yün-kuang was a Liang dynasty monk (reign of Wu-ti, 502–549) who did not maintain the *śīla*. He once bragged to Pao Chih (d. 514—see poem 172): "I fast by not fasting and don't eat by eating." When he died he became an ox. Pao Chih, seeing him dragging a cart through mud, said to him, "Why don't you say you do not drag by dragging!" Hakuin (*Kanzan shi sendai kibun*, Ch. 2, pp. 71–72) cites Lin-ch'üan's *Hsü-t'ang chi* (case 86) as the source of this anecdote. This seems not to be identical with the *Hsü-t'ang ho-shang yü-lu* (brief title *Hsü-t'ang lu*, T.2000, Vol. 47, pp. 984–1064, compiled by Miao-yüan in 1269), though the latter remains an important source of *kōans* (100 are found in *chüan* 6; the present ancedote is not among them). Iritani and Matsumura (*Kanzanshi*, p. 332), seem to know a variant account of the story, but they do not cite their source.

9. *P'ing-teng hsin, p'ing-teng* (*sama*) being the quality of impartiality, seeing all things the same.

10. On the expression *fa-chung wang*, see poem 90, note 4.

Note: The last ten lines are omitted in the *Tse-shih-chü ts'ung-shu* and *Kunaichō* editions. The SPTK text (*Han-shan-tzu shih-chi*, p. 13) has a black parenthetical mark before the last eight lines of the text, seemingly indicating a break, although the following lines are not set off as a separate poem. The last eight lines *are* treated as a separate poem (found between poems 296 and 298) in Hakuin's edition of the text; see *Kanzan shi sendai kibun*, Chapter 4 of *Hakuin oshō zenshū* (Tokyo: Ryūgin sha, 1934), 3: 45.

No. 160*

Valuable indeed! The natural stuff;[1]
It stands all alone, without companion or mate.

You can search for it, but it cannot be seen;[2]
It goes in and out without gateway or door.

Compress it—it will fit inside your heart;[3]
Extend it—it will fill all of space.

But if this is something you neither believe nor accept,
You might run into it and yet never meet.

---

*Pulleyblank: Han-shan II.

1. *T'ien-jan wu.* Tseng P'u-hsin (*Han-shan shih-chieh*, p. 94) is probably right in specifying that what is intended is one's given nature (*hsing*).

2. The language is reminiscent of *Lao-tzu,* Chapter 14. Wing-tsit Chan (*The Way of Lao Tzu,* p. 124), translates the opening lines: "We look at it and do not see it. . . . We listen to it and do not hear it. . . . We touch it and do not find it." The *it,* of course, is the Tao.

3. Han-shan, here and elsewhere, uses the alternate, anatomical name for heart, *fang-ts'un* ("square inch").

No. 161*

In my house there is one cave;
In the cave there is not one thing.

Spotless and pure—empty just like a court;[1]
Dazzling and bright—it shines just like the sun.

Coarse foods nourish this ethereal person;
Cotton-fur robes cover this illusory substance.

I'll let you have your one thousand sages appear,
For *I* have the true Buddha inside.[2]

---

*Pulleyblank: Han-shan II.

1. *T'ang-t'ang* normally means "dignified and imposing." But I translate "like a court" (*t'ang* by itself means a courtyard) to parallel the next line, where *jih-jih* seems to mean "like the sun."

2. The *t'ien-chen fo*, *bhūtatathatā*, is another name for *dharmakāya*, the law body of the Buddha, the ultimate reality underlying all things.

Note: Surely the opening two lines are intended metaphorically—his "house" is his body, and the "cave" is his mind.

No. 162*

Gentlemen, Gentlemen—all you great men;[1]
In doing things never be rash.

With vigor maintain your iron and stone heart;
Uprightly hold on to the wisdom road.[2]

The road of perversion is useless to walk;[3]
If you walk it—in vain you will bitterly toil.

There's no need to seek the Buddhahood fruit;[4]
Just know and hold on to the Dharma Master and King.

*Pulleyblank: Han-shan II.
1. Mencius, in 3B:2 (p. 22), defines the "great man" (*ta chang-fu*), but such special meaning seems unnecessary here.
2. Literally, the "bodhi" (*p'u-t'i*) road.
3. The *hsieh-lu; hsieh-tao* (*mithya-mārga*) is the incorrect way, the heterodox way, incorrect views.
4. *Fo-kuo* (*Buddhapāla*)—i.e., the state of Buddhahood.

No. 163*

Since I have lived on Han-shan,
I've already passed through several ten-thousands of years.

Complying with fate, I escaped to the forests and springs,
And here I tarry and stay, contemplating that which exists
    on its own.[1]

Cold cliffs—people do not come;
White clouds—always dense and obscure.

Downy grass I use for my mattress;
The blue sky is my cover and quilt.

Happy and alive, I pillow my head on a rock;
Heaven and Earth, I let transform and change.

*Pulleyblank: Han-shan II.
1. *Tzu-tsai* (*vaśitā*) describes the mind free from obstruction and
delusion.

No. 164[†]

Of great value! It is, this Han-shan;
White clouds always at their ease.

The screeching of monkeys resounds through her paths;
The roaring of tigers is outside the realm of men.

Alone I traverse the walkable rocks;
Solitarily chant, on the vines that are easy to climb.

Wind through the pines, so pure—sigh, sigh;
The chatter of birds, the sound—in harmony tweet, tweet.

[†]Missing from the *Tse-shih-chü ts'ung-shu* and *Kunaichō* Library editions.

No. 165

At my leisure, in person I go to look for an eminent monk;
Mountains in mist—ten thousand, ten thousand tiers.

The Master himself points out the way to return;
The moon hangs in the sky—a single circular lamp.

Note: The poem is symbolic of the Zen quest for enlightenment. One might paraphrase as follows: Line 1, one must search on one's own for the truth, and one must have the leisure to do it; Line 2, the initiate is lost in the fog, and the ascent to the truth seems unending; Line 3, in Zen it is the Master who points (*chih*) out the way, by directly pointing to one's true mind and original nature; Line 4, my mind is enlightened, pure, bright, and complete, just like the full moon.

In Zen, the transmission of the truth is sometimes called "the transmission of the lamp" (*ch'uan-teng*). Moreover, the word I translate as "circular" is *lun*, which means "wheel," and the preaching of the Buddha is known as "turning the wheel of the Law."

Also of interest—there is a well-defined group of poems in the T'ang on the subject of "looking for" (*hsün* or *fang*) this or that monk or recluse, the theme we have here. In many of these poems the poet does not succeed in finding the monk or recluse that he seeks (*pu-yü*, "looking for so-and-so but not finding him in").

No. 166

At my leisure I stroll to the top of Hua-ting;[1]
The sun is bright, the daylight dazzling and gay.

Into the four directions I gaze—into the clear sky and void;
White clouds flying together with cranes.

1. Hua-ting, "Flower Peak," is the highest mountain in the T'ien-t'ai range.

Note: A symbolic poem much like the last. Again, bright light at the top seems to stand for the enlightened mind. So too does the "clear sky and void" (*ch'ing-k'ung*), "void" being the same word that translates *śūnyatā*, "emptiness," the Mahāyāna qualifier of all phenomenal things— they are "empty" of own-being, any permanent stuff. The enlightened mind joins the clouds and the cranes who soar free of the world in the purity, transcendence, and light of the sky.

No. 167*

In this world there are people of many affairs,
Widely learned in all sorts of knowledge and views.[1]

But they don't know their original true natures;
Thus they are turned from and far from the Way.

If they could understand the true mark,[2]
For what use this display of false hopes?

With one thought understand your own mind,
And you open the Buddha's knowledge and views.[3]

*Pulleyblank: Han-shan II.
  1. "Knowledge and views" *(chih-chien)* means knowledge of mind and knowledge from perception.
  2. The *shih-hsiang*, "true *lakṣaṇa*," the one mark of reality underlying all phenomenal appearance—i.e., *bhūtatathatā*.
  3. i.e., as soon as you understand your true mind, you then have the knowledge of the Buddha, which is far superior to the learning of men. Underlying this is the T'ien-t'ai and Zen tenet that one's original mind is the one mind underlying and containing all things and thus all-knowing.

No. 168*

On Han-shan there's only one house;[1]
In this house there are neither railings nor screens.[2]

Six doors lead both left and right;[3]
In the courtyard one can see the blue sky.[4]

Room after room is empty, deserted and bare,
From the wall on the east to the wall on the west.

Inside there is not one thing;
In this way I avoid having others come borrow them away.

When the cold arrives, I burn soft wood for heat;
When hunger comes, I cook up some vegetables to eat.

I don't imitate the old farmers,
Who place cattle in their village homes.[5]

All this makes *karma* that leads one to hell;
Once you've entered—when will it ever end?

Carefully, carefully—think it over real well;
If you think, you'll then know the rule.

*Pulleyblank: Han-shan II.
1. The "one house" (*i-chai*) is the "one mind."
2. i.e., the original mind knows no distinctions; there are no fixed boundaries between things.

3. The "six doorways" *(liu-men)* are the six sense organs: eyes, ears, nose, tongue, body, and mind. See, for example, *The Platform Sutra*, section 31 (p. 153 in Philip Yampolsky, translator, *The Platform Sutra of the Sixth Patriarch* [New York: Columbia University Press, 1967] and his note 151).

4. Again, the open, blue sky is symbolic of the enlightened mind.

5. There is a variant of field *(t'ien)* for cattle *(niu)*.

No. 169*

Once for a short while I went down the mountain,
Went inside the walls and the moat.[1]

I ran into a flock of young ladies,
Upright and proper, beautiful in countenance and face.

On their heads they wore Southern-style flowers,[2]
Yen-rouge daubed on cheeks, powder glossy and smooth.[3]

Bracelets of gold, engraved silver earrings,
Robes of thin silk, purple and scarlet red.

Peachy complexions, just like immortals and gods;
Fragrant sashes, heavy aroma of good fortune and wealth.[4]

Men of the times all ogled and leered,
Blindly in love—unclean, the thoughts on their minds.

They said, "The world has no equal";
With soul and shadow they followed behind.

When dogs bite into dry bones,
In vain do they lick teeth and gums![5]

If you don't understand that you must repeatedly think things
    through,
In what way do you differ from beasts?

And now they've turned into white-haired old hags,
Old and ugly, just like witches and spooks!

If from beginningless time you follow your dog's heart,
You'll never ascend to the realm of release.

*Pulleyblank: Han-shan II.

1. i.e., he went into the city.

2. *Shu-yang hua:* Shu, modern Ssu-ch'uan, was known for a special embroidery style.

3. A special rouge made from the juice of the safflower, produced in the northeastern kingdom of Yen.

4. Though Iritani and Matsumara *Kanzanshi,* p. 235) seem to understand *tai* as a verb—"Their perfume *carries with it* the air of the prosperous and rich."

5. i.e., the beauty of these women is equally lacking in substance, in meat.

No. 170*

Ever since I escaped to Han-shan,
I've nourished my life by eating mountain fruits.

All my life through—for what should I be concerned?
The world passes according to fate.[1]

Days and months go by like a swift-flowing stream;[2]
Bright light and shade—like a spark in a rock.

I'll let *you* change with Heaven and Earth;
My delight is sitting here in these cliffs.

*Pulleyblank: Han-shan II.
1. Literally, "in accord with causes," *sui-yüan*.
2. Another allusion to the words of Confucius—see poem 49, note 3.

No. 171

I've seen the people in this world;
Far and wide, they race about in the dust on the roads.

If they don't understand the affairs in this realm,
How will they know to go on to the ford?[1]

Glory and honor you can keep a few days;
Family members, for a brief moment are kin.

Though you might have one thousand catties of gold,
It's not as good as poverty here in the woods.[2]

1. i.e., how will they know to go on to the more important concern with salvation, the "ford" being the place where one can cross over to the other shore of *nirvāṇa*. There is an allusion here to *Analects* 18: 6 (p. 38), where Confucius sends his disciple Tzu-lu to ask two recluses where he might find the ford.

2. "In the woods," *lin-hsia*—really "at the bottom of the woods"—is an expression that means to retire.

No. 172*

I have myself heard of the days of the Liang;[1]
For their "four supports" they had many worthy men.[2]

Pao-chih[3] and Master Wan-hui,[4]
The Four Immortals[5] and Mahāsattva Fu.[6]

They displayed and made known the "teachings of an age,"[7]
Being Tathāgata emissaries[8] for their time.

They built and established monasteries and parks;[9]
Sincere minds clinging to Buddhist truths.

But although their accomplishments were like this,
When there is action, there are many troubles
    and cares.[10]

From the Way—this is extremely distant and far;
It's simply breaking it off from the west and sticking it
    on to the east.

This can't reach to the merit of taking "no action";
It's simply reducing the many to increase the few.[11]

That which has sound but no form;
To the present—where has it gone?[12]

*Pulleyblank: Han-shan II.

1. Emperor Wu of the Liang (r. 502–549) was one of the great early supporters of Buddhism in China. For a summary of his actions, see, for example, Kenneth Ch'en, *Buddhism in China: A Historical Survey*, (Princeton, NJ: Princeton University Press), 124–128.

2. Lists of the "four supports" *(ssu-i)* vary. The standard gloss notes that there are four kinds of support—those of "practice," of "doctrine" or *(dharma)*, of "men," and of "speech"—the four supports of practice, for example being those of "rag clothes, begging for food, sitting under trees, [and] purgatives and diuretics as moral and spiritual means" (William Soothill and Lewis Hodous, *A Dictionary of Chinese Buddhist Terms* [Taipei: Southern Materials Center, 1979], p. 170). Ch'en Hui-chien *(Han-shan-tzu.* p. 257), citing the "Ta-chih-tu lun" as his source, says the "four supports" (or four reliances) mean: (1) to rely on the *dharma* and not to model oneself on men; (2) to rely on understanding the meaning of the *sūtras;* (3) to rely on the meaning and not on the words; and (4) to rely on wisdom and not on mere intellection. Chapter 6 of the *Nirvāṇa-sūtra* (T. 374, Vol. 12, pp. 396 bottom–397 top), on the other hand, seems to say that the "four supports" are four types of people on whom people in the world must rely, those who "give peace and joy to both men and gods." That seems most relevant here. Specifically, the four are: (1) those who have left behind all things in the world of *kleśa* nature (? *ch'u-shih chü fan-nao hsing);* (2) the *srotāpanna* ("stream-winners") and *sakrdāgamin* (once-returners); (3) the *anāgamin* ("non-returners"); and (4) the *arhant* (nobles—those who have attained *nirvāṇa).*

3. Pao-chih (d. 514) was a Buddhist monk arrested in the Ch'i by Emperor Wu (r. 483–494) for deceiving the masses with his strange actions and remarks. He was well received under Wu in the Liang and has come to hold a place in Zen tradition because of a number of cryptic remarks he made in response to questions from Emperor Wu. His biography is recorded in *Kao-seng chuan ch'u-chi,* Chapter 11 (pp. 280–285 in the Taipei, Yin-ching-ch'u 1970 edition). But also note *Ching-te ch'uan-teng lu,* Chapter 27, pp. 150–151, and the *Pi-yen lu,* cases 1 and 67 (T. 2003, Vol. 48, pp. 140–141 and 197; translated into English in J. C. Cleary, *The Blue Cliff Record* [Boulder, Co: Shambhala, 1977], Vol. 1 pp. 1–9, and Vol. 2 pp. 424–428).

4. Master Wan-hui ("Master Ten Thousand Return") is presumably the Fa-yün kung (lay surname was Chang), whose biography we find in *Ching-te ch'uan-teng lu,* Chapter 27, p. 158. Master Wan-hui was so named after he travelled a great distance overnight and then returned (i.e., ten thousand li) to check on the welfare of an older brother. (See Ch'en Hui-chien, *Han-shan-tzu.* p. 239; the *Ch'uan-teng lu* account is slightly different.) He was favored by Empress Wu (r. 684–705) and well received by other royalty at the capital. Iritani and Matsumura *(Kanzanshi.* p. 240) point out that there is a problem with this identification. Fa-yün's dates are 632–711; thus he was not a monk in the Liang. There was, however, another Fa-yün who lived in Kuang-chai ssu in Liang times (his dates are 467–529). Thus,

they argue that originally Han-shan's poem said "Fa-yün"—meaning the Fa-yün of the Liang—and that a later editor, knowing that "Wan-hui" was the more popular name for the T'ang Fa-yün, changed the name to Wan-hui.

5. Iritani and Matsumaura (*Kanzanshi*, p. 240) and Tseng P'u-hsin *Han-shan shih-chieh*, p. 98) agree in identifying the "Four Immortals" (*ssu-hsien*) as four Taoists of the Liang: the Perfected of Hua-t'ao, T'ao Hung-ching; P'ei the Perfected of Purity and the Void; Chou the Perfected of Purple Yang; and the Perfected of T'ung-po, Wang Tzu-ch'iao (for documentation, see the *Fo-tsu t'ung-chi*, Chapter 37, pp. 350–351; T. 2035, Vol. 49). This is clearly problematic. If the "four immortals" refers to four men, then there are "seven supports" in the Liang, not four. Iritani and Matsumura also note this problem and suggest that the group as a whole is intended or that the "four" means only one of the group. In any event, T'ao Hung-ching (456–536) seems to be the only *real* person in the group.

6. Mahāsattva Fu (Fu ta-shih) was Fu Hsi (497–569), another monk greatly favored by Emperor Wu of the Liang. He called himself "The Great Scholar with the Good Wisdom of Future Release" but was dubbed Mahāsattva Fu for short. He figures in cases 1 and 67 of the *Pi yen lu*; the title of case 67 is "Mahāsattva Fu Expounds the Scripture" (Cleary, *The Blue Cliff Record*, Vol. 2, pp. 424–428).

7. The *i-tai chiao*—i.e., everything the Buddha taught from his *nirvāṇa* until his death.

8. *Ju-lai shih; Tathāgata-dūta.*

9. *Seng-chia-lan* transliterates *saṅghārāma*, the monastery with its parks and gardens attached.

10. *Yu-wei*, as opposed to *wu-wei*, "acting without action."

11. This seems to be an allusion to Chapter 77 of the *Lao-tzu*, but in the *Lao-tzu* this is seen as something good. Wing-tsit Chan (*The Way of Lao Tzu*, p. 234) translates the line in question: "The Way of Heaven reduces whatever is excessive and supplements whatever is insufficient."

12. The point being—I think—that these men were all praised, but they have no lasting accomplishment. Where are their deeds today?

No. 173

Alas! Poor, and on top of that ill;
I'm a man cut off from both friends and kin.

Inside my jug—always empty of rice;
My pots—constantly covered with dust.[1]

My thatch cottage doesn't keep out the rain;
My wet bed—too small to hold my [large] frame.

No need to wonder why I'm at present so haggard and worn;
Many worries clearly waste a person away.

1. *Tseng-chung sheng-ch'en* (literally, "inside my jug, dust is produced") is a set expression, descriptive of utter poverty—i.e., there is no food to cook, so the pots go unused.

No. 174

As for raising girls—I'm afraid there just are too many,[1]
And once they are born, they must be instructed and led.

Pat their heads—chase away their small fears;
Whip their behinds—teach them to keep their mouths shut!

If they don't understand how to operate shuttle and loom,
How can they serve you with dustpan and broom?

Old lady Chang said to the young donkey's foal,
"When you grow up, you won't be as good as your mother!"[2]

1. In *Yen-shih chia-hsün* (1. 13b), the words of T'ai-kung are quoted: "The girls who are raised are too many; it's a complete waste."
2. i.e., if you don't learn how to behave when you are young.

No. 175

I maintain my resolve—it can't be rolled up;
You must know that I'm not some mat![1]

Unrestrained I arrived at this mountain wood;
All alone I recline on a large and firm rock.

Skilled talkers come to urge me to leave,
Invite me to accept gold and circlets of jade.[2]

Boring holes in walls to plant daisies;[3]
Just like this—it's something that does little good.

1. Apparently alluding to the lines in stanza 3 of poem 26 in the *Shih*. Karlgren (*The Book of Odes*, p. 15) translates: "My heart is not a stone, you cannot turn it; my heart is not a mat, you cannot roll it; my dignified demeanour has been perfect, you cannot measure it."

2. Probably another allusion to the anecdote noted above, in note 1 to poem 102, where King Hsiang of Ch'u sent messengers with gold and jade to get Chuang-tzu to serve as prime minister.

3. An allusion to *Chuang-tzu*, Chapter 23 (p. 61, line 13). Watson (*The Complete Works*, pp. 249–250) translates the phrase: "And as for those two you mentioned—Yao and Shun—how are they worthy to be singled out for praise? With their nice distinctions they are like a man who goes around willfully poking holes in people's walls and fences and planting weeds and brambles in them, like a man who picks out which hairs of his head he intends to comb. . . . Such bustle and officiousness—how can it be of any use in saving the age?" I.e., this is something useless, of no value—the skilled talkers are wasting their time.

No. 176

The place where I tarry and stay;
Secluded and deep—difficult indeed to describe.

Without any wind, creepers move on their own;
There is no fog, yet the bamboo's always dark, in a haze.

Valley streams—for whom do they weep?
Mountain clouds—suddenly on their own they pile up.

At noon, I sit inside my hut;
Just then I'm aware that the sun has started to rise.

No. 177

I remember before, all the places I went to see.[1]
Among men, I chased after the very best sights and scenes.

Delighting in mountains, I climbed peaks eighty thousand feet
      high;
Loving the waters, I floated on one thousand streams.

I saw off guests at P'i-p'a Valley,[2]
Carried my lute to Parrot Isle.[3]

How could I know I'd end up at the base of some pine,
Arms wrapped 'round my knees, as the cold wind sighs and
      moans?

   1. Preferring the variant *kuo* ("pass by, experience") to *yü* ("encounter"), though either word will do.
   2. P'i-p'a Valley (*p'i-p'a ku*) once formed the boundary between
Liang-chou and I-chou (prefectures located in present-day northern Szech-
wan and southern Shensi); through it runs the Han River, which then emp-
ties into the Yangtze in the vicinity of Wu-han. (See *Shui-ching chu* 29 [p.
933] and Iritani and Matsumura [*Kanzanshi*, p. 248].)
   3. There is a "Parrot Isle" (*ying-wu chou*) in the Yangtze River southwest of Han-yang District in modern Hupeh.

No. 178*

I declare to you followers of the Way;
To go forth and search[1]—in vain do you labor your souls.

People [inside] have something vital and alive;
There's no word to describe it; moreover, there's neither
      sentence nor phrase.[2]

When you call it, it very distinctly responds;
Yet it dwells hidden; it doesn't stay or remain.[3]

I tell you again and again, carefully protect and preserve;
Don't let it have blemish or stain.

---

*Pulleyblank: Han-shan II.
1. For the Buddha—looking outside.
2. The syntax suggests that it is the "vital and alive thing" (*ching-ling wu*) that "has no word and has neither sentence nor phrase." But surely the meaning is that no words can adequately describe or name this thing.
3. Meaning that even though it responds when you call, it is not forever in front of your face.

No. 179

Last year in spring I heard the birds sing;
At that time I thought of my brothers.

This year in the fall as chrysanthemums fade;
At this time I think of things sending forth shoots.[1]

Green waters choked up in one thousand domains;[2]
Yellow clouds, level on all four sides.[3]

Sad it is! In this life of one hundred years,
It tears my insides to remember the capital Hsien.[4]

1. Iritani and Matsumura (*Kanzanshi*, p. 250) point out the poignancy of the contrast in these two lines: in fall he is thinking of spring (*fa-sheng*, "sending forth shoots," is what happens in spring).

2. Choked up with tears.

3. Ch'en Hui-chien (*Han-shan-tzu*, p. 180) cites a number of T'ang verses to show that "yellow clouds" are associated with warfare in the border regions.

4. Hsien-ching would normally mean Hsien-yang (in northwest Shensi), the capital of China during the Ch'in (B.C. 221–209). But it also stands for Ch'ang-an, the capital during the T'ang. As a result, Iritani and Matsumura (*Kanzanshi*, pp. 250–251) argue convincingly that the poet is thinking back to the "springtime" of the T'ang dynasty, before the fall of Ch'ang-an during the An Lu-shan rebellion (755–763).

No. 180*

The many who live on T'ien-t'ai
Do not recognize Master Han-shan.

None of them knows my true thoughts;
They simply call it "idle talk."

*Pulleyblank: Han-shan II.

No. 181**

Once you live on Han-shan, all matters come to an end;
Moreover, there are no confusing thoughts to
    hang up your mind.

At my leisure, on stone walls I write down poetic lines;
Letting fate go its way, together with it I turn—
    I do not tether my boat.[1]

**Seven-character lines.
1. The unattached boat can "go with the flow," floating freely with
life's ups and downs. For more on the "unmoored boat" image in Chinese
poetry, see Eugene Eoyang's "The Solitary Boat: Images of Self in Chinese
Nature Poetry," *Journal of Asian Studies* XXXII, No. 4 (August 1973): 593–621.

No. 182*

Pitiable! This house of one hundred years;
The left side toppled down—the right side also atilt.

Walls split open, scattered and gone;
Boards in chaos, heaped about in great disarray.

Roof tiles in bits and pieces fall off;
Rot and decay that cannot be stopped.

Were a violent wind to blow, it would abruptly collapse;
To stand it up firmly again, would in the end
    be difficult to complete.

*Pulleyblank: Han-shan II.
Note: Han-shan may be developing a metaphor first noted in the
Nirvāṇa-sūtra (Chapter 23, T. 374, Vol. 12, p. 499 top). There we read: "It can
be compared to a rotten house, a building about to collapse: our lives are
also like this."

No. 183

Spirit and soul, extraordinary—far above the rest;
Form and appearance, extremely imposing and grave.

Able to shoot an arrow through seven planks;[1]
In reading books, comprehending five lines at a glance.

Accustomed to sleeping on tiger's head pillows;[2]
At night, sitting on ivory beds.[3]

But if you have none of "this thing,"[4]
You'll simply be treated as cold as the frost.

1. Literally, the seven *cha*, *cha* being thin strips of wood used for writing. Yang Yu-chi, the great archer of Ch'u in Spring and Autumn times, is said to have accomplished this feat. See the *Tso-chuan*, Duke Ch'eng, year 16 (Vol. 1, p. 242).

2. An inventory of the imperial treasury in 265 revealed that it contained a jade tiger's head pillow used by King Chou Hsin of the Yin (r. B.C. 1154–1122). See the *Shih-i chi*, 7: 5ab.

3. For the story of the priceless ivory couch that was offered to Meng-ch'ang chün by the king of Ch'u, see *Chan-kuo ts'e*, "Ch'i ts'e," part 3 (10: 6ab). For Crump's translation of the anecdote, see *Chan-kuo Ts'e*, pp. 187–189.

4. *A-tu wu* was colloquial in the T'ang for "money." Wang Yen of the Chin, in response to the greed of his wife, refused to say the word "money" *(ch'ien)*, always calling it "this thing." See his biography in *Chin shu* 43 (Vol. 4, p. 1237); also *Shih-shuo hsin-yü* 10: 9 (p. 423). Mather (*A New Account of Tales of the World*, p. 281) translates: "Wang Yen had always esteemed the Mysterious and Remote *(hsüan-yüan)*, and being continually vexed by the avarice of his wife, Lady Kuo, and by her worldly contamination, he never let the word "cash" *(ch'ien)* pass his lips. Desiring to test him, his wife had a female slave surround his bed with cash, so that he could not walk past it. When Yen awoke in the morning and saw the cash obstructing the way, he called in the slave and said, "Get these objects *(a-che wu)* out of here!"

No. 184

They laugh at me like some farm boy;
Head and cheeks drooping down like a timid,
    stuttering bumpkin.[1]

My turban has never been high,[2]
And the belt at my waist is always tight.[3]

It's not that I've not "seized the moment";
When you are poor, you might "seize," but you will not succeed.

But if one day I have money and wealth,
I'll stand a *stūpa* on top of my head![4]

1. Translation is tentative. No one seems to know what to make of
chih-se as a compound (see Iritani and Matsumura, *Kanzanshi*, p. 256, and
Ch'en Hui-chien, *Han-shan-tzu*, p. 257). I follow Ch'en in reading *chih* in the
sense of *chü-chin*, "restrained and courteous" or "timid," and *se* means to
"talk haltingly" or "lacking in polish."
2. Iritani and Matsumura (*Kanzanshi*, p. 256) make the interesting observation that a "high head turban" (*kao-t'ou chin-tzu*) was presented to
honored officials (*kuei-ch'en*) during the T'ang, from the reign era *Wu-te*
(618–629) to the reign of Wu Tse-t'ien (690–704).
3. i.e., he's always hungry.
4. Tseng P'u-hsin (*Han-shan shih-chieh*, p. 105) finds this attitude
unbecoming of Han-shan and considers the poem, therefore, to be a later
addition.

No. 185

When you buy meat, blood oozes and drips;
When you buy fish, they jump around—flippity flop.

You invite for yourself the burden of sin,
So that wife and child can be happy.

You'll no sooner die than she'll remarry;
Of others—this deed who would dare to prevent?

One morning, like a broken bed,[1]
The two before your own eyes will be taken away.

1. That quickly, with that much of a shock.

No. 186*

A guest criticized Master Han-shan;
"Sir, your poems make no sense at all!"

[To which I replied] "When I look back at the ancients,
Poverty and low station were no cause for shame."

In responding, he laughed at these words;
"Your remarks—how vague, distant, and imprecise!

I want you, sir, to be up to date;
Money's the only urgent matter."

*Pulleyblank: Han-shan II.
    Note: I have translated the poem assuming that lines 3–4 are by Han-shan and 5–8 by his critic. Iritani and Matsumura (Kanzanshi, pp. 259–260) read lines 2–4 as against Han-shan and 5–8 as his reply, though they note this is problematic. Watson (Cold Mountain, p. 91) reads lines 7–8 as again from the mouth of Han-shan, expressed with resignation—i.e., "Go ahead, you may as well be like everyone else."

No. 187

From birth, I have not come and gone;[1]
Until death, I'll have no Benevolence and Right.[2]

Since when you speak there are already branches and leaves.[3]
What you cherish in your heart will be evil and mean.

If you open up the small roads,[4]
Great hypocrisy by this is produced.[5]

[Others] may craftily urge you to make a cloud ladder,[6]
[But my advice is] pare it away, 'til it turns into briars and
     thorns.[7]

1. Tseng P'u-hsin (*Han-shan shih-chieh*, p. 107) points out the probable allusion here to *Lao-tzu*, Chapter 80. There, in the ideal society, people will "value their lives highly and not migrate far. Even if there are ships and carriages, none will ride in them. . . . [They will] relish their food, beautify their clothing, be content with their homes, and delight in their customs. Though neighboring communities overlook one another and the crowing of cocks and barking of dogs can be heard, yet the people there may grow old and die without ever visiting one another" (translation by Wing-tsit Chan, *The Way of Lao Tzu*, p. 238). "Without ever visiting one another" is literally, "not *come and go* with one another."

2. A way of saying he will remain one with the Tao. One is again reminded of the *Lao-tzu*. The first line of Chapter 18 goes: "When the great Tao declined, the doctrine of humanity and righteousness arose" (translated by Wing-tsit Chan, *The Way of Lao Tzu*, p. 131). "Humanity and righteousness" are the same *jen* and *i* that I translate as "Benevolence and Right."

3. i.e., you break away from what is essential—the root.

4. The "small roads" (*hsiao-tao*) are normally understood to mean minor arts—things like husbandry, medicine, divining, and so forth—things not properly done by a gentleman. In *Analects* 19: 4 (p. 39) Tzu-hsia is quoted as saying (translation by D. C. Lau, *Confucius: the Analects*, p. 153): "Even minor arts are sure to have their worthwhile aspects, but the gentleman does not take them up because the fear of a man who would go a long way is that he should be bogged down."

5. Again, an allusion to *Lao-tzu*. Chapter 18 begins: "When the great Tao declined, The doctrine of humanity and righteousness arose. When knowledge and wisdom appeared, There emerged great hypocrisy." Note that "small roads" (*hsiao-tao*) are the opposite of the "great Tao" (*ta-tao*).

6. A "cloud ladder" (*yün-t'i*) was a scaling device used for attacking city walls. For an illustration, see E. T. C. Werner, *Chinese Weapons* (Los Angeles: O'Hara Publications, Inc., 1972), pp. 78–80. Well known is the crafty speech of Kung-shu Pan, who urged the king of Ch'u to attack the state of Sung using cloud ladders (see *Chan-kuo ts'e* 32: lab; Crump, *Chan-kuo ts'e*, pp. 562–563). This line might also be read: "Crafty speech creates a cloud ladder" (i.e., it makes something that leads nowhere).

7. I think the contrast of cloud ladders and thorns is one of culture and nature. Culture, as the *Lao-tzu* lines suggest, leads to craftiness, deceit, and war. Better to remain one's natural self. To paraphrase: "Others might urge you to develop into a crafty, devious person, one who takes advantage of and causes harm to others. But I say return to your natural stuff, even though it might be insignificant and small." This represents yet another *Lao-tzu* theme—in Chapter 48 we read: "The pursuit of learning is to increase day after day. The pursuit of Tao is to decrease day after day" (translation by Wing-tsit Chan, *The Way of Lao Tzu*, p. 184).

No. 188

One vase, by the casting of metal completed;
Another produced by the molding of clay.

Both vases I let you, sir, see;
Which vase is solid and real?

If you want to know why there are two different vases,
You must know that the trade's not the same.

If you use this to examine the causes of life,
You'll start to practice on this very day.

Note: An allegory on the workings of *karma*. The word "trade" in line 6 is *yeh*, which also means *karma* in Buddhist parlance. The word *yeh*, with its double meaning, therefore marks the transition between allegory and moral. Iritani and Matsumura *(Kanzanshi,* p. 263) point out that in the *Nirvāṇa-sūtra* (Ch. 5, "Ju-lai hsing"; T. 374, Vol. 12, p. 392 bottom) a comparison is made between an earthenware vase and one made of diamond. The text reads: "True liberation *(mukti)* is none other than *tathāgata*. It's just like the fact that when an earthenware vase breaks, it sounds like broken pottery. But with a diamond vase it is not like this. Liberation also does not have the sound of breaking. The diamond vase is a symbol for liberation. True liberation is none other than *tathāgata*."

No. 189*

Dilapidated, in ruins, this cottage of weeds;
Inside, mushrooming fire and smoke.

May I ask you, you many small children,
You've been alive a total of how many days?

Outside the gate there are three carts;
He invites them to take them, but they're unwilling
    to leave.

Full of food, stomachs distended and fat;
All of them stupid, obstinate fools!

*Pulleyblank: Han-shan II.
Comment: In Chapter 3 of the Lotus-sūtra (T. 262, Vol. 9, pp. 10–19)—
"Pi-yü p'in" (Parable)—the Buddha mentions the parable of the burning
house to illustrate the ultimate truth of the One Vehicle (Ekayāna—Buddha
Vehicle or Great Vehicle) teaching. There a rich father tries to save his children from their burning house (i.e., from life in this world, where we are
consumed by the passions), tricking them into leaving the house with the
promise of goat carts, deer carts, and bullock carts waiting for them outside
the door. When they come out, there is only one carriage there, a large,
richly adorned carriage which they all mount. Just so in Buddhism, though
it may appear that the vehicles are three—the ways of the śrāvakas, the
pratyeka-buddhas, and the bodhisattvas—in reality there is only the One Vehicle, that of the Buddha.
    For a translation of the passage in question, see Leon Hurvitz, trans-
lator, Scripture of the Lotus Blossom of the Fine Dharma (The Lotus Sutra) (New
York: Columbia University Press, 1976), pp. 49–83, especially pp. 58–62.

No. 190

There is a body—there is not a body;
This is me—then again it is not.

In this way, carefully I think it through;
Putting off my decision, I sit leaning against this cliff.

Midst my feet green grass starts to grow;
On my head the red dust descends.

Having seen me, some common folk
Present fruit and wine at my funeral bier.[1]

1. i.e., he sits without moving that long. Hakuin (*Kanzan shi sendai kibun*, pp. 106–107), on the last two couplets, cites the text *Kuan-Fo san-mei hai ching*, which says: "At that time the bodhisattva sat down beneath a tree and entered 'extinction of thought' (*samādhi*). The realm of this *samādhi* is called 'tranquility of the senses.' The various deities wept, their tears falling like rain, as they urged and requested the bodhisattva to get up and eat and drink. But at the time they made this request, the bodhisattva was unaware of sound anywhere in the three thousand worlds. There was one Son of Heaven named 'Pleasing Thought,' who saw that the grass growing on the ground had penetrated the bodhisattva's flesh, growing up to his elbows. Thus he said to the various gods: 'Rare indeed! Good sons. To practice austerities like this. To not eat for so much time; to not hear when others call to you; for grass to grow [around you] and be unaware.'"

No. 191

Yesterday I saw the trees by the side of stream;
Smashed up, destroyed—they can't be described.

Two or three remnants of trunks were still there;[1]
A thousand, ten thousand axe and knife scars.[2]

Stripping of frost had withered and faded the leaves;
Pounding of waves had rotted and decayed the roots.

The lot of things born must be like this;
What use in blaming Heaven and Earth?

1. For "trunks still there" *(kan-tsai)*, there is a variant reading of "buds and plants" *(jui-hui)*.

2. Or "hatchet blade" scars—*fu-tao*.

Note: Han-shan seems to be aware of Mr. Kuei-ku's letter reprimanding his students Su Ch'in and Chang I (cited in Yüan Shu's *Chen-yin chuan* [*I-wen lei-chü* 36, p. 640]). That text reads: "People like my two lords—can it be you've not seen the trees by the side of the stream?! Drivers and charioteers break off their limbs; breakers and waves wash against their roots. Above they have not one circular foot of shade; their trunks covered with several thousand scars. These trees—how could they bear a grudge against heaven and earth? [Their situation] is the result of where they live."

No. 192* ** 1

I've seen Seng-yu, by nature rare and unique;[2]
Skillful and clever, "born in-between," at the
time of the Liang.[3]

[The paintings of] Tao-tzu, airy and graceful—that was
his special mark;[4]
The two Masters so good at drawing, when with their
hands they wielded the brush.[5]

At ease when they painted, their paintings so real, with
spirit and feeling distinct;
Their dragons flew, their goblins ran, their gods were
majestic and stern.

Even though, of the distant and void, they could depict
the traces and tracks,
They lacked the means to successfully paint
Master Chih-kung.[6]

*Pulleyblank: Han-shan II.
**Seven-character lines.
1. The two inner couplets are omitted in the *Tse-shih-chü ts'ung-shu*
and *Kunaichō* editions.

2. Chang Seng-yu (c. 470–550) was one of China's great painters. He was hired a number of times by Liang Wu-ti (r. 502–550) to do paintings for temples. His paintings are reported to have been so real that when he painted in the eyes of a dragon on one of them, the dragon broke free and flew away. William Acker (*Some T'ang and Pre-T'ang Texts on Chinese Painting* [Leiden: E. J. Brill, 1954], pp. 49–50) translates the *Hsü Hua-p'in* entry on him. See also Max Loehr, *The Great Painters of China* (Oxford: Phaidon Press, 1980), pp. 26–29.

3. My translation of *chien-sheng* as "born in-between" is tentative and follows the interpretation of Iritani and Matsumura (*Kanzanshi*, p. 266) that every one hundred or one thousand years a Buddha or sage is born. But I wonder if it might not mean "scholars at their leisure" (like *hsien-chü*).

4. Wu Tao-tzu (c. 698–792) being another great Chinese painter who lived in the T'ang. He painted in the tradition of Chang Seng-yu, and the *Hsüan-ho hua-p'u* (cited in Ch'en Hui-chien [*Han-shan-tzu*, p. 262]) says that when he painted dragons, their scales shook.

5. Chang Seng-yu and Wu Tao-tzu are often cited together with Ku K'ai-chih (344–405) and Lu T'an-wei (c. 440–500) as China's four great masters of painting. Thus Iritani and Matsumura (*Kanzanshi*, pp. 266–267) feel that the "two masters" (*erh-kung*) refer to Ku and Lu. I see no reason not to see these as referring once more to Seng-yu and Wu Tao-tzu.

6. For Master Chih-kung, see poem 172, note 3: he is the same as Pao-chih. On Seng-yu's inability to paint this portrait, Hakuin (*Kanzan shi sendai kibun*, Chapter 3, p. 63) cites the *Fo-tsu kang-mu* as saying the following: "Emperor Wu of the Liang once commissioned the painter Seng-yu to draw a portrait of Master Chih. Yu started to draw but was suddenly undecided. Chih then using his finger cut open his mouth and separately revealed the appearances of the twelve-faced Kuan-yin. Some faces were compassionate, others were stern. Yu in the end was unable to draw."

No. 193**

For a long time I've lived on Han-shan; altogether
    now several autumns;
All alone I hum my ballads and songs, completely
    without any cares.

My bramble door I don't shut, yet it's always secluded and
    still;
The spring bubbles forth its sweet broth—
    constant, its natural flow.

Chamber of stone, earthen hearth—my cinnabar caldron
    bubbles and boils;[1]
Yellow pine, tea made from cypress, frankincense in a bowl.[2]

When I'm hungry for food, I have one grain of *agada* herb;[3]
The seat of my mind harmonious, at peace, I lean
    up against a big rock.

**Seven-character lines.
    1. Agreeing with Iritani and Matsumura (*Kanzanshi*, p. 268) in their
conclusion that *sha-ting* here means *tan-sha ting*, "cinnabar caldron," the caldron in which cinnabar was refined.

2. Iritani and Matsumura *(Kanzanshi,* p. 268) say that eating "yellow pine" *(sung-huang)* makes the body light. Stuart *(Chinese Materia Medica: Vegetable Kingdom,* p. 334), qualifying *sung-huang* as the "flowers" of the pine tree, says they "are considered to have especial action on the heart and lungs, and to be astringent." He adds, "They are distilled into a sort of 'wine,' which is used in 'fullness in the head' and post-partum fever." A tea can be made from the shoots of the cypress *(po-ya).* For the identification of *ju-hsiang* as "frankincense," see Shiu-ying Hu, *An Enumeration of Chinese Materia Medica* [Hong Kong: The Chinese University Press, 1980], p. 50. On the medicinal uses of frankincense, see Stuart, *Chinese Materia Medica: Vegetable Kingdom,* pp. 71–72.

3. *Chia-t'o* = *a-chia-t'o,* "*agada,*" a universal remedy for all diseases.

No. 194**

Cinnabar Mound lofty, erect, standing even
    with the clouds;[1]
There in the void the Five Peaks—seen from afar
    they seem low.[2]

Wild Goose Pagoda pushing up high, out beyond
    the blue cliffs;[3]
"Meditation grove" and old halls, merging
    with the rainbow.[4]

Wind shakes the leaves on the pines—
    Red Wall, exquisite, refined![5]
The mist spews forth at mid-cliff—
    the road to the immortals indistinct and unseen.

Against backdrop of blue, one thousand mountains,
    each eighty thousand feet high here appear;
While wistaria vines intertwine, one to
    another attached in the valleys below.

**Seven-character lines.
    1. Standard reference works gloss Cinnabar Mound (*tan-ch'iu*) as one
of the T'ien-t'ai peaks, located 90 li south of Ning-hai county seat in Chekiang. In the *Ch'u-tz'u*, Cinnabar Mound is the site of immortals. In the
"Yüan-yu" we read (translated by David Hawkes, *The Songs of the South*, p.
196): "I met the Feathered Men on the Hill of Cinnabar; I tarried in the
ancient land of Immortality." Iritani and Matsumura (*Kanzanshi*, p. 264) understand Cinnabar Mound to be just another name for T'ien-t'ai and cite

Sun Ch'o's "Roaming on T'ien-t'ai" (Wen-hsüan 11: 6a, p. 148), where, they feel, *he* makes this identification. Richard Mather ("The Mystical Ascent of the T'ient'ai Mountains," *Monumenta Serica* 20 [1961]: 238) translates the relevant lines: "Then 'Join the winged men upon Tan-ch'iu,' To search for immortality's delightful halls!"

2. Tseng P'u-hsin (*Han-shan shih-chieh*, p. 178) identifies *wu-feng* ("Five Peaks") as one of the peaks in the T'ien-t'ai range and the site of Kuo-ch'ing Temple. Iritani and Matsumura (*Kanzanshi*, pp. 264–265), on the other hand, feel the "five peaks" are the five sacred mountains in China (see poem 112, note 2) which here, in contrast to Cinnabar Mound, seen from afar seem low. They point out that Sun Ch'o, to his "Roaming on T'ien-t'ai," explains why T'ien-t'ai is not ranked with the Five Peaks. He says (*Wen-hsüan* 11: 4a, p. 147; translated by Watson, *Chinese Rhyme-Prose*, pp. 80–81): "The reason that Mount T'ien-t'ai is not ranked among the Five Sacred Peaks, that records of it are lacking in the classical texts—is it not that it stands in such a remote and out-of-the-way place that the road there is so long and hard to trace?"

3. Iritani and Matsumura (*Kanzanshi*, p. 265) point out that there was (and still is) a famous "Great Goose Pagoda" (*Ta-yen t'a*) in Ch'ang-an during the T'ang. But that could hardly be the pagoda intended here.

4. "Meditation grove" (*ch'an-lin*) is a generic term for a Zen temple.

5. "Red Wall" is one of the peaks in T'ien-t'ai. Its location is given as 6 li north of T'ien-t'ai County (in Chekiang). It was known as one of "Two Wonders," the other being Cascade. Richard Mather ("The Mystical Ascent of the T'ient'ai Mountains," p. 238) comments: "the 'Two Wonders' are the Red Wall and Cascade in the south and southwestern part of the range. The Red Wall, a rocky cliff rising perpendicularly several hundred feet, is marked with horizontal stratification, eroded in some cases into low caves, giving the appearance from a distance of layered brick."

No. 195**

One thousand lives, ten thousand deaths;
    When will it come to an end?[1]
Life and death, they come and they go—'round and 'round
    [spin our] deluded feeings.[2]

To not know in the heart, there is
    this priceless jewel[3]
Is like a blind ass going forward
    just trusting his feet!

**Seven-character lines.

1. Preferring the variant reading of *ho-shih i* to *fan chi-sheng*. With the latter reading, the line would be, "One thousand births, ten thousand deaths; altogether how many lives?"

2. Or is it, "we turn around in the midst of deluded feelings"? The Chinese is *chuan mi-ch'ing*.

3. The "priceless jewel" *(wu-chia pao)* presumably means Buddha-nature in this context. But there is a story in the *Lotus-sūtra* (Chapter 8, "Wu-pai ti-tzu shou-chi"; T. 262, Vol. 9, p. 29 top), where the priceless jewel is compared to the thought of attaining All-Knowledge. The passage is translated by Hurvitz *(Scripture of the Lotus Blossom of the Fine Dharma* [New York: Columbia University Press, 1976], pp. 164–165) as follows: "There is a man who arrives at the house of a close friend, where he gets drunk on wine, then lies down. At that time, his friend, having official business, is on the point of going away, when he sews a priceless jewel into the interior of the first man's garment and departs, leaving it with him. The first man, laid out drunk, is unaware of anything. When he has recovered, he sets out on his travels, then reaches another country, where he devotes every effort to the quest for food and clothing. He suffers such hardship that he is content with however little he may get. Then, his friend, encountering him by chance, speaks these words to him. 'Alas, Sir! How can you have come to this for the sake of mere food and clothing? Once I, wishing to afford you comfort and joy, as well as the natural satisfaction of your five desires, in such-and-such a year, on a certain day of a certain month, sewed a priceless jewel into the inside of your garment. Surely it is still there. Yet you, not knowing of it, have suffered pain and grief in quest of a livelihood. How foolish you have been! Now you need only take this jewel, exchange it for what you need, and have things always as you wish, suffering neither want nor shortage.'

The Buddha is also thus. When he was a bodhisattva, he taught and converted us, inspiring in us the thought of All-Knowledge, but later we forgot, and thus neither understood nor were aware of anything. . . . We were so hard-pressed to support life that we were satisfied with what little we got, though the vow concerning All-Knowledge, still there, had never lost its effect."

On the "priceless jewel" and the "treasure inside your robe," see also poem 283.

No. 196* ** [1]

Old and sick in my final years,
    already one hundred and more;
Face yellow, hair white—but I love
    living here in the mountains.

Cotton-fur robes wrapped 'round my substance—
    I pass my time in accordance with fate;[2]
Why should I covet those crafty models
    found out there among men?

Mind and spirit used to exhaustion
    for the sake of profit and fame;
One hundred kinds of avarice and greed
    serve only to advance one's own self.

This unstable world of illusion and change
    is like snuff on the end of a wick;
When in a grave they bury your body
    then is this having something or not?[3]

*Pulleyblank: Han-shan II.
**Seven-character lines.

1. In the *Tse-shih-chü ts'ung-shu* and *Kunaichō* editions this poem is divided in two: the first four lines are poem 195; the second four lines are poem 186.

2. i.e., he wears the poorest of clothes. "Cotton-fur robes" (*pu-ch'iu*) are robes or coats with hide on the outside and cotton on the inside.

3. *Shih yu-wu.* The body will be like the ash of a lamp.

No. 197**

In this world what is the thing most lamentable?
It's nothing but the three paths, creating a raft made of sin.[1]

No one imitates the sojourner, in the white clouds
    at the base of the cliff;
One cold, monk's robe—this is the shore where I live.[2]

Autumn arrives—so let it!—the trees in the woods
    drop their leaves;
Then spring comes—as you please!
    and the trees open in bloom.

The "three realms" I lay 'cross to sleep,
    at ease, no affairs on my mind;[3]
The bright moon with a cool breeze—this is indeed my home.

**Seven-character lines.
1. The "three paths" (*san-t'u*) are the paths that lead to existence in hell, rebirth as an animal, or existence as a hungry ghost. They are also known as the paths of fire, blood, and knives in accordance with the fate that results. The raft is needed to get over the river of life.
2. *Sheng-yai* here meaning, I think, his lot in life—i.e., it's as a Buddhist that he chooses to live. *Sheng-yai* can also mean one's surroundings.

3. Classical Buddhist cosmology pictures a world made up of three realms *(san-chieh, triloka)*—the "realm of desire" *(kāmaloka)*, the "realm of form" *(rūpaloka)*, and the "formless realm" *(arūpaloka)*. These can be charted vertically as roughly equivalent to earth (and the underworld), heaven, and beyond, the "formless realm" being a state of mind only realized in meditation. The cosmic mountain, Mt. Meru (or Sumeru), stands between heaven and earth at the center of this cosmos. Han-shan—at the top of the mountain Han-shan—sees himself, I think, in a sense above the "three realms"; he lies across them to sleep *(heng-mien)*. But note that Han-shan is not only in a place that transcends all of space, he is also beyond changes in time; seasonal change means nothing to him. Note also that the poem begins with the "three paths" of sin in the world and ends up beyond the "three realms."

No. 198** †

In former years I once travelled
    on an excursion to the great sea;
For the sake of collecting the *maṇi*[1]
    I vowed in earnest to seek.

I went directly to the dragon palace,
    to the place most secret and deep;[2]
At the golden gates I broke off the lock—
    the master's spirits all grieved!

The Dragon King to protect his treasure
    had placed it inside his ear;
Soldiers brandished their weapons, sparks flew!
    there was no way to get close and peek.

But when this merchant, to the contrary,
    withdrew from inside the doors,
He discovered that bright pearl had been all along
    right there inside of his mind.

†Missing from the *Tse-shih-chü ts'ung-shu* and *Kunaicho* Library editions.

**Seven-character lines.

1. The *maṇi* being a jewel—normally a bright pearl—symbolic of the Buddha and his teaching. Here it seems specifically to equate with Buddha-nature.

2. Tseng P'u-hsin (*Han-shan shih-chieh*, p. 174) equates the "dragon's palace" with the eighth consciousness, the *ālaya-vijñāna* or "storehouse consciousness."

No. 199**

The numerous stars are spread out and arranged
  on a night that is both bright and deep;
Here in the cliffs I light just one lamp—
  the moon has not yet gone down.

Round and full, radiant and light;
  no need to polish this gem;[1]
Hanging there in the blue sky, that indeed is my mind.

**Seven-character lines.
1. "Round and full" (*yüan-man*)—i.e., perfect—is a phrase used in the T'ien-t'ai school to describe one of four kinds of doctrine taught by the Buddha (the others being *Pitaka* [or *Hīnayāna*], common, and special). See, for example, Kenneth Ch'en, *Buddhism in China: A Historical Survey* (Princeton, NJ: Princeton University Press, 1964), p. 309.

No. 200* **

On top of rocks one thousand years old,
    footprints of ancient men;
In front of a one hundred thousand foot cliff,
    one spot that is empty and void.

When the bright moon shines,
    it's constantly spotless and pure;
No need to be troubled to look for someone
    to ask which way is west and which east.

*Pulleyblank: Han-shan II(?)
**Seven-character lines.
Note: Meaning, I think, in good Zen fashion, that we need no guide
in our search for enlightenment. We have the record of what others have
done (their footprints), and we have that small spot inside—the original
mind—that, so long as it shines, will always keep us on course.

No. 201**

Above the peak of Han-shan, the moon—
[round like] a wheel and alone;
Shining, it shows through the clear sky;[1]
[in the sky] there is not one thing.

The valuable, natural, priceless jewel[2]
Is concealed within the five *skandhas*,
submerged in this body, this self.[3]

**Seven-character lines.
1. *Chao-hsien* might also be read as *chao-chien*, which would mean "Looking at the [moon] as though at a mirror, [I perceive that] in the sky there is not one thing." In any event, it is clear that the moon here, as later in poem 277, "enlightens" Han-shan about the nature of his true mind.
2. i.e., Buddha-nature, the original mind. On the "priceless jewel" see poem 195, note 3.
3. The "five skandhas" *(wu-yin* here, though normally *wu-yün)* are the five components of life, the five elements which combine to produce the compound of "self." They are form, feeling, perception, will, and consciousness.

Comment: The first couplet serves as a metaphor for the second. The true mind should shine through the *skandhas* just as the moon does through the sky, for in reality, the *skandhas* are void: they have no true substance.

No. 202* **

I face toward the front valley,
    look at myself in that emerald-green flow;
Or I look toward the side of the cliff,
    sitting on rocks large and firm.

My mind is like a lone cloud,
    having nothing to use for support;[1]
Distant, distant the affairs of the world—
    why must they be pursued?

*Pulleyblank: Han-shan II.
**Seven-character lines.
    1. "Having nothing to use for support" *(wu so-i)* is a good thing; the
mind is unattached, not clinging to any object or perception.

No. 203**

Right from the start I've lived on Han-shan;
Stone cliffs, on these I nest and rest,
    far apart from the causes of delusion.[1]

When it's[2] submerged, the ten thousand forms
    disappear without mark or trace;
When it unfolds, it spreads all around,
    reaching to all parts of space.[3]

Light rays and shadows, leaping and glowing,
    shine from the seat of my mind;[4]
There's not one single thing, at times like these,
    that shows up in front of my face.

It's then that I know the *maṇi*[5]—that one single pearl—
When understood and used, has no corners,
    in all places it's round and complete.[6]

**Seven-character lines.
    1. *Fan-yüan*, the causes of *kleśa* (*fan-nao*), affliction, delusion, and pain.
    2. i.e., original mind.
    3. Literally, reaches to all the "great thousand," the *ta-ch'ien*—that is to say, "the three-thousand ten-thousand world" (*Tri-sahasra-mahā-sahasra*), the huge universe of 1,000,000,000 worlds (1000 x 1000 x 1000) that is part of the Mahāyāna view. The mind in itself is tranquil and pure, devoid of one single thing, but when it is active, all things are there. There is not one thing in all the world that is not contained in the mind as thought.

4. It could be the light rays shine *on* his mind *(chao hsin-ti)*. But I think the point here—as in poem 277—is that the mind is like the moon which shines, but which shines *on* nothing at all.

5. On *maṇi* as pearl and symbol of Buddha-nature, see poem 198, note 1.

6. A mind with corners *(fang)* would be, I think, a mind with aspects and therefore limitations. The mind is round *(yüan)*; it embraces all things.

Note: Iritani and Matsumura *(Kanzanshi,* p. 281) point out that this poem is cited in Chapter 12 of the early Sung collection *Tsung-ching lu* (completed in 976; T. 2016, Vol. 48, p. 481 middle). The poem there cited contains a number of interesting variants. Lines 1 and 2 there read: "I live in this place—I call it Han-shan; In the mountain cliffs I rest and nest, far apart from the bother and noise *(fan-hsüan)*. Lines 7 and 8 there read: "It's then that I know that the *maṇi*—that one single treasure; If profoundly used is without exhaustion *(miáo-yung wu-ch'iung)*—in all places it's round and complete."

No. 204**

The people of this world—what is the thing
    that makes them sigh and lament?
Sorrows and joys, in turn, burn their insides
    without limit or end.

Life and death—they come and they go
    for how many eons of time?
East, West, South, and North—
    this is whose home this time?

Chang, Wang, Li, Chao—a surname
    just for a short while;
The "six ways" and the "three paths";[1]
    affairs tangled and twisted like hemp.

Only because the "master"[2] they have not completely
    renounced;
As a result, they invite change and decline
    and chase after delusion and sin.

**Seven-character lines.
1. The "six ways" (liu-tao) are the six destinies (gatis) possible after
death—i.e., to be punished in hell, become a preta (a hungry ghost), to be
reborn as a demon (asura), a human being, an animal, or a god (deva). The
"three paths" (san-t'u) are the three evil destinies—viz., existing in hell, as
a hungry ghost, or as an animal.
2. Chu-jen here meaning, I think, the ātman, the self or soul.

No. 205**

In the beginning I lived on T'ien-t'ai;
A path through the clouds—mist and fog dense,
    cut off from the coming of guests.

Eight thousand feet high the cliffs and the peaks,
    deep—[a place to which one] can flee;
Ten thousand layers of valleys and brooks;
    boulders as large as a tower or stage.

With kerchief of birch bark and clogs made of wood,
    I follow the course of the stream;
In cotton-fur coat, with staff of pigweed,
    I circle the slopes and return.

Aware on my own that this floating life[1]
    is a matter of illusion and change.
I ramble untrammelled in joy and delight;
    truly wonderful indeed![2]

**Seven-character lines.
   1. *Fou-sheng;* drifting and floating like a cloud or a bubble on water,
life has no real substance and will eventually dissipate.
   2. Reading the variant *ch'i* for *shan*. With *shan*, the line would be
"truly great indeed."

No. 206

The thing to be pitied is this disease of all living things;
They taste and they eat—but they generally never get full.

They steam the piglet—soaking it in garlic sauce;
Roast up the duck—add a dash of pepper and salt.

They take out the bones, making "raw slices of fish;"
Leave the skin on, cook up the face meat.[1]

They don't know the "bitterness" of other's lives;
Only hold on to the "sweetness" of their own homes.

1. Since *yü-kuai* ("sliced or diced fish") is a set phrase, *jou-lien* might
be as well, but I can find nothing on it. Chinese do, however, eat the face
skin of certain animals. Iritani and Matsumura (*Kanzanshi*, p. 276) feel that
jou-lien is a meat soup.

No. 207

By reading books can you avoid death?
By reading books can you avoid being poor?

For what reason do we delight in recognition of words?[1]
Through recognition of words we defeat other men!

If a great man does not recognize words,
There is no place where he'll be secure.

When golden thread is soaked in garlic sauce;
You forget that it's bitter as can be![2]

---

1. Literacy, that is.
2. i.e., we tend to forget the bitter realities of life through knowledge and job security. On *huang-lien* as "golden thread," see Read, *Chinese Medicinal Plants*, p. 170 (item 534). The *Shen Nung pen-ts'ao ching* (1.25a, SPPY ed.) explains that "if golden thread is consumed for a long time it causes people not to forget."

No. 208

I've seen people who deceive others;
It's like running with a basket of water.

Though you might rush home with it, all in one breath;
In the basket—what will you have?[1]

I've seen people *being* deceived by others;
They're just like the leeks in the garden.

Day after day they're cut by the knife,
But what they were born with by nature
    is something that still remains.[2]

1. Meaning their deception of others is something that gains them nothing, despite what they might think.
2. Leeks are like chives—each day you can cut off the green tops, but the white root is unharmed, and new, green shoots will appear. One's true nature, true self—Buddha-nature—is never harmed by what others might say.

No. 209

Have you not seen the dew that descends in the morn?
With the sparkling rays of the sun, of itself it dispels
    and is gone.

Man's life is also like this;
Jambudvīpa[1]—this is just where we stop over awhile.[2]

Never, never pass your time just going along;
Moreover, you must cause the three poisons to leave.[3]

Wisdom must take the place of delusion;[4]
You must totally make this so—let no delusion remain.

1. Jambudvīpa is the Indian name of the continent on which we live.
One common Buddhist cosmological scheme has the giant mountain Mt.
Meru in the center of the earth; around it we find a large ocean with four
island continents, one in each of the four cardinal directions. Jambudvīpa is
the southern continent, and Bhāratavarṣa—the Indian name for India—is
found on the southern half of that isle.

2. *Chi-chü* meaning the temporary lodging of a traveller on a long
trip.

3. The "three poisons" *(san-tu)* are anger, greed, and ignorance. See
poem 88, note 1.

4. Literally, the line says, "*bodhi* is none other than *kleśa*" (*p'u-ti chi fan-nao*).

Note: Iritani and Matsumura (*Kanzanshi,* p. 284) point out how the opening lines mimic the middle of poem 13 of the "Nineteen Old Poems" (*Wen-hsüan* 29:6ab, p. 399). Watson's translation of the relevant lines (*Chinese Lyricism,* p. 29) reads: "Times of heat and cold in unending succession, but the years Heaven gives us are like morning dew. Man's life is brief as a sojourn; his years lack the firmness of metal or stone." That poem ends with advice that differs considerably from Han-shan's—"Ten thousand ages come and go, but sages and wise men discover no cure. Some seek long life in fasts and potions; many end by poisoning themselves. Far better to drink fine wine, to clothe ourselves in soft white silk!"

No. 210

Water that's clear, calmly still, and transparent;
All the way to the bottom, one can naturally see.

When in the mind there is not one thing,
The ten thousand realms cannot make it turn.[1]

If the mind does not falsely arise,[2]
For endless eons there'll be no change.

If you can know the mind in this way,
This is knowledge that has no back side.[3]

1. That is, the phenomenal world, the ten thousand *dharmas*—differentiated things. I prefer the variant line of *wan-ching pu-neng chuan* to the reading of *shui ch'ing chung-shou hsien*. "In clear water, the hosts of animals' [reflections] will appear."
2. Or, with the variant *chi*. "Since the mind. . . . "
3. i.e., knowledge that is non-dual.

No. 211** †

From the time I arrived in this realm of T'ien-t'ai
'Til the present—I've passed here
    a number of winters and springs.

The mountains and streams do not change—
    man alone becomes old;
I've seen retreat [from this place] a good
    many young men.

**Seven-character lines.
†This poem is omitted from the *Tse-shih-chü ts'ung-shu* and *Kunaichō* Library editions. The poem is attributed by some to Shih-te.

No. 212

Speaking of food in the end will not make you full;
Speaking of clothes will not keep out the cold.

If you want to eat your fill, the thing you must have is rice;
Put on clothes—*then* you will keep out the cold.

Yet you don't understand, that you must carefully think all
    things through;
You just speak of the difficulties in looking for the Buddha.

Turn your mind 'round—*that's* the Buddha!
Never look for him facing outside.

No. 213*

Frightful! The bitter pain of *saṁsāra;*
We go and return, like dust blown in the wind.

An ant going 'round a bracelet's edge never stops;
The "six ways"—chaotic, in great disarray.[1]

You can change your head and get a new face,
But you'll not get away from the person you were before.

Quickly! Be done with the darkness of Hell;
Don't let your mind and your nature be confused.

*Pulleyblank: Han-shan II.
1. For the "six ways," see note 1 to poem 204. The six destinies of transmigration make up one big circle—like the bracelet the ant goes around.

No. 214*

Frightful! Rotation in the three realms;[1]
It continues from moment to moment[2]—never once has
    it ceased.

Just when you start thinking you might get out,
Again you fall back and find yourself sunk and submerged.

Even if you reach the realm that's Neither Thought nor
    No Thought[3]
And produce much strength for future good fortune,

Can this compare with knowing the true source?
Once you attain it, you have it for good.

---

*Pulleyblank: Han-shan II.
1. On the three realms, see above, note 3 to poem 197.
2. Literally, "thought after thought" (nien-nien).
3. Fei fei-hsiang abbreviates fei hsiang fei fei-hsiang—naivasaṁjñānā-saṁjñānāyatana—the fourth heaven in the "Formless" realm and thus the highest point in the cosmos. It is commonly mistaken by heretics for nirvāṇa.

No. 215*

Yesterday I roamed to the top of a peak;
Below, peered over a thousand foot cliff.

On the brink of disaster—one lonely tree;
Swayed by the wind, it split into two.

Tossed about by the rain, the leaves scattered and fell;
Dried out by the sun, they turned into ashes and dust.

I sigh to see this luxuriant growth
Has today become a big pile of dirt.

*Pulleyblank: Han-shan II.
Note: In the *Nirvāṇa-sūtra* (Ch. 38; T. 374, Vol. 12, p. 589 bottom) we read: "Those who are wise look upon this life just like a large tree on the edge of a cliff by the side of a stream."

No. 216*

From of old there have been many sages
Who have time and again urgently taught belief in oneself.

But people, fundamentally, by nature are not the same;
Some are high and some low, some are sharp and some dull.

If the true Buddha you're unwilling to acknowledge,
You put all your strength into uselessly enduring
    hardship and pain.

You don't know that the clear and pure mind
Is precisely the seal of the true Dharma-king.[1]

---

*Pulleyblank: Han-shan II.
1. The "seal" is the proof of the Buddha.

No. 217*

I have heard of the mountain T'ien-t'ai;
That in this mountain, there are trees of white jade.[1]

For a long time I've said I want to climb it,
But no one knows the path that crosses Stone Bridge.[2]

For this reason I let out a sad sigh;
My good fortune in living here—already in its decline.[3]

Today I looked into a mirror;
Unkempt and disheveled[4]—my temple hair hangs down
    in strands.

*Pulleyblank: Han-shan II.

1. *Ch'i-shu* are trees one finds in Paradise, in the realm of the immortals. Sun Ch'o mentions the *ch'i-shu* on T'ien-t'ai in his "Yu T'ien-t'ai fu" (*Wen-hsüan* 11: 8a, p. 149). Richard Mather ("The Mystical Ascent of the T'ient'ai Mountains," p. 242) translates as follows: "The Standing Tree effaces shadows for a thousand *hsün*, while "alabaster orchards" [*ch'i-shu*] gleam and glow with hanging pearls." (Also see Watson, *Chinese Rhyme-Prose*, p. 84).

2. This probably alludes to a line in the early part of Sun Ch'o's rhapsody. Mather ("The Mystical Ascent of the T'ient'ai Mountains," p. 237) translates: "The farers, since the road is cut, none understand"; for the Chinese text see *Wen-hsüan* 11: 5b, p. 148. On the "Stone Bridge," see poem 44, note 2.

3. Reading the variant of *mu* ("sunset," "closing years of one's life") for *mu* ("admire," "long for").

4. *Sa-sa* normally means the sound of wind or the sound of rain. Here it appears to describe the scattered, thin appearance of Han-shan's hair.

Note: Han-shan's poem is allegory as well as description. To him, as to Sun Ch'o, the ascent of T'ien-t'ai is the mystical ascent to enlightenment. The "narrow bridge" crosses a stream to the "other shore" of *nirvāṇa*, but in good Zen fashion, Han-shan says that no one knows where the path is that crosses the bridge.

No. 218

In raising sons, if they don't study with a teacher,[1]
They won't measure up to the city park rats![2]

Have they ever once seen good men?
Do they listen to the words of their elders?

If you want something dyed, put it with plants that are
    fragrant or foul;[3]
For your sons, you must pick their companions and mates.

If in May you peddle fresh fish,
Never let others ridicule you![4]

1. Or possibly, "if they don't study the classics with a teacher"—*pu ching shih*—but I think the *ching* here means to pass through or experience.
2. Literally, "city pavilion rats" *(tu-t'ing shu)*. Iritani and Matsumura *(Kanzanshi*, p. 293) have found the following line in the *Shih-liu kuo ch'un-ch'iu*: "Rats in the city pavilions often get to hear words of elders." Given line 4 below, rats have the advantage.
3. The compound *hsün-yu* ("fragrant plants and foul-smelling plants") is a stock metaphor for people who are good or bad. Read *(Chinese Medicinal Plants*, p. 34, item 134a) identifies the *hsün-ts'ao* as *O. basilicum*: for *yu*. Hu Shiu-ying *(An Enumeration of Chinese Materia Medica* [Hong Kong: The Chinese University Press, 1980], p. 182) has the botanical name *Caryopteris incana*.
4. The point is that fish in the fifth month easily spoil, just like boys when they are young. Parents must be careful; their sons can easily and quickly turn bad.

No. 219

In vain I close my bramble door and sit down,[1]
Repeatedly going through changes that endure
    like the spark of a flint.[2]

I've only heard about people turning into ghosts;
I've never seen the crane-transformed immortals.[3]

When I think of this—how can I bear to speak?
When you live following fate[4], you must
    take pity on yourself.

I turn and gaze out beyond the suburbs and walls;
"Ancient tombs now ploughed into fields."[5]

1. On *p'eng-men* ("bramble door") see poem 29, note 4. "Bramble door" is a set expression for describing the humble abode of a recluse.
    2. There is a variant of *sui-yüeh*, "years and months" for "the spark produced by striking a flint" (*shih-huo*).
    3. i.e., people who become immortals by turning into—or riding to the sky on—cranes.
    4. Literally, live "in accord with karmic conditions" (*sui-yüan*).
    5. A direct quote from poem 14 of the "Nineteen Old Poems" of the Han (*Wen-hsüan* 29: 6b, p. 399).

No. 220*

When people of this age see Han-shan,
They all say, "This is some nut!"

"His face—not fit to be seen by human eyes;
His body wrapped only in cotton-fur robes."

But my words they don't understand,
And *their* words are things that I wouldn't say!

My response to these visitors is,
"You too can come look at Han-shan!"[1]

---

*Pulleyblank: Han-shan II.
1. Possibly meaning to "look at" *(hsiang)* Han-shan in the way that Bodhidharma is said to have looked at *(mien)* a wall for nine years—sitting in meditation.

No. 221

Independent and free[1]—at ease in the white clouds;
But from the beginning, it's not that I purchased
    these hills.[2]

To get through the passes below, you must
    support yourself with a cane;
For the precipitous peaks up above—
    grab on to creepers to climb.

At the bottom of the valley, the pines are always
    kingfisher green;
By the side of the brook, the rocks are by nature mottled.

Though friends and campanions are impeded, cut off,
When spring arrives the birds peacefully sing out
    "tweet, tweet."

1. *Tzu-tsai* translates *īśvara*, "sovereign" or "king." Literally, the Chinese means "to exist on one's own"—thus to be free from any resistance to one's movement.
2. Probably an allusion to a story that is told of the Buddhists Chih Tun (314–366) and Chu Tao-ch'ien (286–374). Chu Tao-ch'ien's biography in *Kao-seng chuan* 4 (*ch'u-chi* pp. 97–99) records that Chih Tun once sent someone to Tao-ch'ien to buy from him a small ridge on Yang-shan on which to retire. Tao-ch'ien's response was: "If you want to come, then I will give [it to you]. Have you ever heard of [the recluses] Ch'ao [Fu] and [Hsü] Yu buying mountains and retiring?" A similar anecdote is recorded in *Shih-shuo hsin-yü* 25:28 (Yang Yung, *Shih-shuo hsin-yü chiao-chien* [Hong Kong: Ta-chung shu-chü, 1969], pp. 601–602: Mather, *A New Account*, pp. 412–413).

No. 222

I live in a little country village,
Where everyone praises me as someone without compare.

But yesterday I went down to the city,
Where, to the contrary, I was looked up and down by the *dogs!*

Some complained that my trousers were too tight;
Others said that my shirt was a little too long!

If someone could draw off the eyes of the hawk,
Little sparrows could dance with dignity and grace!

No. 223

"Life and death from the beginning are fixed by Fate;
Wealth and rank originally come from Heaven."

These are the words of the ancients;[1]
My words now are not some false report.

But the wise and the clever "enjoy" their short lives,
While the stupid and foolish, to the contrary,
     live out their long years.

And the dull creature has abundant treasures and wealth,
While the sharp, alert man has no money at all.

1. Han-shan seems to have in mind—indeed, virtually quotes—the words of Tzu-hsia found in *Analects* 12: 5 (p. 22). D. C. Lau (*Confucius: The Analects*, p. 113) translates: "Ssu-ma Niu appeared worried, saying, 'All men have brothers. I alone have none.' Tzu-hsia said, 'I have heard it said: "life and death are a matter of Destiny; wealth and honor depend on Heaven." The gentleman is reverent and does nothing amiss . . . and all within the Four Seas are his brothers. What need is there for the gentleman to worry about not having any brothers?'"

Comment: One is reminded of poem 2 in T'ao Ch'ien's famous series, "Twenty Drinking Wine Poems," where a similar bitterness about the injustice in life is expressed. Hightower (*The Poetry of T'ao Ch'ien*, p. 126) translates the opening lines of that poem: "Do good, they say, and your reward will come—Po-i and Shu-ch'i found theirs on West Mountain. Since good and evil go without reward, what's the point of all the cant they talk?" Po-i and Shu-ch'i (see note 4 to poem 8) were the two recluses who died of starvation, refusing to serve the founder of the Chou dynasty, whom they regarded as a usurper—in this way preserving their integrity.

No. 224

For the country, it's the people that are fundamental;[1]
It's just like the tree that depends on the soil.

If the soil is rich, the tree will flourish and spread;
If the soil is poor, the tree withers and decays.

You must never leave its roots bare;
When the branches dry up, the seeds are the first things
    to fall.[2]

To breach the dam to get the fish—
This is to seize but momentary profit.

1. Iritani and Matsumura (*Kanzanshi*, p. 300) see an allusion here to a line in the "Wu-tzu chih ko" (Songs of the Five Sons) in the *Shu* (*Shang-shu K'ung-chuan* 3: 9b). Legge/Waltham (*Shu Ching: Book of History* [Chicago, IL: Henry Regnery, 1971], p. 58) translates that line: "The people are the root of a country." The Chinese is *min wei pang-pen*; Han-shan's text is *kuo i jen wei pen*. Iritani and Matsumura further argue that Han-shan changes *min* to *jen* to avoid the taboo on T'ang T'ai-tsung's name (Li Shih-min; r. 627–649).
   2. But what are the seeds in the allegory? Future possibility? Wealth?

No. 225

Sentient beings—they're not worth discussing!
What's the meaning of their allowing the upside-down
    and perverse?

On their faces, the two evil birds;[1]
In their hearts, three poisonous snakes.[2]

These pose for them hindrances and obstructions;
They cause you to serve defilement and pain.[3]

Raise your hand high and snap your fingers!
[Let's just sing,] "Namaḥ Buddha."[4]

1. The identity of the "two evil birds" *(liang-o niao)* is uncertain. Iritani and Matsumura *(Kanzanshi,* pp. 301–302) say they stand for two kinds
of *kleśa, chien-ssu fan-nao (kleśa* of perception and thought?), on the one
hand, which is confusion about the true mark of things, and *wu-ming fan-*
nao (kleśa of ignorance) on the other, which is fundamentally lacking the
ability to know. However, they cite no textual authority for this interpretation. Tseng P'u-hsin *(Han-shan shih-chieh,* p. 119), on the other hand, explains "the two evil birds" as the obstacles of seeing and hearing. The "two
evils," unlike the "three poisons," does not seem to be a set expression in
Buddhism.
    2. i.e., the three poisons—greed, anger, and ignorance.
    3. *Fan-na* here seems to mean the same thing as *fan-nao,* which is *kleśa*
("defilements," "passions"), even though the syllable *na* by itself is thought
to be a sound that *dispels* the defilements.

4. Following the interpretation of Iritani and Matsumura (*Kanzanshi,* p. 302), who feel that to raise one's hand high and snap one's fingers is a sign of joy—i.e. "Forget them! Let's have a good time." Another interpretation of these last two lines might be made. Since the words "Namaḥ Amitābha" (here *na-mo fo-t'o-yeh*)—meaning "I bow down to Amitābha"—are chanted at the moment of death by believers in the Pure Land, it could be that the author is saying, "By the time it takes to snap your fingers (that fast), you'll be chanting "Namaḥ Amitābha" (i.e., you'll be dead). In support of this *t'an-chih* (to snap the fingers) is used above in poem 34 in this way—to mean "that fast."

No. 226

I find my joy in the Everyday Way;[1]
Midst mist and vines and stone caves.

Delighting in the wilds—great is my unrestraint;
My constant companions—white clouds at their ease.

There are roads—but they don't reach through to the world;
I have no mind[2]—who can pull me away?

On my rock bed, alone I sit in the night,
While the round moon climbs up Han-shan.

1. In *kōan* 19 in the *Wu-men kuan* (T. 2005, Vol. 48, p. 295 middle), the Zen master Nan-ch'üan replies in a similar way to a question from Chao-chou. Chao-chou asks, "Like what is this Way?" To which Nan-ch'üan replies, "The everyday mind is the Way" (*p'ing-ch'ang hsin shih tao*). For an English translation of the whole, see Paul Reps, *Zen Flesh, Zen Bones* (New York: Doubleday, 1957), p. 105.

2. *Wu-hsin*, like *wu-nien*, is the desired Zen frame of mind, a mind in which there is no intentional or deliberate thought.

No. 227*

The great ocean—water without any shore;
Fishes and dragons—ten thousand, ten thousand thousand.

Taking turns, they eat and they chew one another;
All mixed together—one stupid lump of flesh.[1]

Because the mind isn't completely cut off,[2]
False thoughts arise like smoke.

Your nature is like the moon—pure and clear, it is bright;
Far and wide it shines without end.[3]

*Pulleyblank: Han-shan II.
    1. Han-shan is obviously talking about the "sea" of sentient beings.
    2. The active mind being that which thinks on purpose for some selfish end.
    3. *Wu-pien;* without an end spatially, the same words end the first line, there translated as "without any shore." In this way Han-shan identifies the true nature with the phenomenal realm.

No. 228*

In person[1] I see the top of T'ien-t'ai;
Alone in its height—standing above the common crowd.

Swayed by the wind, pines and bamboo sigh in harmony;
When the moon shines, the ocean and tides incessantly roll.

Below I look out to the edge of green hills;
To discuss things profound, I have the white clouds.

My delight in the wilds agrees with these mountains and
   streams;
My original ambition—to admire fellow followers of the way.[2]

*Pulleyblank: Han-shan II.
1. There is a variant of *mu* ("With my own eyes I see") for *tzu* ("in person").
2. The same line occurs at the start of poem 278.

No. 229

Three or four[1] stupid youngsters!
In the things they do, neither genuine nor sincere.

They've not yet read ten volumes,
Yet in their presumption, they pick up the "editing pen."[2]

They take the chapter "Conduct of Scholars"[3]
And call it "regulations for robbers and thieves!"

They metamorphose—like they're silverfish—
Then chew up and destroy others' books.

1. Literally, "three or five" (*san-wu*).
2. The "editing pen" is literally the "yellow ochre pen" (*tz'u-huang pi*). Yellow ochre was used in ancient times to blot out words, since the color of the paper was yellow.
3. Chapter 40 in the *Li-chi* (Record of Rites).

No. 230*

A mind as high as some mountain peak!
Maintaining the distinction between self and other,
    he does not yield to other men.[1]

He knows how to lecture on the Vedas,
Can discuss the writings of the Three Schools.[2]

In his heart there's no sense of shame or disgrace;
Even though he has broken the precepts,[3] gone against
    Vinaya lore.[4]

He himself says this is the teaching for the highest of men
And claims that he himself's number one!

Those who are stupid all praise him and sigh;
Those who are wise, clap their hands together and laugh.

Dust in sun's rays—spots in the air;[5]
Can he avoid life and old age?

This does not compare to understanding nothing at all,
To silently sitting,[6] cutting off vexation and grief.

---

*Pulleyblank: Han-shan II.

1. Following Iritani and Matsumura (*Kanzanshi*, p. 307) in understanding *jen-wo* in this way—the distinction between self and other. Ch'en
Hui-chien (*Han-shan-tzu*, p. 240) understands it to mean that he is subjective or biased. In Buddhism, *jen-wo* technically is the erroneous view that
there is a permanent self, an *ātman*. The line thus might also read: "He
believes in true self—he will not yield to others."

2. The "Three Teachings" *(san-chiao)* are Confucianism, Taoism, and Buddhism.

3. The "precepts" are the moral rules of laymen and monks, *śīla (chieh)*. The ten precepts upheld by all monks are—quoting from Soothill and Hodous, *A Dictionary of Chinese Buddhist Terms*, p. 239—"(1) not to kill, (2) not to steal, (3) not to commit adultery, (4) not to speak falsely, (5) not to drink wine, (6) not to use adornments of flowers, nor perfumes, (7) not to perform as an actor, juggler, acrobat, or go to visit and hear them, (8) not to sit on elevated, broad, and large divans (or beds), (9) not to eat except in regulation hours, and (10) not to possess money, gold or silver, or precious things."

4. *Lü-wen*, the Buddhist writings on training and discipline—all moral and administrative rules for monastic life.

5. i.e., life is like this; it is something that is not really real. On "flowers/spots in the air" *(k'ung-hua)*, see also poem 297.

6. In meditation—*ching-tso*.

No. 231

It's like having many fine treasures;
In the ocean, riding a broken-down tub!

In the front part you've lost your mast;
To the rear there's also no helm.

Twisting and turning, blown about by the wind;
High and low, you bob with the waves.

How can you get to that shore?
You must work hard and never sit still.

Note: An allegory of what life is like: with Buddha-nature inside (the "many fine treasures"), we strive to reach the other shore of *nirvāṇa* with this "broken-down tub" (i.e., our bodies). The metaphor of the broken-down boat is mentioned in the *Nirvāṇa-sūtra*, Chapter 27 (T. 375, Vol. 2, p. 674 bottom). Whatever *nu-li* ("work hard," "exert all your strength") might mean elsewhere in these poems (see the comment on poem 53), here it surely means to work hard in a Buddhist way.

No. 232*

I've seen common dumb men;
They store up large amounts of riches and grain.

They drink down their wine and eat living things,
Saying, "Ah, now I'm rich and content."

None of them knows the depths of Hell;
They only seek the good fortune of mounting to Heaven.

But their sinful *karma* is like Mount Vipula;[1]
How can they avoid disaster and harm?

When this rich master suddenly dies,
His kin will compete in weeping in front of his corpse.

They'll make offerings to monks to read sacred prayers;
In vain, this money paid to spirits and ghosts!

If you have not even one blessings field,[2]
It's useless to bring forth a crowd of bald [monks and nuns].

This can't compare to being early enlightened;
To never doing[3] that which leads to the dark and black Hell.

When wild winds do not shake the tree,
The mind that is real[4] has neither blessings nor sin.

I send these words to you bewildered men;
I urge you to read them two or three times.

*Pulleyblank: Han-shan II.

1. Mount Vipula (p'i-fu for p'i-fu-lo) is a large mountain near Kusāgārapura in Magadha. The claim that the bones of sentient beings passing through countless lives pile up this high is made in Chapter 25 of the Nirvāṇa-sūtra (T. 375, Vol. 12, p. 739 bottom). See also poem 280.

2. Fu-t'ien, an area of good works that will result in blessings.

3. This might also be read as direct exhortation—"Never do [things that lead to]. . . . "

4. Hsin-chen; the mind is bhūtatathatā.

No. 233*

I urge you people in the three realms,[1]
Never do things that go against reason.[2]

If your powers in reason are weak, you'll be cheated
    by others;
If they are strong, they'll not tolerate you.

In this world, people impure and excessive,
Are just exactly like burdock.[3]

They don't see that the man unconcerned with affairs,
He alone is set free—there is no one who can compare.

Early on, you must return to the original source;
The three realms, following causes, arise.

The pure and unsullied—enter it just like a stream;
Never drink from water that is unclear.[4]

*Pulleyblank: Han-shan II.
1. On the three realms, see poem 197, note 3.
2. Or such the Chinese seems to say. But the point is unclear, given the text that follows.

3. For *shu-nien-tzu* as "Great Burdock" *(Arctium lappa)* see Read, *Chinese Medicinal Plants*, p. 1 (item 2). But what is the point? Does Han-shan mean to say they stick fast to you no matter which way you turn? Or is it that, having come into contact with the external, phenomenal world, they stick fast to it, unable to tear themselves free? (this seems to be Iritani and Matsumura's interpretation *[Kanzanshi*, p. 313]). Ch'en Hui-chien *(Han-shan-tzu*, p. 238) feels it simply stands for bad people in the world.

4. That is, from *avidyā*, "ignorance" *(wu-ming shui)*, the basic cause of existence in the three realms.

No. 234

Men in the three realms,[1] like millions of insects
    wiggle and squirm;
Men in the six paths[2]—a limitless mass.

They covet their wealth and cherish their lustful desires;
Hearts evil, like those of the jackal[3] and wolf.

Off to Hell they will go, like the shot of an arrow;
Extreme misery, as though right in front of one's face.[4]

Confused, in a muddle they pass nights and days,
None distinguishing virtue and good.

Goodness and evil they never recognize,
As though they were swine and sheep.

Talking with them is like talking to trees or rocks;
Jealous and envious, as if they were stark-raving mad.

They themselves don't see their own faults,
Like pigs asleep in their pens.

They don't know they must pay;
To the contrary, they laugh at the ox pulling
    the mill.[5]

1. On the "three realms," see poem 197, note 3.
2. The "six paths" are the six possible fates that await one at death.
See poem 72, note 2.

3. Read *(Chinese Materia Medica: Animal Drugs,* item 379) identifies the *ch'ai* as the "ch'ai wolf" *(Canis lupus tchiliensis).*

4. i.e., it will come that quickly. Or possibly, "as though it were fit" *(jo wei tang).*

5. i.e., they are as dumb and as trapped in this existence as the ox who goes 'round and 'round to move the millstone for grinding grains.

Comment: In the *Tse-shih-chü ts'ung-shu* and *Kunaichō* editions of the text, this poem is combined with the preceding (233) to form one poem (no. 231 in that count). Though both poems describe people in the three realms, there seems to be no other connection; the rhyme in each case is distinct (see Pulleyblank, "Linguistic Evidence for the Date of Han-shan," in Ronald C. Miao, *Studies in Chinese Poetry and Politics,* Vol. 1. San Francisco: CMC, 1978, p. 188).

No. 235

Man's life in this blanket of dust
Is just like [that of] a bug in a bowl.

All day long he goes 'round and 'round
And never gets out of his bowl.

Immortality he cannot attain;
Delusions he counts without end.

The months and the years flow by like a stream;[1]
In a moment he's become an old man.

1. See poem 49, note 3.

No. 236*

Han-shan sets forth these words;
I repeat them, like some crazy man.

When I have something to say, I say it right to your face;
Hence, I have earned the resentment of men.

If the heart is sincere[1], the words set forth are direct;
With a direct heart, there is no behind.[2]

When you draw near to death and cross the river Nai-ho,[3]
[Then you will ask,] "Who was that babbling fool?!"

Dark, dark is the road to the grave;
By your *karma* you're tied and detained.[4]

---

*Pulleyblank: Han-shan II.
1. Preferring the variant of *chen* ("sincere") to *chih* ("direct").
2. i.e., what he says is not two-sided, or he does not say one thing
and mean another.
3. The river that is crossed as one enters the underworld.
4. Like a criminal in jail.

No. 237* †

I've seen these men of great knowledge;
All day long they use up their spirits and minds.

At each fork in the road, they show off with their prattle,[1]
Cheating and deceiving all other men.

All they produce is the dregs that will lead them to Hell;
They do not practice the means to conduct upright and correct.

Suddenly death[2] will arrive;
Then their set knowledge will be thrown into confusion,
    chaotically scattered about.

---

*Pulleyblank: Han-shan II.
†Missing from the *Tse-shih-chü ts'ung-shu* and *Kunaichō* Library editions.
1. i.e., where others would hesitate about which direction to go.
2. *Wu-ch'ang* translates *anitya* "impermanence," but it is also commonly used for death.

No. 238*

I send these words to you many benevolent lords;
Time and again, what is it that you should hold dear?

Exhaust the Way and see your own nature;
Your own nature is none other than Tathāgata.

Your Heaven-given endowment, from the beginning,
      is sufficient and complete;
And when through practice you experience the truth, you
      will turn 'round and head home, your mission fulfilled.[1]

To reject the root and, to the contrary, pursue the branch
Is simply to maintain a position that's dumb!

*Pulleyblank: Han-shan II.

1. *Ch'ai-hui* is an expression used in official life. It means to return to one's home office, having been far away for a long time on a mission that is now complete. The task completed in the present case is the Buddhist task of knowing one's true self. That too is a return home with one's mission complete.

No. 239*

In this world there's one kind of person;
He's not really bad—he's also not good.

He does not know the Lord who is master of men,[1]
So he follows the guest, turning first here then there.[2]

Just letting things slide, he passes his time;
Bemuddled! This stupid piece of sliced meat!

'Though he has his sacred terrace,[3]
It's only like the guest that he is a man.[4]

*Pulleyblank: Han-shan II.

1. "Lord who is master of men" *(chu-jen kung)* is a name for Buddha-nature.

2. In some Zen sects (especially the Ts'ao-tung Sect), the opposition of subjective and objective reality—or the true Buddha-nature inside versus an objectively real world outside—is discussed in terms of the relationship of Host *(chu)* and Guest *(k'o)*. Someone who "follows the guest" still believes in the reality of an objective, external realm and does not know the true Buddha-nature inside. On the five possible relationships of host and guest, see, for example, Heinrich Dumoulin, *A History of Zen Buddhism* (New York: McGraw-Hill, 1963), pp. 112–118; also Charles Luk, *Ch'an and Zen Teaching*, Vol. 2, pp. 127–157.

3. *Ling-t'ai*, "sacred terrace," is a name for the mind. It is also something a "ruler" would have, and King Wen of the Chou dynasty is famous for building one.

4. i.e., he has not yet realized his true mind and thus become one with the "host"—or his own Buddha-nature—inside.

No. 240*

I've often heard that Śākyamuni Buddha
Previously received acknowledgement from Dīpaṁkara.[1]

With Dīpaṁkara and Śākyamuni,
We're simply discussing a case of former and latter wisdom.

Former and latter in *essence* were not in any way different;
In what is distinctive there's nothing distinct.[2]

In one Buddha and in all Buddhas,
The mind is the locus of the "thus come."[3]

---

*Pulleyblank: Han-shan II.

1. Dīpaṁkara Buddha—"Lamplighter Buddha" *(Jan-teng fo)*—was the twenty-fourth predecessor of Śākyamuni. The *Jui-ying ching* (T. 185, Vol. 3, pp. 472–473) records that Śākyamuni (not yet a Buddha) met Dīpaṁkara when the latter was Buddha and scattered seven lotus flowers in front of him, five of which stood still in mid-air. Moreover, he threw his hair over mud and let Dīpaṁkara walk across it. As a result, he was recognized by Dīpaṁkara as a future Buddha and informed that he would become a Buddha in 91 *kalpas*.

2. One cannot pull off in English what Han-shan does in Chinese. In what is *i*—"different," but also "rare," "unique," hence "distinct"—there is nothing *i*.

3. i.e., Tathāgata, Buddha-nature.

No. 241*

I've often heard of these great ministers of state;
Robes purple and red, hair pins, chin straps and salary![1]

Wealth and rank—one hundred, one thousand kinds;
They lust after glory, never knowing disgrace.

Servants and horses fill their houses and sheds;
Gold and silver overflow in their treasury rooms.

Stupidly blind to the fact that good fortune is but a temporary
    support,
They bury their heads, doing things that will lead them to Hell.

Suddenly they die—all matters then come to an end;
Sons and daughters in front of them weep.

They didn't know there would be this calamity and disaster;
The road out in front—how fast it went by![2]

The family in ruins—cold winds sigh and moan
For food—not one kernel of grain.

Freezing and hungry, bitter, pathetic and sad;
Truly this is because they went along unaware,
    bumping into this and then that.

*Pulleyblank: Han-shan II.
1. All symbols of high-ranking nobles. The "hair pins" (*tsan*) and "chin straps" (*ying*) keep on their official caps.
2. i.e., their future.

No. 242

The highest of men have minds that are sharp and quick;
They hear things just once and know the best part.

Those in the middle have minds that are pure and clear;
When they think it over with care, they can tell you
    what's most important to know.

Gents at the bottom are dull, stupid, and dumb!
Obstinate and perverse, they're the hardest to crack.[1]

They simply wait 'til the blood drips from their heads;
Only then do they *start* to know they've been defeated, destroyed!

You've all seen—we can take, for example, the thief
    with wide open eyes,[2]
Who is executed in the bustling market where people have
    gathered.

His corpse thrown away like it's dust;
At this time to whom will he speak?

A great man, a truly great hero,
With one stroke will be cut into two.

People with human faces but hearts of birds and beasts;
Their crafty deeds—when will they ever end?

---

1. One hears in the background the words of Confucius in *Analects*
16: 9 (p. 34). D. C. Lau (*Confucius: The Analects*, p. 140) translates: "Confucius said, 'Those who are born with knowledge are the highest. Next

come those who attain knowledge through study. Next again come those who turn to study after having been vexed by difficulties. The common people, in so far as they make no effort to study even after having been vexed by difficulties, are the lowest."'

2. It is not clear if his eyes are "open" because he now recognizes his wrong or if they're wide open in fear.

No. 243

I have six older and younger brothers;
In the lot there's one that is evil.

Though you strike him, you can't really touch him;
Though you scold him, you will not succeed.

With all of his traits, there's just no hope;
Addicted to wealth, he loves to be lewd and cause harm.

When he sees what he likes, in his craving he has
      thoughts of only one thing;
His greedy mind is worse than those of the demons.[1]

Our father hates to see him;
Our mother detests him; she's not at all pleased.

Last night he was apprehended by me;
I berated him, telling him he must restrain these wild feelings.

I used this chance to confront him with his inhuman traits;[2]
Speaking to him about each of them one by one.

"You must immediately change your conduct;
'If the cart overturns, you must alter the track.'[3]

If you don't believe me and accept this advice;
I'll share in your evil—together we'll be put to death.

If you accept my advice and calm and subdue your passions,
Together with you I'll seek life."

From that time on, he's been completely agreeable and pleasant,
And now he's even surpassed the bodhisattvas!

To study his new occupation, he applied himself at the forge,[4]
And when his refining was through, he had fashioned three
      mountains of iron.[5]

And now he is tranquil and calm;
Everyone praises him and is pleased.

1. The *rākṣasas (lo-ch'a)*.

2. Translation is tentative. The line might also mean, "I took advantage of this situation to go to a place where there were no people," or "He's headed in a direction where there are no other people." The line is *ch'en hsiang wu-jen ch'u* ("take advantage towards without people place").

3. A common saying cited in the biography of Chia I (*Han shu* 48; Vol. 8, p. 2251) is relevant here: "If the cart in front overturns, carts behind should beware."

4. "Study his new occupation" (*hsüeh-yeh*) also means "cultivate his *karma*."

5. Iritani and Matsumura (*Kanzanshi,* p. 328) cite evidence from *P'ang chü-shih yü-lu* to show that "three mountains of iron" (*san-shan t'ieh*) means the three kinds of *karma*—those of word, thought, and deed.

Note: Iritani and Matsumura (*Kanzanshi,* p. 327) follow Hakuin (*Kanzan shi sendai kibun.* 3: 11–12) in identifying the six brothers as the six senses or first six consciousnesses (eye consciousness, ear consciousness, nose consciousness, tongue consciousness, body consciousness, and thought or idea consciousness (*i-shih*). It is the sixth consciousness that is bad and needs to be reformed. Tseng P'u-hsin (*Han-shan shih-chieh,* pp. 131–132) goes even further, arguing that the "father" is the "seventh" consciousness (*manas-vijñāna*—intellection, reason, thought center) and the "mother" would then be the "eighth consciousness" or *ālaya-vijñāna,* the storehouse of all the seeds of experience. (For a full discussion of the eight consciousnesses and how they interact according to the Consciousness-Only School, see Fung Yu-lan [translated by Derk Bodde], *A History of Chinese Philosophy,* Vol. II, pp. 299–338.) Though this interpretation is very appealing, the culprit in "Consciousness-Only" terms is the "seventh" consciousness, which always clings to the reality of self and things; here the "evil" brother is one of the six.

No. 244*

In former days I was extremely impoverished and poor;
Night after night, I'd count up the treasures of others.[1]

But today I've thought it over with care;
I myself must build up my own stock of wealth.

Digging, I found a real treasure store,
Filled completely with crystal pearls.[2]

But a full-grown, blue-eyed barbarian[3]
Secretly planned to buy it and take it away.

Then I replied to him with these words:
"These pearls have no price you can set."[4]

---

*Pulleyblank: couplets 3, 4, and 5—Han-shan II.

1. Tseng P'u-hsin (*Han-shan shih-chieh,* p. 132), correctly points out that in terms of the allegory of the poem, this means that he was reading about the enlightenment experiences of others instead of having his own—he was looking for the truth outside instead of looking inside.

2. i.e., Buddha-nature.

3. The "blue-eyed barbarian" (*pi-yen hu*) in Zen texts normally means Bodhidharma, the founder of Zen in China. It can also simply mean a foreigner from Central Asia.

4. On the "priceless jewel," see poem 195, note 3.

No. 245*

All my life I've been lazy and lax about work;
Hating the heavy, I only find fit what is light!

Others might study for a trade or career,
But I hold on to only one book.

I'm of no mind to mount it as a scroll;
In going and coming, this saves me from carrying it around.

In accord with the disease, we prescribe the medicine;[1]
Using the expedient method[2], we save all living things.

If one's mind is simply unconcerned with affairs,
In what place will it not be enlightened?

---

*Pulleyblank: Han-shan II.
  1. A common Buddhist saying (normally *ying-ping yü-yao*) referring to the way in which the Buddha tailors his message to the capacity of the listener.
  2. The term is *fang-pien (upāya)*; this line means essentially the same as the one before.

No. 246*

I've seen these people who've "left home";[1]
They don't really get into their "leaving home" studies.

If you want to know what it means to *really* leave home,
It's to have a pure mind with no attachments or ties.

Clear and calm, completely sublime and profound;
Like-so like-so[2], relying on none for support.

Through the three realms he moves at his will,[3]
    back and forth, up and down;
The four forms of birth cannot make him stay.[4]

The person who does not act, who's unconcerned with affairs,
Is free, unrestrained, and truly knows happiness and joy.

*Pulleyblank: Han-shan II.
    1. *Ch'u-chia (pravraj)*, to leave home and become a monk or a nun.
    2. *Ju-ju* means the same as *chen-ju, tathatā, tathatā* being that level of reality that's really real. It is what it *is* in itself, depending on nothing for its existence.
    3. On the "three realms" in Buddhist cosmology, see poem 197, note 3.
    4. The "four forms of birth" *(ssu-sheng, catur-yoni)* are: (1) things that are born from the womb; (2) things that are born from an egg; (3) things that are born from water (e.g., fishes and worms); and (4) things that are born by transformation/metamorphosis (e.g., moths and butterflies).

No. 247*

Yesterday I went to an abbey up in the clouds,
Where I suddenly met an honored immortal.

With his starry cap¹ and his moon cape draped over
      his shoulders,
He spoke to me in great detail about living in the mountains
      and streams.

I asked about the method for becoming an immortal;²
He replied, "The Way—to what does it compare?

We call it the Powerful, the Supreme;
The Profound Drugs are the heart's divine secret.

Maintaining the Way until death, we wait for our cranes
      to come,
Though everyone says we depart riding on fish."³

I then repeatedly thought this through;
Upon investigation, it made no sense at all!

Just look at an arrow shot into the air;
In a short while, it still falls back to the ground.

Even if you're one of those people who attains immortality,
You're just like a ghost holding on to his corpse.⁴

The mind like the moon, in itself is pure and bright;
The ten thousand forms—how can they compare?

If you want to know the method for compounding
      the immortal elixir
Inside your body, the original soul—this is it!⁵

Never study the arts of Master Yellow Turban;⁶
Holding fast to your ignorance and obstinately maintaining
      your determination.

*Pulleyblank: Han-shan II.

1. The "star hats" (hsing-kuan) worn by Taoist adepts are described by Edward Schafer in his Pacing the Void: T'ang Approaches to the Stars (Berkeley, CA: University of California Press, 1977), pp. 224–227. No pictures of them remain. But some are noted with the twenty-eight "lunar lodges" depicted on them; others have the sun and moon and five planets. Typically the Taoist wears a "feather cloak" that goes along with his "star hat," but Schafer cites lines from a poem by Li Hsün (p. 225) where a Taoist is "moon cloaked," as in the line we have here.

2. A "divine immortal" (shen-hsien)—which is what the text says—normally means just an immortal. However, in some cases a distinction is drawn between Heavenly Immortals, Earthly Immortals, and Water Immortals: one who can transform into any one of the three is a "divine immortal."

3. Apparently alluding to the story of Ch'in Kao (Lieh-hsien chuan 5b–6a; Max Kaltenmark, Le Lie-sien Tchouan [Beijing: Centre d'études sinologiques de Pékin, 1953], pp. 104–107), who, on entering the waters of the Cho River, told his disciples to fast and wait for him at a temple they should set up on the shores of the stream. He appeared, at the appointed time, riding out of the river on a red carp.

4. Han-shan has a clever comeback to the Taoist who said, "Maintaining [the Way] until death [shou-ssu] we wait. . . . " Such people to Han-shan are "ghosts who hold on to their corpses [shou-shih kuei]."

5. Han-shan seems to have in mind the Taoist practice of nei-tan, "inner alchemy," where the adept, in meditation, identifies various parts of his body with the various ingredients and apparatuses used to produce an actual chemical elixir and thus refines an inner elixir inside his body. Han-shan's point is that we have that immortal soul from the start—the Buddha-nature inside.

6. "Master Yellow Turban" (Huang-chin kung) is presumably Chang Chüeh, founder of the T'ai-p'ing tao (Way of Great Peace) sect in the second century A.D. and leader of the Yellow Turban revolt in 184. It is with the Way of the Celestial Master (T'ien-shih tao), founded by Chang Chüeh's contemporary Chang Tao-ling, that we associate the beginnings of organized Taoism. Perhaps the most thorough account of the activities of Chang Chüeh in English is Barbara Kandel's book, Taiping Jing: The Origin and Transmission of the 'Scripture on General Welfare'—the History of an Unofficial Text (Hamburg: Gesellschaft für Natur und Völkerkunde Ostasiens e.V., 1979).

There is a variant of Huang-shih kung—Master Yellow Stone—for Huang-chin kung. Master Yellow Stone was a Ch'in (B.C. 221–209) recluse who gave Chang Liang a book on military tactics that helped him go on to be the great general who helped to establish the Han dynasty in 206. See Shih-chi (Vol. 6, pp. 2034–2035).

No. 248*

In my village there is one house;[1]
In this house there is no true lord.[2]

Here the ground grows one inch of grass,
And the water descends in one drop of dew.

Fire consumes the "six thieves";
Wind blows away the black clouds and rain.

If you look closely for the inhabitant;
It's just that true pearl wrapped in coarse cloth.[3]

*Pulleyblank: Han-shan II.
1. Preferring the variant of *hsiang* ("village") to *chia* ("family").
2. The symbolism seems to be that the house is here the body: the true lord *(chen-chu)* would then be an *ātman*.
3. i.e., Buddha-nature. The "inhabitant" is literally, the "original man" *(pen-jen).*

Comment: Iritani and Matsumura *(Kanzanshi,* p. 342) confess that while there is no difficulty in understanding each individual line in this poem, it is not clear what the whole means. Ch'en Hui-chien *(Han-shan-tzu,* p. 211) is the only commentator I know to see that Han-shan is talking about the "four constituent elements of reality" *(ssu-ta, mahābhūta):* earth, water, fire, and wind; these are the things that make up one's body. That is not all; the symbolism of the poem is rich in other ways. "One square inch" *(fang-ts'un)* is another name for the mind; in addition, in Taoism all things start in the beginning with the Tao, from the "one square inch." Secondly, a number of Zen texts speak of a "one drop of water Zen" *(i-ti ch'an),* with the idea that all truths are contained in a single drop of water. Next, the "six thieves" mean the six senses in Buddhism—or rather, the activities of the senses—i.e., seeing, smelling, tasting—because they lust after beautiful sights, smells, and so on. And finally, the clouds blown away are most likely the clouds of ignorance that keep us from seeing the truth.

No. 249*

I send along these words to the various sons of the rich;
You've all heard tell of Shih Ch'i-nu.[1]

Of servants and slaves—he had eight hundred people;
Water-driven mills in thirty locations.[2]

Beneath his cottage, they raised fish and birds;
Upstairs, they blew on the *sheng* and the *yü*.[3]

Still he stuck out his head as he drew near the smooth blade;
Blindly in love, for the sake of Green Pearl.

*Pulleyblank: Han-shan II(?).

1. Shih Ch'i-nu was Shih Ch'ung (A.D. 249–300), Ch'i-nu being the name he was called as a young boy. He was a man who enjoyed great wealth and power, but he was executed in 300 for plotting against the Prince of Chao, Ssu-ma Lun. He had earlier offended Sun Hsiu, who was on good terms with Ssu-ma Lun, by refusing to give Sun Hsiu one of his female entertainers, the beautiful Green Pearl. For these events, see *Shih-shuo hsin-yü* 36: 1 and accompanying notes (Yang Yung, *Shih-shuo hsin-yü chiao-chien*, pp. 692–693; Richard Mather, *Shih-shuo Hsin-yü: A New Account of Tales of the World*, pp. 489–491). See especially, the note cited from Kan Pao's *Chin-chi*.

2. Specifically, mills for hulling his rice.

3. The *sheng* is a kind of mouth organ with bamboo pipes of varying lengths—thirteen pipes in all. The *yü* is a similar instrument with a total of thirty-six pipes.

No. 250*

Why am I always so disappointed and sad?
Man's life is like that of the morning mushroom.[1]

How can we bear it, that within several tens of years,
Relatives and old friends get old, decline, and vanish?

Thinking of this makes me sad;
Sad feelings I cannot endure.

What can I do? What *should* I do?
I'll abandon this body[2] and retire to the mountains.

*Pulleyblank: Han-shan II(?).

1. Alluding to the lines in *Chuang-tzu*, Chapter 1 (1: 1:10), "The morning mushroom knows nothing of twilight and dawn; the summer cicada knows nothing of spring and autumn" (translated by Burton Watson, *The Complete Works of Chuang Tzu*, p. 30). These are things that only live a short time.

2. Reading the variant of *t'o* ("abandon," "take off") for *t'o* ("entrust to").

No. 251

These worn-out clothes are connected to previous *karma*
Never blame the bodies we have today.

If you say these come from the grave,
You're all just the dumbest of men!

If in the end you turn into a ghost;
Could you make sons and daughters be poor?

This is clear—a matter that's easily understood;
Why are you lacking in spirit?

Note: Reflecting the common Chinese belief in geomancy—that the location of one's grave (and one's home) in relation to surrounding geographic features can determine good or bad fortune for one's descendants. Iritani and Matsumura *(Kanzanshi,* pp. 345–346) also see this poem as a Buddhist criticism of geomancy. For a good account of geomancy in English, see Stephan Feuchtwang's *An Anthropological Analysis of Chinese Geomancy* (Taipei: Southern Materials Center, 1982).

No. 252

I've seen the water in the Yellow River;
Altogether it's cleared just a few times.[1]

Water flows like a fast-flying arrow;
Human life is like floating duckweed.

To belong to things stupid—this is our basic *karma*;
Ignorance is *kleśa's* pitfall.[2]

Transmigration through several *kalpas*
Simply makes us deluded and blind.

1. See poem 64, note 1.
2. i.e., if we fall into ignorance, then we are totally immersed in *kleśa* (delusion and pain).
   Note: Note how the parallel between water and human life established in couplet two is pulled apart at the end. Though the water of the Yellow River (which is naturally muddy) might nonetheless on occasion clear (i.e., the silt settles), our ignorance is made worse as we pass through time (last couplet).

No. 253

The Two Forms having opened and spread,[1]
Mankind thus lives in between.

If he wishes to lead you astray, he spews forth mist;
If he wants you to be enlightened, he blows out the wind.

If he takes pity, you'll enjoy wealth and rank;
If he snatches away, you'll be needy and poor.

Oh, you common untalented masses of people,
All matters come from Lord Heaven.[2]

1. The "Two Forms" (*erh-i*) are the two principles of creation—Yin and Yang.

2. Lord Heaven (*T'ien-kung*) no doubt means "Nature" or the natural forces of Yin and Yang, not a deity.

Note: In the second couplet, Han-shan seems to allude to the Chinese belief—much developed by the Neo-Confucians—that one's nature can be determined by the atmospheric conditions at the time of one's birth. For more on this, see, for example, the words of Chu Hsi (1130–1200) translated by Wing-tsit Chan (*A Source Book in Chinese Philosophy* [Princeton, NJ: Princeton University Press, 1963], pp. 624–625). More complete—and more interesting—are the words of Chia Yü-ts'un at the beginning of the great Chinese novel *Dream of the Red Chamber*: see David Hawkes' translation, *Cao Xueqin: The Story of the Stone*, Vol. 1 (New York: Penguin Books, 1973), pp. 76–80. Iritani and Matsumura (*Kanzanshi*, p. 350) note that this is a completely Chinese view of fate; it is not Buddhist. See also poem 112.

No. 254

I urge all of you children,
Quickly get out of that burning house!

The three carts are sitting outside of the gate;
Riding them, you can avoid the life of the homeless drifter.

When you sit in an open place at the crossroads,
That very day, all matters will be empty and void.

The ten directions have no above or below;
In coming and going, it matters not if you go east or west.

If you attain the mind that's inside,[1]
This way or that—you can move everywhere.

---

1. On *ke-chung i* as "the mind that's inside," see poem 105, note 4.
    Note: On the parable of the burning house in the *Lotus-sūtra*, see the comment to poem 189. Here lines 2 and 5 virtually quote from the original text (for which, see T. 262, Vol. 9, p. 12 middle and bottom). Parallel to line 5 in the original is: "At this time, the great man, seeing that his children have contrived to get out safely and *that all are seated in an open space at a crossroads* is no longer troubled" (translated by Hurvitz, *Scripture of the Lotus Blossom*, p. 59; emphasis added).

No. 255*

Lamentable! The men in this floating life;
It goes on and on—on what day will it end?

Day after day, they have no leisure time;
Year after year—unaware that they're getting old.

All of this done for the purpose of seeking
    clothing and food,
Making their minds produce delusion and pain.[1]

Confused and perplexed for one hundred, one thousand years,
They come and they go through the three evil ways.[2]

---

*Pulleyblank: Han-shan II.
1. *Kleśa* (*fan-nao*).
2. That is, the three evil destinies—to be reborn as an animal, become a hungry ghost, or suffer in hell.

No. 256*

Men in these times search for the road through the clouds,
But the cloud-road's obscure—there's no trace.

The mountains are high, with many steep narrow passes;
The streams are broad, with little brightness of day.

Emerald-green cliffs in front and behind;
White clouds, to the west and, what's more, to the east.

If you want to know where you find the cloud-road,
The cloud-road is here in the sky.[1]

---

*Pulleyblank: Han-shan II.

1. *Hsü-k'ung* being the "sky" but also *śūnya* ("Emptiness"), the general Mahāyāna qualifier of all things—i.e., the "way" to enlightenment (to get above the clouds) lies in the realization of the emptiness of all things; there is no set path that one must follow.

Comment: The poem is an allegory on the Zen quest for enlightenment, symbolized by reaching the top of the peak, beyond the clouds (of ignorance), up with the sun and the moon in the clear sky. There is no set path for us to follow, and/or that "way" is obscure (couplet 1). And when we set out, the obstacles (mountains to climb and rivers to cross) seem insurmountable (couplet 2). But when we realize the truth, we find that we have been at the top all along (i.e., we look out at the peaks and clouds down below [couplet 3]): such realization comes from perceiving the "emptiness" of all things (couplet 4).

No. 257

Han-shan is a place that is hidden away,
Cut off from impure men passing by.

At times I encounter some birds in the woods,
And together with them sing mountain songs.

Auspicious grasses connect valleys and dales;[1]
Old pines, pillowed against jagged peaks.

And here you can see a traveller who's free from all cares,
At rest at the foot of a cliff.

1. *Jui-ts'ao* are plants that one seldom sees; when you see them it is a sign of good things to come. They are literally "omen grasses."

No. 258*

The five sacred mountains have all turned to dust;¹
Sumeru's a "peak" one inch high.

The great ocean's no more than one drop of water,
which I imbibe and take into the field of my mind.²

Give birth to, develop, your *bodhi* seeds;³
Everywhere cover the God among gods.⁴

I tell you admirers of the Way,
Be careful to never get entangled in the Ten Cords.⁵

---

*Pulleyblank: Han-shan II.

1. On the "five sacred peaks" (*wu-yüeh*) see poem 112, note 2.

2. *Hsin-t'ien*: the mind is a field in which one can plant the seeds of good or evil deeds. On "one inch" and "one drop of water," see poem 248. Note that here the "one drop of water," *ch'an*, having watered the field of his mind, gives birth to and develops the *bodhi* seeds.

3. *P'u-t'i tzu*, the seeds of enlightened wisdom. Note how this connects with line 4. One of the ways to establish the equality of things in Buddhism is to realize that all things are nothing but thoughts, and as thoughts, Mount Sumeru and—for example—a small seed are the same. As thoughts, they occupy the same space in the mind. This way of understanding things seems to lie behind the lines of this poem. For the equality of Mount Sumeru and a mustard seed, as this is explained in the T'ien-t'ai school, see, for example, Fung Yu-lan (translated by Derk Bodde), *A History of Chinese Philosophy*, Vol. 2, pp. 370–375.

    4. The "God among gods" (*t'ien-chung t'ien*, *devātideva*) is Śākyamuni.
This is a title given to him when he went to a temple and all the statues of
the gods in the temple bowed down to him. The "cover" (*kai*) is the canopy
or parasol which is over the Buddha. One might also read, "[Let them]
everywhere cover the God among gods," meaning that one should develop—let grow—his *bodhi* seeds until they become the great *bodhi* tree of
wisdom that "covered" the Buddha in his night of enlightenment.
    5. The "Ten Cords" (*shih-ch'an*) are explained by Soothill and Hodous
(*A Dictionary of Chinese Buddhist Terms*, p. 52) as the "ten bonds that bind
men to mortality—to be shameless, unblushing, envious, mean, regretful,
torpid, drowsy, absorbed, angry [and] secretive (of sin)."

No. 259

When you lack clothes, you must search for some on your own;
Never scheme with the fox how to get furs.

When you lack food, you must gather some on your own;
Never scheme with the lamb how to get rich things to eat.

If the fox loans you its hide and the lamb loans you its meat,
They will harbor regrets and, what's more, harbor
          feelings of grief.

This is because justice has lost its right place;
Clothing and food can never be just "handed out."

Comment: Similar in tenor and language to poem 212. Here too the message is that you must seek enlightenment on your own. The "fox and the lamb" stand for Buddhist masters who already have what the beginner wants (i.e., rich furs and rich foods = enlightenment). But for them to give these things away would be like giving away their very own bodies. Enlightenment—unlike food and clothing—cannot simply be distributed, handed out to the needy (the meaning of *chou*). "Scheme" is *mou*, in the sense of *mou sheng-huo*, "plan out how to make a living."

No. 260

I truly delight in the joys that I find in the mountains;
I wander here unrestrained—relying on nothing, with no support.

Day after day I nourish this decrepit frame,
Think idle thoughts—there's nothing I *have* to do.

From time to time I unroll some old Buddhist books;
Frequently climb up to some rocky hall.[1]

Below I peer out over thousand foot drops;
Above me, there's the vast expanse of the clouds.

Cold moon so chilling—it's light, crisp, and cool;[2]
My body—like that of a lone flying crane.

1. i.e., that big—as big as, or in the shape of, a pavilion.
2. *Sou-sou* is normally glossed as either the sound of wind or the sound of rain. But it also refers to the "crisp and cool" light of the moon.

No. 261*

I've seen the Cakravartī king;[1]
His one thousand sons, constantly circle 'round.[2]

His Ten Good Traits[3] transport him to the Four Heavens,[4]
August and stately, adorned with the Seven Jewels.[5]

The Seven Jewels weigh him down, on his body
    wherever he goes;
August and stately, truly exquisite and fine.

But then one day his blessed reward[6] will be all used up,
And he'll be like the birds who nest in the weeds.[7]

Or perhaps he'll be a bug on the neck of an ox;[8]
In the six kinds of rebirth,[9] he will enjoy
    the effects of his karmic ways.

All the more will this be true for all common men;
Being impermanent[10]—how can they preserve life for long?

Life and death are like spinning flames;[11]
Our lives in transmigration, as numerous[12] as hemp
    plants or rice.

If you don't understand that you must early become enlightened,
You'll be a man who becomes old in vain.

*Pulleyblank: Han-shan II.

1. A "Cakravartī-rājan" (*chuan-lun wang*) is a universal ruler, literally—Soothill and Hodous tell us (*A Dictionary*, p. 469) "a ruler, the wheels of whose chariot roll everywhere without hindrance." He justly rules the entire world.

2. Having one thousand sons who surround or circumambulate (*wei-jao*) him is one of the marks of a Cakravartī-rājan.

3. The "Ten Good Traits" (*shih-shan*) result from not committing the Ten Evils, which are (Soothill and Hodous [*A Dictionary*, p. 50]): "killing, stealing, adultery, lying, double-tongue, coarse language, filthy language, covetousness, anger, and perverted views."

4. Iritani and Matsumura (*Kanzanshi*, p. 358) understand the "Four Heavens" to mean the "Four Kings of Heaven" (*ssu t'ien-wang*)—i.e., the guardians of the four directions. One who fervently upholds the ten rules will, in his next life, become one of these kings.

5. The "Seven Jewels" (*ch'i-pao, saptaratna*) are the seven treasures possessed by a Cakravartī. There are two lists. The treasures that specifically go with the Cakravartī are (from Soothill and Hodous, *A Dictionary*, p. 12): "(1) the golden wheel, (2) elephants, (3) dark swift horses, (4) the divine pearl or beautiful pearls, (5) able ministers of the Treasury, (6) jewels of women, and (7) daring generals." The other list of Seven Jewels is more general. In that list the seven are gold, silver, lapis lazuli, crystal, agate, white and red pearls, and cornelia. The "Seven Jewels" in our line are something the Cakravartī wears. This might make the second list more relevant. But the author might still mean the first list, speaking in a figurative way.

6. *Fu-pao*; his fortunate rebirth as a Cakravartī is a reward for his previous good deeds.

7. In Seng Chao's "Pao-tsang lun" (T. 1857, Vol. 45, p. 144 top), "sick birds that nest in the weeds" (*ping-niao ch'i-lu*) are cited as examples of things that "reject the great and seek for the small"; they are "not known in the forests" and "rest content with small contentment."

8. Such insects are easily crushed when the oxen are yoked to pull carts.

9. The "six kinds of rebirth" (*liu-ch'ü*, six *gatis*).

10. *Wu-ch'ang, anitya*.

11. A *hsüan-huo* is a spinning flame that *seems* to be a real wheel but is not.

12. Following Iritani and Matsumura's interpretation.

No. 262

Across open fields—the waters broad and wide;
Cinnabar Mound linking up with Four Brights.[1]

Immortal City[2]—most high and sublime;
Its many peaks soar above kingfisher-blue screens.

Far off, far off I gaze—where does it end?
Jagged, uneven—its appearance beckons to me.

Alone it towers beyond the edge of the sea;
Spread everywhere is its fine name.

1. For "Cinnabar Mound (*tan-ch'iu*), see poem 194, note 1. Han-shan seems to mean by it just another name for T'ien-t'ai. The location of an *actual* "Cinnabar Mound" 90 li south of Ning-hai County seems to place it outside of the T'ien-t'ai range. The "Four Brights" (*ssu-ming*) is the name of a mountain range located southwest of Yin County in Chekiang. The Taoists regard Four Brights as the locus of one of their "cavern heavens," named Cinnabar Mountain Red Water (*tan-shan-ch'ih-shui*). There is thought to be a gate above the mountain that leads to the sun, the moon, the planets, and stars—hence its name. The northwest tip of the T'ien-t'ai range is contiguous with the southwest tip of the Ssu-ming range.

2. "Immortal City" (*hsien-tu*) can simply mean a place where immortals are found, but Sun Ch'o does come to an "Immortal City" when roaming T'ien-t'ai ("Ascending and descending, I have passed two days and nights, and come at last to Hsien-tu, City of Immortals"—translated by Richard Mather, "The Mystical Ascent of the T'ient'ai Mountains," p. 241). Mather implies that this mountain is not an actual peak in T'ien-t'ai, however, noting that in legend it is "located in the Ts'ang-hai part of the North China Sea (note 90, p. 241)."

There was an *actual* mountain named "Immortal City" in Chekiang to the east of Chin-yün County. The original name of this mountain was Chin-yün, but the name was changed to Hsien-tu in the seventh year of T'ien-pao (748). The Taoists regard Hsien-tu as "cavern heaven" 29. This mountain would seem, however—like the Cinnabar Mound noted above—because of its location, to be outside of the T'ien-t'ai range. (Chin-yün County is southwest of T'ien-t'ai.)

No. 263* †

Estimable! This "one name" mountain;[1]
The Seven Jewels—how can they compare?[2]

The moon through the pines—crisp and cool its cold [light].
White and pink clouds—bit by bit they arise.

To go all the way 'round—several layers of mountains;
To make the trip back—a good many li.

Valley streams, tranquil—so still and bright;
My happiness here knows no end.

---

*Pulleyblank: Han-shan II.

†Missing from the *Tse-shih-chü ts'ung-shu* and *Kunaichō* library editions.

1. I.e., it's name is number one—it is the best. However, the "one name" (*i-ming*) is also the one truth or one reality in Buddhism. There is only one truth (and thus only one true name)—*nirvāṇa*. But the one reality is, on occasion, called many different things—e.g., *wu-wei* (acting without taking action), *wu-hsiang* (the markless), and so forth.

2. On the "Seven Jewels"—see poem 261, note 5. The point would seem to be that to realize the one truth of Buddhism is of much greater value than becoming a mere Cakravartī.

No. 264*

I've seen the men in this world;
They live for a while, and then they return to death.

Yesterday morn—like being sixteen;[1]
Young gents in their prime, filled with energy and ambition.

But as for today—already past seventy years;
Strength all used up—in appearance haggard and worn.

They're just like flowers on a spring day;
In the morning they bloom—at night they simply fall and decay.

*Pulleyblank: Han-shan II.
1. Literally, "two eights" (*erh-pa*).

No. 265

Lofty, erect, reaching up far away—beyond the
     boundary of heaven;[1]
The road in the clouds—distant and steep.

The cascading stream drops ten thousand feet,
Like a strand of spread-out, softened white silk.

Below is "Rest Your Mind" Cave;
Set firmly across is "Fate is Set" Bridge.[2]

Of imposing sights that overpower the world,
The name of T'ien-t'ai alone rises above all the rest.

1. *Hsiao-han* can also mean the Milky Way.
2. Iritani and Matsumura (*Kanzanshi*, p. 362) feel that "Rest Your
Mind" Cave (*ch'i-hsin k'u*) and "Fate is Set" Bridge (*ting-ming ch'iao*) were
two of the natural wonders in the T'ien-t'ai mountains. They add that, according to one source, "Fate is Set" Bridge was a natural rock on the top of
T'ien-t'ai which fell down during the Yüan, and they seem to identify this
with the Stone Bridge noted in poem 44.

No. 266

I sit here on top of this large and firm rock;
Streams in the valleys—cold, icy and chilled.

For my quiet amusement I prefer the exquisite and fine;
Empty cliffs—wrapped in mist, dim and vague.

Happy, contented—I rest in this place;
With the sun's last slanting rays tree shadows grow low.

As for me, I look into[1] the base of my mind,[2]
And a lotus blossom emerges from the filthy mud.[3]

1. *Kuan* ("look into") translates *vipaśyanā*—contemplation or insight—and is normally paired with *chih* (*śamatha*), the stillness of mind which precedes insight.
2. *Hsin-ti*, the mind as the ground of all thought (and therefore all reality).
3. The image is common enough in Buddhism to require no documentation. But one does find almost exactly these same words (there, *lien-hua ch'u tzu wu-ni*) in the *Ta-chih-tu lun* (Ch. 14; T. 1509, Vol. 25, p. 163 middle).

No. 267*

When recluses escape from life among men,
Many go to the mountains to sleep.

Bluish-green creepers—sparsely placed, in profusion
    they grow;[1]
Emerald-green mountain streams—their tinkling sounds
    unbroken go on.

Steady and slow[2]—moreover, contented with joy;
Unhurried, at ease—they keep themselves both calm and pure.

Avoiding contact with the tainted affairs of the world,
Their hearts remain spotless like white lotus blooms.

---

*Pulleyblank: Han-shan II (?).
   1. "In profusion" is a guess at the meaning of *lu-lu*. By itself, *lu*
means "the foot of a mountain" or "a large forest," but *lu-lu* must describe
shu ("coarse")—i.e., the way in which the creepers are far apart. Note that
there is a homophone *lu-lu* that does mean "luxuriant" or "flourish."
   2. *T'eng-t'eng* ("steady and slow") can also mean "as though asleep."

No. 268

I send these words to you meat-eating men;
Your time for eating will not long remain.

For this present life, you planted the seeds in the past;
For lives not yet come, you cultivate *karma* today.

You only hold on to the present day's beauty,
Not fearing the woes of lives yet to come.

When the old rat gets into the rice jar,
Though he may eat his fill, he'll find it hard
        to get his head out![1]

1. I.e., we pay for our present gluttony by being trapped in this kind
of life; we cannot get out of *saṁsāra*.

No. 269*

Ever since I "left home,"[1]
Bit by bit I've acquired an interest in nourishing life.[2]

I've stretched and drawn back[3], making my four limbs whole;
With diligence listened, making my six senses complete.[4]

My coarse woolen robe is with me winter and spring;
Unpolished rice sustains me morning and night.

Today, earnest and eager, I practice,
Hoping to run into the Buddha.

*Pulleyblank: Han-shan II (?).
1. Ch'u-chia (pravraj) is the formal ceremony of going off to a monastery to become a monk or a nun.
2. Yang-sheng, "nourishing life," refers to a set of practices we normally associate with Taoists. To nourish one's life in hope of living a very long time, one normally does certain breathing exercises, avoids consuming meat, wine, and grains, and eats instead certain long-life minerals and herbs. For a thorough discussion, see Henri Maspero, "Methods of 'Nourishing the Vital Principle' in the Ancient Taoist Religion," in his Taoism and Chinese Religion, translated by Frank A. Kierman, Jr. (Amherst, MA: The University of Massachusetts Press, 1981), pp. 445–554.
3. Shen-su, "stretched and drawn back," refers to the calisthenics done by "life-nourishing" adepts in conjunction with their breathing exercises.
4. The "six roots" (liu-ken) are, for Buddhists, the six sense organs—the eye, ear, nose, tongue, body, and mind. When these are perfected, their functions can be interchanged. Iritani and Matsumura (Kanzanshi, p. 366) feel that to "listen with diligence" refers to training all senses, not just hearing.

No. 270

Of five-character poems, I've written five hundred;
With seven characters, seventy-nine.

In three-character lines, twenty-one;
Altogether that comes to six hundred *shou*.

All are the same, written on the cliff rocks;
I praise myself saying, "You've got a good hand!"

If you can understand my poems,
You're truly Tathāgata's mother.[1]

1. Or possibly, "You're truly the Tathāgata mother." Tathāgata is called the "mother of sentient beings" in the *Nirvāṇa-sūtra* (T. 375, Ch. 35, Vol. 12, p. 838 top).

Comment: The discrepancy between this number and the actual number of poems in the various Han-shan collections (e.g., the CTS collection has 285 five-character poems, 20 seven-character poems, and 6 three-character poems, giving a total of 311) does not go unnoticed. Iritani and Matsumura (*Kanzanshi*, p. 406, note to poem 298) point out that this may mean that many Han-shan poems are lost. It is also possible, they feel, that Han-shan arbitrarily used these numbers to make the wording sound good, or to end up with the nice round number of 600. They follow the *Wu-shan* edition in placing this poem at the end of the five-character poems, feeling the poem is intended as a summary of what went before.

No. 271

Worldly affairs—how they trouble our thoughts;[1]
Those who thirst after life are never willing to rest.[2]

If you want to grind to extinction this rock of great earth,[3]
When will you have time to lay down your head?

The four seasons go 'round as they transform and change;
The eight festive days[4] speed by like a fast-flowing stream.

To repay the burning house lord,
Out in the open ride on the white ox.[5]

1. Following the variant reading of *ho yu-yu* for *jao yu-yu*. The latter reading would work as well: "Entangled in worldly affairs—our thoughts troubled and anxious."
2. Following the variant reading of *wei-k'en hsiu* for *tsao-wan hsiu*. The latter might be read as, "[Those who] thirst after life, sooner or later [must] rest."
3. That is, the whole world. Han-shan seems to have in mind people who want to understand every single thing, since the words are *yen-chin*, "grind to extinction," but also "examine" or "research" to extinction.
4. The *pa-chieh* are the first days of the four seasons and the equinoxes and solstices.
5. An allusion once again to the "burning house" story in the *Lotus-sūtra* (see poems 189 and 254). The "white ox [cart]" (*pai-niu ch'e*) is the vehicle of Mahāyāna. The ox cart is waiting outside the gate of the house in "uncovered" or "open" land (*lu-ti*).

No. 272*

Laughable! This cave of five shades;[1]
With the four snakes together we live.[2]

Gloomy and dark—we have no bright candles;
The three poisons—in succession by them we're pursued.[3]

For companions and cohorts we have the six thieves,[4]
Who plunder and steal our dharma-wealth pearls.

If you can slaughter and expel the troops of Mara's army,
You'll then feel calm and at peace—clear and deep, as
    though reborn.

---

*Pulleyblank: Han-shan II.
1. The "five shades" (*wu-yin*) are the five *skandhas*, the five aggregates of human life—i.e., form, feeling, will, perception, and consciousness. This is an early translation; later *wu-yün* is preferred.
2. The "four snakes" (*ssu-she*) are the four elements of physical nature—earth, water, fire and wind. See the comment to poem 248.
3. The "three poisons" (*san-tu*) are anger, greed, and ignorance.
4. i.e., the six senses—eye, ear, nose, tongue, body, and mind. See the comment to poem 248.

No. 273

I've often heard of Emperor Wu of the Han,
And as well of the First Emperor of Ch'in.[1]

They both took delight in the "immortal" arts,
But they extended their years, in the end, not very long![2]

Their Golden Terraces—already smashed up and destroyed;[3]
Sandy Mound—subsequently extinguished, wiped out.[4]

Mao-ling and Li-yüeh[5]
Today are covered by weeds far and wide.

1. Han Wu-ti's reign dates are 141–87 B.C.; Ch'in Shih-huang-ti's reign dates are 247–210 B.C.

2. Han Wu-ti's and Ch'in Shih-huang-ti's interest in the arts of immortality are well known. The former employed the magician Li Shao-chün to concoct for him the elixir of immortality; the latter is said to have sent a group of youths off China's east coast to search for the Isles of the Blessed. See, for example, Holmes Welch, Taoism: The Parting of the Way (Boston: Beacan Press, 1957), pp. 97–105, and Ying-shih Yü, "Life and Immortality in the Mind of Han China," The Harvard Journal of Asiatic Studies 25 (1964–65): 80–122.

3. "Golden" is understood to simply mean "beautiful." Han Wu-ti built a famous terrace named Po-liang t'ai (Cypress Beam Terrace), which was situated northwest of Ch'ang-an County in Shensi.

4. "Sandy Mound" (sha-ch'iu) was northeast of the present-day P'ing-hsiang County in Hopeh Province. Ch'in Shih-huang-ti died at Sandy Mound.

5. Mao-ling is the tomb mound of Han Wu-ti, located northeast of Hsing-p'ing County in Shensi; Li-yüeh is the site of Ch'in Shih-huang-ti's tomb, southeast of Lin-tung County in Shensi.

No. 274*

When I think back twenty years,
With slow solemn steps I entered Kuo-ch'ing.[1]

The people in Kuo-ch'ing Temple
All said Han-shan is a fool!

A "stupid man"—what use in my harboring doubts?
Yet my doubts went unresolved, so I pondered the matter
    with care.

I still didn't really understand myself;
How is this something they could know?

I lowered my head—no use in asking them questions;
What's more, if I ask, what good would it do?

Some people came and cursed me,
Clear and distinct, what they knew.[2]

But although I did not reply,
Nonetheless, the advantage was mine!

*Pulleyblank: Han-shan II.
  1. Literally, "returned" (*kuei*) to Kuo-ch'ing. That means this is where Han-shan entered the faith, committed himself to the Three Jewels. On the location of Kuo-ch'ing, see poem 40, note 1.
  2. Equally plausible is Iritani and Matsumura's interpretation (see *Kanzanshi*, pp. 369–370): "Clearly and distinctly, I understood [all that they said]."

No. 275*

I address you, the "leaving home" group;
What is it you call "leaving home"?[1]

Wasteful and extravagant, you seek to maintain your lives,[2]
To continue on without end, your family with its clan names.[3]

With your beautiful tongues and sweet lips,
You flatter and distort, hearts more and more twisted and bent.

All day long you worship at the altar;[4]
Holding *sūtras* in your hands, you establish your studies.

In your stoves you burn incense for gods and Buddhas,
And when the bell's struck, with a loud sound you chime in.

Throughout the six times[5], you study how to bump your
        head on the floor;[6]
Day and night you're unable to sleep.

All of this simply done, because you love money and wealth;
In your hearts, never untrammelled and free.

When you see others, men of the high Way,
These, nonetheless, you despise, slander, and curse.

Like donkey shit compared to the fragrance of musk,
Bitter indeed! Is the Buddha.[7]

I've also seen the "leaving home" crowd;[8]
Some have the strength, and some of them don't.

The very best, those of the highest integrity,
Spirits and gods respect their great virtue.

Rulers of kingdoms sit with them sharing their carriages;
Feudal princes, bowing, welcome them in.[9]

Worthy of being fields of blessings[10] for the whole world,
These, worldly people must protect and tenderly love.

With the lowest of the low—those abysmally stupid;
Deceitful they are in appearance—many the things
    that they seek.

That they are wasteful and corrupt—this then can be known;
Ignorant and stupid—they love women and wealth.

Though they wear their "blessings fields" clothes,[11]
They plant *real* fields to get clothing and food.

Creating debts, they rent oxen and plows;
In what they do, they're neither faithful nor just.

Day after day they do things loathsome and evil;
Time after time making ache their bottoms and spines.[12]

They don't understand how to carefully think things through;
They'll endure Hell's torments and pain without end.

If one day you contract a bothersome illness;
For three years you'll lay on your bed or your mat.[13]

They too have the real Buddha-nature;
Yet they turn it upside down, becoming ignorant thieves.

I devote myself to the Buddha;[14]
Far, far away—we pray to you Maitreya.

    *Pulleyblank, couplets 7, 8, and 9: Han-shan II.
    1. "Leaving home" (*ch'u-chia, pravraj*), again (see poem 269, note 1),
is the formal act of leaving home to be ordained as a monk or a nun.

2. *Yang-huo* means, specifically, taking care of, providing for one's family.

3. A *tsu-hsing chia*—i.e., the lineage of a particular ancestral line. Buddhists borrow Chinese clan terminology to keep track of branches and schools, speaking of "ancestors" (*tsu*), "generations" (*shih*) of disciples, and "descendants" (*szu*). In some cases, the religious surname of the master becomes the religious surname of his disciples.

4. *Tao-ch'ang* is a translation of *bodhimandala*, the seat on which the Buddha sat on the night of his enlightenment. However, it is also the place where one worships the Buddha, making offerings and performing rituals.

5. The "six times" (*liu-shih*) are the Buddhist divisions of the day— morning, noon, evening, beginning of night, middle of night, and the last part of the night. So this means all day long.

6. Translation is tentative. What is studied day and night is *k'o-ch'ung*. *K'o* means being a guest or traveller; *ch'ung* is the action done when hulling rice—i.e. beating it repeatedly to get out all the grain. Iritani and Matsumura (*Kanzanshi*, p. 372) conclude that this means repeatedly bowing in front of the Buddha, prostrate on the floor. Might it not also be read as "hulling rice like a guest"?

7. Iritani and Matsumura (*Kanzanshi*, p. 372) point out that the *yeh* in *Fo-t'o-yeh* is probably added for the rhyme; Buddha is normally just *Fo-t'o*.

8. *Ch'u-chia erh*, monastic companions, the host of disciples as opposed to the master.

9. *Ying-ni*, which one would normally read as opposed actions—"to welcome" and "to oppose"—apparently combine to mean only "welcome."

10. *Fu-t'ien*—i.e., by respecting and honoring such people as these, people build up good *karma*.

11. i.e., the robes of monks and nuns.

12. Do their backs ache from carrying this heavy burden of evil? Iritani and Matsumura (*Kanzanshi*, p. 375) say that *t'ung t'un-chi* ("making ache their bottoms and spines") refers to a form of punishment in which the buttocks and back are struck with a cane.

13. The point is—I think—that we will suffer a long time in Hell for what we do in this "one day" of life.

14. The phrase is *Na-mo (namah) Fo-t'o-yeh; namah* being the word— meaning to "submit to," "bow to," "to devote oneself to"—that is constantly used in liturgical incantation.

Comment: Iritani and Matsumura (*Kanzanshi*, p. 370–375) treat this as two poems, breaking between couplets 9 and 10 (i.e., "I've also seen the 'leaving home' crowd" begins poem 2). They note that this is only one poem in the *Kunaichō* and *Tse-shih-chü ts'ung-shu* editions (*Kanzanshi*, p. 371) but choose to follow the *Wu-shan pen*. Hakuin (*Kanzan shi sendai kibun*, 3: 35–37) also treats this as two poems. Moreover, there is a mark between couplets 9 and 10 in the SPTK text which indicates some sort of break.

No. 276*

Cold cliffs—the deeper you enter, the better they seem;
Yet nobody walks on this road.[1]

White clouds calmly idle about lofty peaks;
Up on a green ridge, one lonely ape cries and howls.

Even greater than these[2], what is it that I hold dear?
To grow old, completely fulfilling my will, doing that
    which is fitting for me.

Appearance and form may change with the cold and
    the heat,[3]
But the pearl that's my mind—this can be firmly preserved.

---

*Pulleyblank: Han-shan II.
1. "Nobody follows this *Way*."
2. Or possibly, "in addition to these" (*keng*).
3. i.e., the seasons or years—moving from summer to winter.

No. 277

In front of a cliff, all alone I silently sit;
The round moon brightly beams in the sky.

The ten thousand forms, as vague shadows appear
    in its midst,[1]
But that one wheel—fundamentally, there is nothing
    on which it shines.[2]

Free, empty, unbounded—my soul in itself it is pure.
Embracing the Void[3], I penetrate the mysterious and
    profound.[4]

By using a finger we see the moon;
The moon is the hinge of the mind.

1. The *wan-hsiang*, meaning all phenomenal forms. Given the identification of mind and moon that follows, the "vague shadows" are probably the marks we see on the moon. Alternatively, this might be a way of saying that all things external to the moon (= mind) have only this shadowy, unsubstantial kind of existence.

2. The "one wheel" (*i-lun*) is the moon.

3. *Hsü*, *śūnya*, the empty state of all things—that they have no true reality.

4. *Hsüan-miao* always brings to mind the last lines of Chapter 1 in the *Lao-tzu*: *hsüan chih yu-hsüan, chung-miao chih men*. Chan (*The Way of Lao Tzu*, p. 97) translates: "Deeper and more profound, the door of all subtleties!"

Comment: The symbolism in the poem is discussed in the Introduction.

No. 278

My original ambition was to admire fellow
     followers of the Way;[1]
With fellow followers of the Way,
     one can often get close.

To run into, from time to time, guests who can
     stop up the source,[2]
To welcome in every day visitors with whom
     one can talk about Zen.

To discuss the abstruse on bright moonlit nights;
To search for the truth on morns as the sun starts to rise.

When the ten thousand shoots[3] are all wiped
     out without trace;
Then you'll know the original man.[4]

1. The same line occurs as line 8 in poem 228.
2. Ch'en Hui-chien (*Han-shan-tzu*, p. 205) explains "stop up the source" (*tu-yüan*) as "to stop up the source of life and death." "Ignorance" is normally the original fault that involves us in the wheel of *saṃsāra*.
3. *Wan-chi*, the "ten thousand shoots" or "ten thousand beginnings," is a phrase used to refer to the deeds the ruler controls. He handles all matters at their start. This would mean something like the roots of all phenomenal things, the "ten thousand *dharmas*."
4. *Pen-lai jen*—i.e., the true Buddha inside.

No. 279

Those who, from the beginning, are not [*true*] retired scholars
Simply *call* themselves "men of the mountains and woods."[1]

Taking up service in Lu[2], they cover their heads
    with their turbans of silk;
Still they "love" wrapping up in coarse linen kerchiefs.[3]

They say they have the restraint of Ch'ao Fu and Hsü Yu;[4]
They'd be ashamed to be ministers to Yao and Shun.

Monkeys putting on hats![5]
Imitating others—in their flight from the dust and the wind.[6]

1. *Shan-lin* ("mountains and woods" or "a wooded hill") means "recluse" by association: it is in this kind of place that recluses live.
2. A way of saying they are true Confucians at heart, since Lu was the home state of Confucius.
3. *Shu-chin*, the kind recluses would wear.
4. According to the *Chuang-tzu* (Ch. 1, p. 2, line 22), Hsü Yu was offered the empire by Yao (traditional reign dates 2356–2255 B.C.), but he was so insulted by the offer that he went and washed out his ears. On Ch'ao Fu, who was also by tradition a recluse in Yao's time, see Huang Fu-mi's *Kao-shih chuan* (A: 2ab, SPPY ed.). His name (Nest Father) comes from the fact that he slept in a tree, and it was after Hsü Yu reported Yao's offer to Ch'ao Fu, according to the *Kao-shih chuan*—and as a result was criticized by Ch'ao Fu for not "hiding his form and concealing his light"—that he went off and washed out his ears.
5. *Mi-hou*, the *Macacus* monkey, to be exact.
6. i.e., the confusion and turmoil of life in the world.

No. 280*

From of old, with the many wise men,
I've never seen one who had long-lasting life.

They live, then they go back to death,
Completely transformed into ashes and dust.

Piled up bones like Vipula Mountain;[1]
Parting tears that turn into a sea.

All they have is an empty name that remains;[2]
Can they avoid life and death's wheel?

*Pulleyblank: Han-shan II.
1. Vipula Mountain is a large mountain near Kuśāgārapura in Magadha (see poem 232, note 1).
2. The *"have* an empty name" of this line seems to contrast with the *"have* long-lasting life" of line 2.

No. 281

Today I sat in front of a cliff;
I sat a long time, until the mist and clouds had cleared.

One clear mountain stream running cold;
For eight thousand feet, rise the tops of emerald-green peaks.

White clouds—in the morning their shadows so still;
The bright moon—at night its rays drift and flow.

When on my body there's no dust or filth,
In my heart—how, besides, could there be any woe?

No. 282*

One thousand clouds blended with ten thousand streams;
In their midst, one gentleman at his ease.

In the bright light of day, he rambles in the green hills;
At night he returns, to sleep at the base of a cliff.

Swiftly pass the autumns and springs;
Silent and still, he has no polluting cumbersome ties.[1]

Happy indeed! On what does he rely?
Tranquil, at peace—like the water in a fall stream.

---

*Pulleyblank: Han-shan II.
1. "Polluting, cumbersome ties" (*ch'en-lei*) in Buddhism is a metaphor
for *kleśa* and *karma*, which soil us and tie us to the world.

No. 283

I urge you, put an end to your comings and goings;
Never vex him—old Yama.[1]

Lose your footing, and you'll fall into the three evil paths;[2]
Your bones will be ground into powder, having been
          pounded one thousand times!

For a long time you'll be a person in Hell;
Forever cut off from the ways of this life.[3]

I exhort you—believe in my words;
Recognize, hold on to, the treasure inside your robe.[4]

1. *Yen-lao*, the king of Hell.
2. The *san-t'u*, the three evil destinies: to suffer in hell, become a hungry ghost, or be reborn as an animal.
3. Or the "path" of this life (*sheng-tao*)—i.e., the *gati*, or destiny, to be a human being.
4. On the "treasure inside your robe" (*i-chung pao*), see poem 195, note 3.

No. 284*

In this world there's one group of people;
Truly able to give the rest of us all a good laugh.

"Leaving home"[1], they exhaust their own bodies;
Deceiving lay masses—this they take as their "Way."

Though they wear their "free from dust robes,"[2]
Inside those robes, they nourish a good crop of lice!

This can't compare to returning,[3]
To knowing and holding on to the mind that is king.

*Pulleyblank: Han-shan II.

1. For "leaving home," see poem 246, note 1.

2. *Li-ch'en i* is another name for the monk's robe, normally called the *chia-sha* (*kāsāya*).

3. Iritani and Matsumura (*Kanzanshi*, p. 383) note that *kuei ch'ü-lai* is a much-used phrase in Buddhism, where it means to return to and rely on the Truth. See poem 124, note 2, for additional comments on this phrase.

No. 285

High up! High up! On the very top of the peak;
Looking out in all four directions—to the limit
    no boundary [I see.]

I sit alone—there's no one who knows;
The single moon shines on a cold spring.

But in the spring, in truth, there's no moon;
The moon itself is in the blue sky.

And although I sing this one song,
What's in this song is not Zen.[1]

---

1. Following the variant of *chung*, "in" for *chung*, "end."
Note: The Zen message is that words—the teachings of a master, the words of a *kōan*—can *reflect* the truth, just as the spring reflects the moon, but they must not be taken as the real thing. The source of the reflection in the spring is the one moon itself in the sky; the source of all Zen words is the one Mind inside. That must be *experienced*, not simply understood.

No. 286

There's a Mr. Wang the *hsiu-ts'ai*,[1]
Who laughs at my poems for containing so many errors.

He says I'm unfamiliar with the "wasp's waist,"
And again, I don't comprehend the "crane's knee."[2]

"Level and slanted"[3]—I don't understand where they should go;
Common words are selected and repeatedly used.

[But I reply,] "I laugh at the way *you* write poems;
Like some blind man singing about the sun!"

---

1. *Hsiu-ts'ai*, "Elegant Talent," was the first of three degrees (i.e., like the B.A.) in the imperial civil service examinations during the Ming and the Ch'ing and was the *highest* degree given in the Sui and early T'ang. The degree was abolished in the T'ang in 651 (see Denis Twitchett, *The Cambridge History of China*, Vol. 3, [Cambridge: Cambridge University Press, 1979], p. 275). Charles Hucker notes, however, that even after 651 the title remained an "unofficial reference to a Presented Scholar (*chin-shih*)." (See his remarks on "Cultivated Talent" in *A Dictionary of Official Titles in Imperial China*, p. 248, item 2633).

2. The "wasp's waist" (*feng-yao*) and the "crane's knee" (*ho-hsi*) are two of eight errors that can be made in *lü-shih* (regulated verse) versification. The "wasp's waist" is the mistake of having the second and fifth character in a five-character line be the same tone; the "crane's knee" is the fault committed when the fifth and the fifteenth characters in a five-word poem are the same tone.

3. *P'ing-ts'e* (more commonly *tse*) "level and slanted" are the two basic tone categories used in "regulated verse" versification. "Level" tones correspond to modern tones one and two; the "slanted" tones are modern tones three and four, plus a fifth tone equal to the p, t, k endings in present-day Cantonese.

Note: As the reader might well expect, Han-shan in this poem—
surely deliberately—commits the two faults of versification mentioned in
lines 3 and 4. The tonal sequence in the poem, line by line, is: (1) TTPTP,
(2) TTPPT, (3) PTTPP, (4) PTTTT, (5) PTTTT, (6) PPTTT, (7) TTTTP, and (8)
PPPTT. Since tones 5 and 15 are the same, he ignores the "crane's knee,"
and he commits the fault of the "wasp's waist" in lines 2, 4, and 5. This
fault is allowed, so long as the basic tonal sequence is proper, but the tonal
sequence in this poem does not correspond at all to proper patterns, and
the rhyme words are all "slanted"; in proper "regulated verse" poems, all
rhyme words must be "level."

No. 287

I live in some country village;
I have no father, no mother as well.

I have no name, also no surname-rank;[1]
People just call me old "Chang" or "Wang."

There is absolutely[2] no one to teach me;
Poverty and low station—this is my constant lot.

What I tenderly love is the truth in my mind,
Solid and firm like a diamond.

1. *Hsing-ti* is a number denoting one's place among the sons in the family—e.g., "Chang the second" would be the second-born son in the Chang family.
2. Or, "Moreover, there is no one to teach me" (*ping-wu*).

No. 288

Han-shan sends out these words,
But these words nobody believes.

Honey is sweet—pleasing to people's taste;
Yellow oak[1] is bitter and hard to get down.

When things accord with our feelings, they produce
    joy and delight;
When they counter our wills—many the feelings
    of anger and hate.

But just look at that puppet of wood—
Exhausted! From performing this one act on stage.[2]

---

1. For "Yellow Oak" (*huang-po, Phellodendron amurense*), see G. A. Stu-art, *Chinese Materia Medica: Vegetable Kingdom*, pp. 316–317. Stuart says the inner, yellow bark is used in medicine, and "the taste is very bitter." He also notes that the root is "said to relieve the hundred diseases of the heart and abdomen, to quiet the soul, to relieve hunger and thirst, and if taken for a long time, to prolong life and permeate the spirit." One assumes it is mere coincidence that one of the T'ang Zen masters was Huang Po: that is, Hsi Yün, who lived on Huang Po mountain in Fukien and took this as his name. His sayings are translated into English by John Blofeld.

2. Han-shan might have in mind—and might here allude to—a four-line poem by Liang Huang (fl. 742–756—the poem is attributed by some to Ming-huang, r. 713–756) which goes like this: "Carve the wood, attach some pull strings to make an old man; use chicken [flesh?] for the skin, crane [feathers] for hair, it will look just like the real thing. But in just a short while, its performance is done; then it will be still with nothing to do; It's just like human life in a dream" (for the text, see CTS, Vol. 3, p. 2116.) Iritani and Matsumura, *Kanzanshi*, p. 388, note this possibility.

No. 289*

I've seen people reciting the scriptures;
Their understanding relies on the words and comments
    of others.

Their mouths may move, but their hearts do not turn;[1]
Hearts and mouths diametrically opposed.

When the heart is sincere, it does not twist and bend;
It doesn't produce the various covers and bonds.[2]

You must simply in person examine yourself;
Never look for others to take your place!

In this way you can, inside, produce and attain
    the true lord;
This is knowledge that has no inside or out.

*Pulleyblank: Han-shan II.
1. The phrase that means to read or recite the scriptures is *chuan-ching*, literally, "turn over the sutras"; in reciting the scriptures one's mouth "rotates" with the page. However, *chuan-hsin*, "to turn the mind," is a set phrase meaning "genuine conversion."
2. *Ch'an-kai* ("covers and bonds") is another name for the passions; they entangle the mind and keep it from seeing the truth.

No. 290

On Han-shan there are only white clouds;
Quiet and still, cut off from the dirt and the dust.

Seats made of straw—mountain families have these;[1]
Their sole lamp, the bright wheel of the moon.

My stone bed overlooks an emerald-green pool;
Tigers and deer—always my neighbors nearby.[2]

I truly covet the joys of this remote life;
Forever to be a man who lives "beyond form."[3]

1. Reading *shan-chia* in its general sense. In Buddhism *shan-chia*, "the Mountain School," is also the name of one branch of T'ien-t'ai, the "authentic branch" developed by Ssu-ming; this stands in contrast to the "sect [developed] away from the mountains" (*shan-wai tsung*) headed by Wu En (d. A.D. 986).

2. The line may be symbolic, though it makes good sense as it is. For deer as symbols of compassion and freedom, see poem 152 and poem 291. Tigers seem to represent inner passions in poem 144.

3. The *locus classicus* for the phrase "beyond form" (*hsiang-wai*)— i.e., one who lives outside the phenomenal/ordinary world—seems to be Sun Ch'o's "Rhapsody on Wandering on Mount T'ien-t'ai." Watson (*Chinese Rhyme-Prose*, p. 85) translates the relevant lines; "Spreading doctrines of what is 'beyond symbol,' expounding texts on what is 'without origination.'"

No. 291

Deer live in the deep woods,
Where they drink water and eat grass.

They stretch out their legs to sleep at the foot of some tree;
How adorable! No distress and no pain.[1]

But tie them up in some splendid hall,
Feed them delicacies and rich foods—the very fattest and best—

And all day long they'll be unwilling to eat;
In appearance and form they'll turn thin and pale.[2]

1. Literally, they have no *kleśa*.
2. One is reminded of Hsi K'ang's (A.D. 223–262) "Letter to Shan T'ao," in which Hsi K'ang breaks off relations with Shan T'ao for recommending him for office. Hsi K'ang, noting how he had grown up free from control and restraint and how he would therefore hate the caged in life of the official, says: "In this I am like the wild deer, which captured young and reared in captivity will be docile and obedient. But if it be caught when full-grown, it will stare wildly and butt against its bonds, dashing into boiling water or fire to escape. You may dress it up with a golden bridle and feed it delicacies, and it will but long the more for its native woods and yearn for rich pasture" (translation by J. R. Hightower in Cyril Birch, ed., *Anthology of Chinese Literature* [New York: Grove Press, 1965], p. 163).

No. 292

Atop the flowers, a golden oriole;
"Kuan-kuan," its sound, oh so sweet![1]

A beautiful woman, complexion like jade,
Facing this way, strums her lute and makes the strings sing.

In this way amused, she can't get her fill;
Tender thoughts in her young age.[2]

But when blossoms fall, the bird too will leave;
Shedding tears, she'll face the fall wind.

---

1. Kuan-kuan, the "harmonious sounds made by birds," are the opening words of poem 1 in the *Shih ching* (see Karlgren, *The Book of Odes*, p. 2). That poem describes a beautiful young maiden about to be wed, and there too the playing of lutes is mentioned.

2. Literally, in her years of shedding milk teeth (*t'iao-nien*).

Note: The oriole in the poem seems to assume the role of the girl's loved one: the oriole loves the blossoms of spring, just as young men are attracted by the girl's youthful good looks. But when her youth is gone (when the blossoms fall), the oriole (her lover) will leave, and she'll be alone to face the fall wind (the remaining years of her life.) The allusion to poem 1 in the *Shih* seems to support this interpretation.

No. 293*

I sojourn here beneath this cold cliff,
With my bias exclaim this spot most secluded and rare!

Taking my basket, I pick mountain roots;
Raising my tray, pluck some fruit and return.

With vegetarian fare spread on thatch I sit down,
Sipping and pecking, purple fungus I eat.[1]

In a clean mountain pool rinse my ladle and bowl;
Mixing and blending, boil sunflowers and mallows.[2]

Facing the sun, I sit wrapped up in furs,
Leisurely reading poems by men from the past.

*Pulleyblank: Han-shan II.
1. On "purple fungus" see poem 19, note 3.
2. The text has *ch'ou-hsi*, "much and little," and Tseng P'u-hsin (*Han-shan shih-chieh*, p. 161) accordingly reads, "Whatever I have [much or little,] I boil." However, Iritani and Matsumura (*Kanzanshi*, p. 394) cite the notes to the *shou-shu* edition of the text, which gloss *ch'ou-hsi* as *chou-hsi*: *chou* is the sunflower, while *hsi* is identified as *Eranthis pirnatifida*; white mallow.

No. 294*

To places I travelled in former days
Today I returned after seventy years.

Of old friends, there are none who still come and go;
All buried deep in their old, high graves.

As for me, my hair's now already white,
But still I stick by this mountain with its layer of clouds.

I makes this report to those who will come later on;
Why don't you read the words of the ancients?

*Pulleyblank: Han-shan II.

No. 295

I've been wanting to go to that eastern cliff,
To the present—for innumerable years.

So yesterday I came and climbed up through the vines,
But halfway there, I was hampered by mist and wind.

The path was narrow—with my clothes it was hard to advance;
The moss was sticky—my shoes could not go on.[1]

So I stay at the base of this red cinnamon tree,[2]
Where with white clouds for my pillow, I sleep.

1. Reading the variant of *ch'ien*, "to go on," for *ch'üan*, though *ch'üan* might make sense as "to keep"—i.e., "I couldn't keep my shoes on."
2. *Tan-kuei*, "red (or vermilion) cinnamon" is defined as a cinnamon (or cassia) tree with red bark.
Note: A number of things signal that the poem should be read as allegory of spiritual quest. In addition to traditional associations of cinnamon trees with recluses and seekers of long life, there is the fact that Han-shan finds the path "narrow" and cannot advance, held back by his "clothes" and his "shoes" (which might symbolize a number of things). Moreover, "mist and wind" (*feng-yen*) make it difficult to see one's way clearly, and the word "vine" (or "creeper"—*ko*) means by extension, "complications," "difficulties," "entanglements." Finally, Iritani and Matsumura (*Kanzanshi*, p. 21) argue—and present evidence for the claim—that in Chinese "field and garden" poetry, the place where one retires is often "eastern X." Thus they understand "eastern cliff" to mean the same as Han-shan—it stands for Han-shan's goal or ideal, enlightenment.

No. 296*

I've seen these men with keen wisdom;
Once they inspect, then they know what it means.

But avail yourself not[1] of this search through written words,
And you'll directly enter the Tathāgata stage.[2]

Let the heart not pursue all the causes[3]
And the mind-sense[4] not falsely arise.

When the heart and mind-sense are not born—
Inside and out—there will be no remaining affairs.

*Pulleyblank: Han-shan II.
  1. *Chia*, "make use of" or "borrow," but also to "pretend" or do something "falsely."
  2. *Ju-lai ti*, the Tathāgata stage or condition. Iritani and Matsumura (*Kanzanshi*, p. 396) locate the expression "directly enter the Tathāgata stage" in Yung Chia's "Cheng-tao ko" (T. 2014, Vol. 48, p. 396 top.) For a translation, see Charles Luk, *Ch'an and Zen Teaching*, Vol. 3 (London: Rider and Co., 1961), pp. 103–145, especially p. 127.
  3. *Chu-yüan*, the "secondary" or "accessory" conditions. *Yüan* (*pratyaya*) are the secondary or circumstantial conditions, as opposed to the direct or primary causes, of all things and events in the phenomenal world.
  4. The *i-ken*, "mind-sense," is the sense organ (*indriya*) which serves as the basis for the sixth consciousness (*mano-vijñāna*), the consciousness that coordinates data from the other five senses (eye, ear, nose, tongue, and body).

No. 297*

On my body I wear "sky-flower" clothes;[1]
With my feet I tread in "tortoise-hair" shoes.[2]

In my hand I hold my "rabbit-horns" bow,
Planning to shoot down the demon of ignorance.

*Pulleyblank: Han-shan II.
1. "Sky-flowers" (*k'ung-hua*) are things that do not exist; they are the flowers—or spots—one sees in the air if one's vision is blurred. See also poem 230.
2. The "hair on a tortoise" (*kuei-mao*) and "horns on a hare" (*t'u-chiao*) are stock metaphors for things that are unreal—they do not exist. See, for example, the *Nirvāṇa-sūtra*, Ch. 35 (T. 374; Vol. 12, p. 570 top).

No. 298

Take a look, sir, at the blooms 'mid the leaves;
For how long can they enjoy the good life?

Today they fear being plucked by men;
Tomorrow morn—just waiting for someone to sweep them
    away.

Pitiable indeed! Our love of beauty and charm;
When years are many, we change, become old.

If we take one's lifespan and compare it
    to that of those blooms;
That rosy complexion—can it be maintained for long?

No. 299

Painted rafters[1]—that's not my house;
The green forest[2]—this is my home.

One's whole life—in a moment suddenly gone;
Concerned with ten thousand affairs, we never
    speak of what's far away.[3]

If, for crossing the stream, you don't build a raft,
You'll drift and then sink, as you try to gather the blooms.[4]

If good roots you now do not plant,
When will you see the sprouting of shoots?

1. A stock phrase for the elaborate, ornate houses of the rich is "painted rafters and carved beams" (*hua-tung tiao-liang*). The SPTK text has *kuei-tung*, "cassia rafters."

2. Reading the variant of *ch'ing-lin* instead of *sung-lin*, "pine forest," which obviously would also make sense. But "green forest" tends to mean the place where a recluse would dwell.

3. i.e., far away in time, the future; we never plan for our fate after death.

4. The couplet contains two allusions to lines in the *Nirvāṇa-sūtra*. In Chapter 20 of that text (T. 375, Vol. 12, p. 741 middle) are the lines, "If you want to cross water, [you need] a boat or raft to protect you well." And in Chapter 29 we find the lines, "One who firmly craves fine lotus flowers, when he goes to pick them, he is tossed about by the water. All sentient beings are also like this. When they crave and long for the five desires, they are tossed about and sunk by the waters of life and death" (T. 374, Ch. 29, Vol. 12, p. 536 bottom).

No. 300

Born thirty years ago;
I've been constantly roaming about—one thousand,
    ten thousand li.

I've walked by rivers where the green grasses merged,
Entered the borders where red dust kicked up.

Refining drugs, in vain I sought to become an immortal;
I read books and wrote poems on historical themes.

But today I've come home to Han-shan[1]
To pillow my head on the stream and wash out my ears.[2]

1. Not in the sense that he has lived there before, but in the sense that this is where he truly belongs—*kuei*.

2. The allusion is to some remarks made by Sun Ch'u (A.D. ?–282) to Wang Chi, when Sun Ch'u wanted to go off and become a recluse. The anecdote—recorded in *Shih-shuo hsin-yü*, 25: 6 (Yang Yung, *Shih-shuo hsin-yü chiao-chien*, p. 588)—goes as follows: "When Sun Ch'u was young, he wanted to become a recluse. Speaking of it once to Wang Chi, he intended to say, 'I'll pillow my head on the rocks and rinse my mouth in the streams.' Instead, he said by mistake, 'I'll rinse my mouth with rocks and pillow my head on the streams.' Wang asked, 'Are streams something you can pillow on and rocks something you can rinse with?' Sun replied, 'My reason for pillowing on streams is to "wash my ears," and my reason for rinsing with rocks is to "sharpen my teeth." ' " (translated by Richard Mather, *A New Account of Tales of the World*, p. 402). The recluse Hsü Yu earlier is reported to have gone and washed out his ears when the Sage-ruler Yao offered to give him the kingdom to rule (see poem 279, note 4).

No. 301

Han-shan is a "no-outflows" cliff;[1]
Its cliffs—most essential for crossing the stream.[2]

The eight winds[3] do not move it when they blow;
From distant years in the past, men have spread word
    of its marvelous traits.

Quiet and still, a good place to peacefully live;
Empty—utterly empty, separated from ridicule and blame.

The lonely moon, throughout the long night always bright;
The round sun, constantly it comes out and shines.

Tiger Mound[4] combined with Tiger Brook;[5]
No need to call back and forth.

In the world there may be tutors to kings,
But never treat them as equal to Chou and Shao.[6]

Ever since I escaped to these cold cliffs,
Happy I've been, forever I sing and I smile.

1. *Lou* (*āsrava*), "outflows," is another name for *kleśa*: the "outflows" are the ignorance and passions that flow out of the unenlightened mind. To "have no outflows" (*wu-lou, anāsrava*) is one of the marks of *nirvāṇa*: it also means to be outside the downward flow that leads to low forms of rebirth.
2. Essential for reaching salvation—the phrase is *chi-yao*.
3. The "eight winds" (*pa-feng*) which stir up the passions are (Soothill and Hodous, p. 41): "gain, loss, defamation, eulogy, praise, ridicule, sorrow, and joy."

4. "Tiger Mound" (*hu-ch'iu*) is one of the beauty spots of Kiangsu; it is a mountain in Soochow. A "Tiger Mound Temple" was established there in A.D. 368, and a number of famous monks preached there in later years, including Chu Tao-i, Chu Tao-sheng, Dharmati, and Hui-yen. The name "Tiger Mound" was briefly changed to "Military Mound" (*wu-ch'iu*) during the reign of T'ang T'ai-tsu (r. 618–627) to avoid the taboo on his name.

5. "Tiger Brook" (*hu-hsi*) is a stream on Mount Lu (in Kiangsi, south of Chiu-chiang County), best known as the place where the Buddhist Hui-yüan (334–416) saw off his guests (see his biography in *Kao-seng chuan, ch'u-chi*, 6: 149). Tradition records that Hui-yüan never crossed this stream; if he did, a tiger would growl.

6. "Chou and Shao" must mean the two great leaders at the beginning of the Chou dynasty (c. 1100 B.C.), the duke of Chou and the duke of Shao. They too were "tutors to kings" (*wang-fu*) in a sense, since they served as regents to young king Ch'eng. I take Han-shan's point to be that one should not confuse the common with the superb; no "common" tutor could compare to the tutors Chou and Shao (and in a similar way, no common mountain could compare with Han-shan). But commentators do not agree on the intent of these lines. Iritani and Matsumura (*Kanzanshi*, pp. 402–403) feel the "king's tutor" specifically refers to Chia I (201–169 B.C.), who had been tutor to the king of Ch'ang-sha. By contrast, Ch'en Hui-chien (*Han-shan-tzu*, p. 216) feels that "*wang*" means the immortal Wang-tzu Ch'iao (on which see poem 6, note 2), and "*fu*" refers to Fu Hsi (on which see poem 172, note 6). Wang and Fu, the *recluses*, thus contrast with the politicians Chou and Shao.

No. 302

Buddhist monks don't keep their rules;[1]
Taoist adepts don't eat their drugs.

From of old a good many worthies
Lie at the foot of green hills.[2]

1. Do not maintain *śīla* (*pu ch'ih chieh*), the rules of monastic discipline.
2. I.e., in their graves.

Comment: The *Ch'üan T'ang shih* (p. 9101) notes that in one text these four lines come at the end of 301—i.e., that poems 301 and 302 are combined. Pulleyblank ("Linguistic Evidence," p. 166n) notes this as true for the *Tse-shih-chü ts'ung-shu* edition; nonetheless, the rhymes he lists for poems 301 and 302 do not agree (?jiew, mjiew, ts'iew, tsjiew, dzjiew, dzjiew, and siew for 301; jiak and kiak for 302—"Linguistic Evidence," p. 191). Supporting the thesis that the two are *separate* poems are the facts that the flow of thought between the two is not continuous, and in the *Tse-shih-chü ts'ung-shu* text (see p. 61), the opening words of poem 302 start at the head of a column.

No. 303

Some people laugh at my poems;
But my poems stand side by side with
    the elegant and refined.[1]

Still I've not troubled Mr. Cheng to add notes,
And what use having Master Mao explain?[2]

I don't regret that those who understand them are few;
It's just that those who know inner thoughts are quite rare.[3]

If you chase and pursue C and D,[4]
With my faults, you'll never come to the end!

But should my poems suddenly meet up with someone
    with a sharp eye,
Then they'll naturally circulate throughout the world.

---

1. I.e., they match the "classics" in style and importance, "elegant and refined" (*tien-ya*), alluding in a way to the *Shu* (*Book of Documents*), which opens with the "Canon of Yao" (*Yao-tien*) and the *Shih* (*Book of Songs*), where two important sections are the "Greater Elegant" (*Ta-ya*) and the "Lesser Elegant" (*Hsiao-ya*).

2. The two earliest commentaries on the *Shih* are the *Mao-shih shih-chuan* in 29 *chüan*, by either Mao Heng or Mao Chang (c. 130 B.C.), and Cheng Hsüan's (A.D. 127–200) *chien* (Supplementary Commentary). Both are contained in the *Mao-shih cheng-i* (see, for example, the *Shih-san-ching chu-shu*). I think Han-shan's point is that his poems are as good as those in the *Shih*, but they are simple and straightforward in meaning and hence need no commentary.

3. "Those who know inner thoughts" are literally, those who "know tunes" (*chih-yin*). Someone who "knows your tune" is someone who knows you very well and can tell from something you do what you really feel. The expression originates in the story of Yü Po-ya and Chung Tzu-ch'i. If Yü Po-ya was thinking of a mountain when he played his lute, Chung Tzu-ch'i knew it, and if he had his mind on a river, Chung Tzu-ch'i knew that as well. The anecdote is recorded in various sources. See, for example, *Lieh-tzu*, "T'ang-wen" (in SPPY ed., 5. 16ab). A. C. Graham translates the relevant passage in *The Book of Lieh-tzu* (London: John Murray, 1960), pp. 109–110.

4. C and D (*kung-shang*) are the first two musical tones in the Chinese pentatonic scale. Here they seem to stand for the tone categories used in regulated verse (see poem 286, notes 2 and 3), *p'ing* (level) and *tse* (deflected). There were also five tones in T'ang Chinese pronunciation. Iritani and Matsumura (*Kanzanshi*, p. 404) translate *kung* and *shang* as *p'ing-tse*.

No. 304[§]

The way to Han-shan;
Nobody arrives.

Can you walk on this road?
You'll be called the Ten Names.[1]

Here there's the chirp of cicadas,
But there's no caw of the crow.[2]

The yellow leaves fall;
The white snow I sweep.

Boulders in piles and heaps;
Mountains hidden and deep.

I live here alone;
My name—the "Good Guide."[3]

You, sir, carefully look;
What are my marks and signs?[4]

[§]Three-character lines.
   1. I.e., you will be a Buddha. The "Ten Names" or "Ten Titles" (*shih-hao*) of a Buddha are (Soothill and Hodous, p. 52): Tathāgata, Arhat, Samyak-saṁbuddha, Vidyācarana-saṁpanna, Sugata, Lokavid, Anuttara, Puruṣa-damya-sārathi, Śāsta-deva-manuṣyāṇām, and Buddha-lokanātha (or Bhagavān).

2. The "chirp of cicadas" is associated with ill-treated men of high virtue in a number of poems. See, for example, Lo Pin-wang's (fl. 680) famous "On the Cicada While in Prison" (*Tsai-yü yung-ch'an*), anthologized in the *Three Hundred Poems of T'ang*: for a translation, see Stephen Owen, *The Poetry of Early T'ang* (New Haven: Yale University Press, 1977), pp. 148–149. Also see Li Shang-yin's (812–858) poem "Cicada," in *Ch'üan T'ang shih*, Vol. 8, p. 6147. Crows are not only common and vulgar, they are sometimes associated with bad luck: see, for example, Read, *Chinese Materia Medica: Avian Drugs*, p. 70, item 302. Read makes the interesting observation that "northerners like crows and dislike magpies; the reverse is true in the south."

3. Iritani and Matsumura (*Kanzanshi*, p. 408) and Tseng P'u-hsin (*Han-shan shih-chieh*, p. 180) point out that "Good Guide" (*shan-tao*) is a name for the Buddha. It is also the name of Shan Tao (613–681), one of the patriarchs of the Pure Land school in China. Iritani and Matsumura see this as possibly pointing to some connection between the poetry of Han-shan and the Pure Land school.

4. "Marks and signs," (*hsiang-hao, lakṣaṇa-vyañjana*) are special bodily features of a Buddha. There are 32 special marks and 80 secondary signs.

No. 305§

Han-shan is cold;
Ice locks in the rocks.

Concealed—mountain's green;
Revealed—the whiteness of snow.

The sun comes out and shines;
In a moment everything melts.

From this time it is warm;
Nourishing this old guest.

§Three-character lines.
Comment: A poem where the connection between weather and spiritual progress seems rather clear. It is the sun of enlightenment that melts the ice and snow of ignorance that hide the green, rich life below.

No. 306* §

I live on this mountain;
Nobody knows.

Up in the white clouds;
Constantly quiet and still.

*Pulleyblank: Han-shan II.
§Three-character lines.

No. 307§

Han-shan is deep;
It matches my mind.

Purely white rocks;
No yellow gold.[1]

Sounds in the spring echo,
As I strum Po-ya's lute.

Were Tzu-ch'i here,
He'd distinguish this tune.[2]

---

§Three-character lines.

1. Iritani and Matsumura (*Kanzanshi*, p. 410) cite a number of lines from biographies of immortals where "white rocks" (*pai-shih*) figure among the things that they eat. "White rocks" is also another name for *Yang-ch'i-shih* (Actinolite), on which see Read, *Chinese Materia Medica: Minerals/Stones*, p. 46 (item 75). Iritani and Matsumura also feel that Han-shan is criticizing the alchemical practice of refining gold.

2. For Yü Po-ya and Chung Tzu-ch'i, see poem 303, note 3.

No. 308[§]

In the midst of layers of cliffs;
Content with the cool breeze.

His fan does not move;
The cold air comes through on its own.

The bright moon shines;
White clouds all around.

Sitting alone by himself,
One venerable old man.

[§]Three-character lines.

No. 309* §

Master Han-shan
Is always "like this." [1]

Alone, by himself he dwells;
He does not live or die.

---

*Pulleyblank: Han-shan II.
§Three-character lines.
1. Always "like this" (*ju-shih, evam*) or "just so." "Like this" are the
words that commonly open each sutra—"Like this have I heard." Han-shan
might be using *ju-shih* as elsewhere he uses *chen-ju*—*bhūtatathatā*—the abso-
lute reality, that which is "really so."

No. 310* [1]

I've seen the men of this world;
Each one contends in a spirited way.

Then one morning they suddenly die;
All they've attained is one strip of land.

Four feet wide,
Twenty feet long.[2]

If you know how to get out of your grave
And come argue with me in this spirited way,

For you, I will
Inscribe a gravestone.[3]

---

*Pulleyblank: Han-shan II.

1. In mixed meter lines. Lines 1–4 are in five-character verse; lines 5–6 and 9–10 are in three-character verse; lines 7–8 are in four-character verse (but see note 3). This poem and the next are noted as additions to the collection in CTS and SPTK editions. Iritani and Matsumura (*Kanzanshi*, p. 413) note that in the original (Yüan dynasty) SPTK, these poems were attributed to Shih-te.

2. Presumably meaning their graves.

3. The poem can be punctuated in a variety of ways. I follow Iritani and Matsumura. The CTS text makes one line of lines 7 and 8, and one line of lines 9 and 10. That presents no problem with rhyme, but it does make line 7 an eight-character line and line 8 a seven-character line. Tseng P'u-hsin's punctuation (*Han-shan shih-chieh*, p. 183) is the same as that of Iritani and Matsumura, with the exception that he splits lines 7 and 8 differently, making line 7 a three-character line and line 8 a four-character line ("If you understand; and come out and argue [with me in this] spirited way"). The poem actually reads best when lines 5 and 6 are added to line 4 and lines 9 and 10 are combined, as they are in the CTS text.

No. 311

If your house has the poems of Han-shan in it,
They're better for you than reading *sūtras*!

Write them down on your screen,
And from time to time take a look.

APPENDICES

Appendix I

[There are a number of poems that seemingly contain datable references. Such information has already been presented in the relevant notes. Here that information is gathered together for convenience in summary form.]

1. *Poem 97:* "You may use all your strength polishing bricks, but can you ever turn them into mirrors?" This would seem to allude to the famous exchange between the Zen master Huai-jang (677–744) and his disciple Ma-tsu (707–786), where meditating in hopes of attaining *nirvāṇa* is likened to polishing a brick or tile in hopes of making it shine—it will never happen. If Han-shan is early T'ang, then the possibility exists that the saying originates with him: alternatively, it might be that the analogy was well known in Zen circles from early on (although the whole thing seems to reflect the negative attitude about meditation that we find in the "Southern Sect" of Hui-neng and Shen-hui [the period 700–750 A.D.]). Poem 97 is classed as Han-shan II by Pulleyblank.

2. *Poem 98:* "Cold or hot, we must judge for ourselves; never believe the lips of the servant." Does this reflect knowledge of the conversation between Chien-ming and the Sixth Patriarch of Zen (Hui-neng, 638–713) where the former says—having realized his own enlightenment—"A Person drinks water and knows himself whether it is cold or warm. May I call you my teacher?" This poem is also classed as Han-shan II.

3. *Poem 120:* "This is what poor scribe, who repeatedly comes to be tested at Southern Court?" The "Southern Court" was established in either 734 or 740 as part of the Personnel Board "responsible for determining," so says Hucker, "seniority and reputation as elements considered in the reappointment or dismissal of an official."

4. *Poem 172:* "I've myself heard of the days of the Liang dynasty; for their 'four supports' they had many worthy men. Pao-chih and Master Wan-hui, the Four Immortals and Mahāsattva Fu." This is one of a number of poems in the collection (see also poems 42 and 192) that show a keen interest in, and knowledge of, the Liang (502–556). Would that support an early T'ang date, not long after the Liang? Whatever our answer might be, there is a problem with "Master Wan-hui." "Master Wan-hui" is normally understood to mean the monk Fa-yün, whose dates are 632–711, someone who lived in early T'ang. Ch'en Hui-chien (*Han-shan-tzu,* pp. 22–24) points out that if this is the intended Wan-hui, then we must assume a death date for Han-shan sometime after 712; Iritani and Matsumura, however, feel that the poem originally said "Fa-yün," intending a Liang monk by that name (467–529), and that the change to "Wan-hui" occurred later on. The opening lines of the poem surely suppose that we are discussing someone who lived in the Liang. The poem is classed as Han-shan II by Pulleyblank.

5. *Poem 179:* "Sad it is! In this life of one hundred years, it tears my insides to remember the capital Hsien." Iritani and Matsumura feel that the "capital Hsien" means Ch'ang-an and that this poem was written during or after the An Lu-shan rebellion (755–763). A number of things in the poem point to a sense of decline and possibly war.

6. *Poem 184:* "My turban has never been high, and the belt at my waist's always tight." Iritani and Matsumura argue that a "high head turban" (*kao-t'ou chin-tzu*) was given to honored officials in the early T'ang from roughly 618–704.

7. *Poem 192:* "I've seen Seng-yu, by nature rare and unique, skillful and clever, 'born in-between,' at the time of the Liang dynasty. [The paintings of] Tao-tzu, airy and graceful—that was his special mark." Chang Seng-yu (470–550) is recognized as one of China's greatest painters, and he worked for Emperor Wu of the Liang (r. 502–550). Wu Tao-tzu, on the other hand, was a great painter in early/mid T'ang (c. 689–c. 758). Some argue that this puts Han-shan in the mid or late T'ang (e.g., see Ch'en Hui-chien, *Han-shan-tzu,* pp. 27–30). However, the inner couplets of this poem, which begin with the words "[The paintings of] Tao-tzu . . . ," are missing from the earliest extant editions of the text, the *Kunaichō* and *Tse-shih-chü*

ts'ung-shu editions. In those texts, this is a four-line poem speaking only of Seng-yu and the Liang monk Pao-chih.

8. *Poem 224:* "For the country, it's the people that are fundamental." Iritani and Matsumura feel that this alludes to a line in the *Shu*— "The people are the root of a country." But in the *Shu*, the word used for "people" is *min*, while here it is *jen*. Iritani and Matsumura think this change was made to avoid the taboo on using the personal name of the early T'ang ruler T'ai-tsung (r. 627–649), Li Shih-min. If they are correct, that would at least establish that this poem was *not* written before the reign of T'ai-tsung, and—could we be sure that the taboo was *only* observed during the lifetime of T'ai-tsung—we would date this poem with some certainty. Unfortunately, such taboos were often in force from the time of accession until the end of the dynasty, and thus this would then help us very little.

9. *Poem 226:* "I find my joy in the everyday Way" (*tzu-lo p'ing-sheng tao*). A similar saying is attributed to the Zen master Ma-tsu (707–786) and to his disciple Nan-ch'üan (748–835): they both said, "The everyday mind—this is the Way" (*p'ing-ch'ang hsin shih tao*). There may be no influence here one way or the other, since such sayings are common in Zen.

10. *Poem 286:* "There's a Mr. Wang, the *hsiu-ts'ai*." According to Twitchett, the *hsiu-ts'ai* degree was abolished in 651. But according to Hucker, *hsiu-ts'ai* remained, even after this date, an "unofficial reference to a Presented Scholar (*chin-shih*)." Therefore this reference would only help in dating this poem if we knew in what sense Han-shan intended "*hsiu-ts'ai*."

11. *Poem 288:* "But just look at that puppet of wood. Exhausted! from performing this one act on stage." Is there an allusion here to the poem attributed to Liang Huang (fl. 742–756)—or by some attributed to Ming-huang (r. 713–756)—about the puppet made of wood?

12. *Poem 304:* "I live here alone; my name—the 'Good Guide' (*shan-tao*)." "Good Guide" here is presumably just a title. But the Buddhist Shan Tao (same characters) was one of the key figures in the Pure Land school in China—his dates were 613–681.

Appendix II

Provided below is a finding list to assist those who would like to check the present translations against the earlier translations of Snyder, Waley, Watson, and Wu. The earlier works can be found in:

1. Gary Snyder, "Cold Mountain Poems," *Evergreen Review* 2: 6 (Autumn 1958): 68–80.
2. Arthur Waley, "27 Poems by Han-shan," *Encounter* 3: 3 (September 1954): 3–8.
3. Burton Watson, *Cold Mountain: 100 poems by the T'ang poet Han-shan* (New York and London: Columbia University Press, 1970).
4. Wu Chi-yu, "A Study of Han-shan," *T'oung Pao* XLV (1957): 392–450.

Numbers in **bold** were not translated by these four men. The original poems can be found on the following pages in Volume 12 of the *Ch'üan T'ang shih*: poems 1–4, p. 9063; 5–12, p. 9064; 13–20, p. 9065; 21–28, p. 9066; 29–36, p. 9067; 37–44, p. 9068; 45–52, p. 9069; 53–60, p. 9070; 61–68, p. 9071; 69–76, p. 9072; 77–85, p. 9073; 86–93, p. 9074; 94–101, p. 9075; 102–109, p. 9076; 110–117, p. 9077; 118–125, p. 9078; 126–133, p. 9079; 134–141, p. 9080; 142–149, p. 9081; 150–157, p. 9082; 158–163, p. 9083; 164–171, p. 9084; 172–179, p. 9085; 180–188, p. 9086; 189–196, p. 9087; 197–206, p. 9088; 207–215, p. 9089; 216–223, p. 9090; 224–231, p. 9091; 232–238, p. 9092; 239–244, p. 9093; 245–251, p. 9094; 252–259, p. 9095; 260–267, p. 9096; 268–275, p. 9097; 276–281, p. 9098; 282–289, p. 9099; 290–297, p. 9100; 298–306, p. 9101; 307–311, p. 9102.

Numbers given are, first, the author's number for the poem itself, then the page number.

Poem No.	Snyder	Waley	Watson	Wu
1				
2	2:72			2:422
3	1:72		48:66	
4				4:422
5				
6				
7			33:51	7:423
8				
9	6:74	6:4	82:100	
10				
11	4:73		29:47	11:423
12				
13			9:27	
14				14:423
15		1:3	1:19	
16		13:5	72:90	
17				
18		14:5		
19				
20	5:73		50:68	20:424
21				
22				
23			5:23	23:424
24				
25		5:4	67:85	
26				
27		2:3	2:20	27:424
28	8:74	8:4	40:58	
29				
30			41:59	
31	9:75	7:4		
32				32:425
33				33:425
34				
35		22:7	3:21	35:426
36			23:41	
37				
38				
39			83:101	
40				40:426

Poem No.	Snyder	Waley	Watson	Wu
41				
42				
43			15:33	
44			42:60	
45				
46				
47				47:426
48			90:108	
49	10:75	24:7	85:103	49:427
50			6:24	
51			97:115	51:427
52				52:427
53			12:30	53:428
54				
55			58:76	55:428
56				
57				
58				
59				
60				
61				61:429
62			31:49	62:429
63				
64				
65				
66			53:71	
67	3:73		47:65	
68			71:89	
69				
70				
71			78:96	
72				
73				
74				
75				
76				
77				
78			43:61	
79				
80			30:48	

Poem No.	Snyder	Waley	Watson	Wu
81	11:75			
82			95:113	
83				
84				
85				
86				
87				87:429
88				
89				
90				
91				
92				
93				
94			27:45	
95				
96				
97				
98				
99		4:4	10:28	
100		27:8	68:86	100:430
101			35:53	101:430
102				
103				
104			34:52	
105				
106		9:5	44:62	
107				
108				
109				
110			13:31	
111		3:3	32:50	
112				
113			19:37	
114				
115				
116				
117			77:95	
118				
119			17:35	
120				

Poem No.	Snyder	Waley	Watson	Wu
121				
122				
123				
124				
125				
126			25:43	
127				
128				128:430
129			22:40	129:431
130	13:76		39:57	
131		25:8		131:431
132				
133				
134		23:7	63:81	134:431
135			11:29	
136				
137			8:26	
138				
139				
140			18:36	
141				141:432
142				142:432
143				
144			98:116	
145				145:433
146			64:82	
147		20:7	51:69	
148			14:32	
149				
150				
151				
152				
153				
154	14:76		45:63	
155			93:111	
156	15:77		79:97	156:433
157				
158			24:42	
159				
160				

Poem No.	Snyder	Waley	Watson	Wu
161			89:107	
162				
163	7:74			
164		15:6		
165		10:5	88:106	166:433
166		12:5		167:433
167				
168	16:77			
169				
170	17:78	17:6		
171				
172				
173			16:34	
174				175:434
175			54:72	
176			46:64	177:434
177			37:55	
178				
179		21:7	52:70	
180	18:78			181:434
181	19:78			
182				
183				
184			26:44	
185				
186	20:78		73:91	
187				
188				
189				
190			96:114	191:435
191			65:83	
192				
193	21:79			
194				
195				
196				
197				
198				
199				
200				

Poem No.	Snyder	Waley	Watson	Wu
201	22:79			
202				
203	23:79			
204				
205				
206				
207			56:74	
208			21:39	
209				
210			86:104	
211				212:435
212			70:88	
213				
214				
215				
216				
217				
218				
219				
220	24:79	16:6	57:75	221:435
221				
222			20:38	223:435
223				
224				225:436
225				
226			49:67	
227				
228			60:78	
229			76:94	
230			84:102	
231				
232				
233				
234				
235			80:98	
236				
237				
238				
239				
240				

Poem No.	Snyder	Waley	Watson	Wu
241				
242				
243				
244			59:77	
245			94:112	
246				
247				
248				
249				
250			36:54	
251				
252				
253			66:84	
254				
255				
256		18:6	69:87	
257				
258				
259				
260				
261				
262				
263				
264				
265				
266				
267				
268				
269				
270				
271				
272				
273			81:99	
274				
275				
276			55:73	
277				
278				
279				
280			74:92	

Poem No.	Snyder	Waley	Watson	Wu
281			92:110	283:436
282			61:79	284:436
283				
284				
285		26:8	62:80	
286			28:46	
287				
288			99:117	
289				
290				
291				293:437
292			4:22	294:437
293				
294				296:437
295		19:6	75:93	297:438
296				
297			91:109	
298			7:25	
299				
300	12:76		38:56	
301				
302			87:105	304:438
303				
304				
305				
306				308:438
307				
308				
309				
310				
311			100:118	

Appendix III

[Note: many poems are listed in more than one category]

Theme	Poem
1. Against greed and the snobbery of the rich (see also 21 below)	36, 37, 76, 84, 86, 104, 126, 151, 196
2. Buddhist themes a. against eating fish and meat	56, 70, 74, 76, 92, 95, 185, 206, 227, 232, 268
b. exhortative/didactic	1, 84, 88, 89, 90, 91, 139, 152, 156, 159, 160, 162, 178, 209, 213, 214, 216, 225, 232, 233, 234, 236, 237, 238, 239, 240, 246, 261, 283, 288, 296
c. *karma* (cause and effect, rebirth and reincarnation)	41, 57, 65, 72, 89, 92, 100, 112, 168, 188, 195, 204, 213, 214, 232, 236, 251, 255, 261, 268
d. message in symbolic form (see also 8.b below)	26(?), 34, 51, 65, 81, 82, 131(?), 144, 155, 161, 182, 198, 231, 243, 244, 245(?),

433

Theme	*Poem*
	248, 252, 258, 295, 297, 299
e. on those who foolishly fail to follow Buddha's Way	21, 29, 54, 57, 74, 75, 89, 90, 91, 98, 105, 136, 138, 167, 189, 204, 216, 225, 232, 234, 239, 242, 310
f. veiled/direct attacks on corrupt/ insincere Buddhists	58(?), 74, 96, 97, 117, 118(?), 139, 157, 159, 172, 230, 246, 274, 275, 279, 284, 289, 302
g. Zen symbols and themes (see also 8.b below)	40, 83, 51, 81, 97, 98(?), 165, 210, 212, 238, 244, 259, 274, 278, 287
3. *Carpe diem* (life is short, enjoy it while you can)	26(?), 53, 64(?), 146
4. Contain biographical clues	5, 6(?), 7(?), 15, 20, 27, 39, 40, 49, 80, 101, 102, 111, 113, 120(?), 134, 177, 179, 196, 204, 205, 269, 270, 294, 300
5. Describing the appearance and lives of aristocratic ladies	12, 13, 14, 35, 42, 60, 61, 62, 169
6. Drinking wine poems	107, 119
7. Han-shan, and his critics, on his poetry	141, 270, 286, 303, 311
8. Han-shan the mountain (also T'ien-t'ai) a. descriptive (the place, and life there as a recluse); see also theme 12	2, 4, 18, 20, 22, 24, 40, 44, 67,

Theme	*Poem*
	78, 106, 123, 130,
	147, 154, 163,
	164, 170, 181,
	193, 194, 196,
	197, 205, 211,
	217, 221, 228,
	257, 260, 262,
	263, 265, 266,
	267, 282, 290,
	293, 300, 301
b. descriptive/symbolic of spiritual	3, 9, 28, 31, 67,
quest (mostly Zen)	68, 154, 165, 166,
	168, 176, 199,
	200, 201, 202,
	203, 226, 256,
	276, 277, 281,
	285, 301, 304,
	305, 306, 307,
	308, 309
9. Joys of the simple life (farming)	5, 15, 18, 27,
	102, 107, 119
10. Love and marriage/raising daughters	50, 52, 56, 115,
and sons	128, 131(?), 174,
	218, 292
11. Miscellaneous	25, 26, 30, 63,
	66, 75, 93, 102,
	108, 121, 133,
	142, 177, 183,
	190, 192, 224,
	229, 253, 291
12. My house/the place where I live	2, 4, 16, 24, 27,
(see also 8a.)	78, 163, 176,
	203, 205
13. Observations on general moral themes	43, 58, 71, 73,
	75, 84, 87, 89,
	94, 98, 103, 110,
	115, 140, 149,
	150, 153, 208,
	222, 229, 237,
	242
14. Other people comment on Han-shan	180, 186, 200

Theme	Poem
15. Poverty/the plight of the poor: sub-theme, the poor scholar	80, 82(?), 99, 114, 116, 120, 125(?), 126, 129, 132, 148, 153, 158, 173, 184, 186, 207, 287
16. Reflections on people and events of the past	108, 127, 137, 172, 192
17. Separation from family and friends	6, 39, 49, 52, 134, 294
18. Taoist themes	
a. comments on the pursuit of long life and immortality	8, 11, 12, 16, 19, 20, 39, 64, 66(?), 68, 77, 79, 122, 157, 193, 219, 235, 247, 260, 273, 280, 300
b. Taoist comments on life: allusions to/ mention of the *Lao-tzu* or *Chuang-tzu*	4, 5, 8, 20, 45, 59, 71, 102, 111, 118, 141, 142, 156, 160, 175, 187, 250, 277
19. The ravaging effects of time on beauty and youth	13, 14, 21, 32, 42, 47, 101, 169, 191, 215, 264, 292, 298
20. The shortness of life and the longness of death: graveyards and the underworld	6, 8, 11, 17, 32, 47, 48, 53, 55, 72, 91, 100, 112, 143, 145, 195, 204, 213, 214, 219, 235, 250, 255, 271, 280
21. The sorrow-filled Han-shan	30, 33, 39, 49, 62(?), 67, 69, 80, 101, 145, 147, 173, 217, 250
22. The vanity of wealth, rank, and government career (see also theme 1)	2, 5, 7, 19, 38, 80, 85, 94, 105, 109, 113, 120, 122, 124, 129,

Theme	*Poem*
	171, 207, 232, 241, 249
23. Themes from and allusions to the "Nineteen Old Poems" of Han	2, 11, 22(?), 50, 52, 80, 94, 131, 135, 146, 209, 219
24. Themes from and allusions to *yüeh-fu* (music bureau) ballads	21, 23, 39, 42, 47, 53, 54, 101, 137
25. *Tristia*: the man of worth overlooked (sub-theme, life is not always fair)	7(?), 10, 59, 69, 127(?), 223

Appendix IV

Buddhist Terms, Metaphors, and Stories

Index to Chinese Terms and Phrases in the Poems

Term	Chinese	Poem Number
1. *ai-ch'en*	埃塵	290
2. *an*	岸	41, 65, 231
3. *ch'an*	禪	278, 285
4. *ch'an-ch'ü*	諂曲	275
5. *ch'an-kai*	纏蓋	289
6. *ch'an-lin*	禪林	194
7. *ch'en (-fen)*	瞋（忿）	88, 152, 157
8. *ch'en-ai*	塵埃	215
9. *ch'en-kou*	塵垢	281
10. *ch'en-lei*	塵累	282
11. *ch'en-shih*	塵世	106
12. *ch'en-su*	塵俗	130
13. *ch'i*	乞	159
14. *ch'i-pao*	七寶	261, 263
15. *ch'ien-sheng*	前生	41
16. *ch'ien-tzu*	千子	261
17. *ch'ih*	癡	41, 89, 90, 91, 94, 125, 138, 157, 169,

Term	Chinese	Poem Number
		189, 223, 227, 229,
		239, 241, 242, 249,
		251, 252, 274, 275
18. *ch'ü* (see *o-ch'ü*)	趣	
19. *ch'u-chia*	出家	246, 269, 275, 284
20. *ch'ü-hsiang*	取相	159
21. *ch'u-li*	出離	90
22. *chan-t'an*	栴檀	83, 96
23. *chang-ai*	障礙	225
24. *chao-ching*	照鏡	139
25. *chen-cheng tao*	真正道	74
26. *chen-hsin*	真心	88, 236
27. *chen-ju hsing*	真如性	97
28. *chen-shih*	真實	155, 229
29. *chen-yüan*	真源	214
30. *chi-tu*	濟渡	41, 299, 301
31. *chia-sha*	袈裟	157
32. *chia-t'o yao*	迦佗藥	193
33. *chieh* (*kalpa*)	劫	204, 210, 252
34. *chieh* (*śila*)	戒	230, 302
35. *chieh-t'o*	解脫	169
36. *chien tzu-hsing*	見自性	238
37. *chien-sheng*	間生	192
38. *chih-chien*	知見	167
39. *chih-hui* (*chien*)	智慧（劍）	156, 159
40. *chin-kang*	金剛	159, 287
41. *chin-kang ching*	金剛經	139
42. *ching*	經	245, 275, 289, 311

Term	Chinese	Poem Number
43. *ching*	境	81, 105, 106, 111, 210
44. *ching-tso*	靜坐	230, 277
45. *chu* (see also *mo-ni*)	珠	102, 198, 203, 244, 248, 276
46. *chuan-ching*	轉經	289
47. *chuan-lun wang*	轉輪王	261
48. *chüeh*	覺	84, 176, 205
49. *chüeh-wu*	覺悟	232, 261
50. *chung*	種	268, 299
51. *chung-sheng*	眾生	159, 206, 225, 245
52. *fa*	法	4, 159, 203, 230, 272
53. *fa-chung wang*	法中王	90, 159
54. *fa-shih, shih*	法師	159, 165, 172, 192
55. *fa-wang*	法王	216
56. *fan-nao* (also *fan-na* and *fan-yüan*)	煩惱 （煩挐, 煩緣）	65, 156, 203, 209, 225, 230, 235, 252, 255, 291
57. *fang-chang*	方丈	83
58. *fang-pien*	方便	245
59. *fei-fei hsiang*	非非相	214
60. Feng-kan	豐干	40
61. *fo* (*chen-* ——, *t'ien-* ——, *shen-* ——)	佛 （真~, 天~, 神~）	74, 97, 136, 138, 152, 159, 161, 162, 167, 212, 216, 240, 269, 275
62. *fo-li*	佛理	172

Term	*Chinese*	*Poem Number*
63. *fo-li*	佛力	63
64. *fo-shen*	佛身	1
65. *fo-shu*	佛書	260
66. *fo-t'o* (*yeh*)	佛陀（耶）	74, 225, 275
67. *fou-sheng*	浮生	196, 205, 255
68. *fou-t'u*	浮圖	184
69. *fu-li*	福力	214
70. *fu-pao*	福報	261
71. Fu ta-shih	傅大士	172
72. *fu-t'ien*	福田	232, 275
73. *fu-tzu*	拂子	83
74. *ho-shang*	和尚	159
75. *ho-t'ung* (?)	合同（？）	40
76. *hsiang*	相	159, 167
77. *hsiang-hao*	相好	304
78. *hsieh* (*chien*)	邪（見）	74, 139, 162, 204, 225
79. *hsin* (Buddhist)	心	1, 9, 44, 51, 74, 84, 85, 88, 89, 139, 152, 159, 162, 172, 195, 198, 199, 202, 210, 212, 213, 216, 226, 227, 230, 232, 236, 237, 240, 242, 246, 247, 255, 267, 275, 276, 281, 287, 289, 296, 307

Term	Chinese	Poem Number
80. *hsin-i*	心意	169, 296
81. *hsin-t'ien*	心田	258
82. *hsin-ti*	心地	193, 203, 266
83. *hsin-wang*	心王	284
84. *hsing (chen- —,* *hsin- —, pen- —)*	性（真~，心~，本~)	1, 167, 213, 216, 227, 275
85. *hsing-p'o*	行婆	74
86. *hsiu*	修	41, 237, 268, 269
87. *hsiu wan-shih* (or *wan-shih hsiu*)	休萬事	78, 85, 181, 241
88. *hsiu-cheng*	修證	238
89. *hsiu-hsing*	修行	89, 188
90. *hsiu-shen*	修身	14, 74
91. *hsiu-tao*	修道	178
92. *hsü*	虛	277
93. *hsü-mi*	須彌	119, 258
94. *hsüan-huo*	旋火	261
95. *Hu-ch'iu*	虎丘	301
96. *hu-ching*	護淨	1
97. *Hu-hsi*	虎谿	301
98. *huan (chih)*	幻（質）	161
99. *huan-hua*	幻化	196, 205
100. *hung-ch'en*	紅塵	111, 137, 190, 300
101. *i-ch'ieh*	衣裓	156
102. *i-ming*	一名	263
103. *i-nien*	一念	167
104. *i-tai chiao*	一代教	172

Term	Chinese	Poem Number
105. *i-ti* (*ch'an*)	一滴（禪）	248, 258
106. *Jan-teng* (*fo*)	然燈（佛）	240
107. *jen-ju*	忍辱	88
108. *jen-wo*	人我	230
109. *jou-yen*	肉眼	138
110. *ju-ju* (?)	如如	246
111. *ju-lai*	如來	172, 238, 240, 270
112. *ju-lai mu*	如來母	270
113. *ju-lai ti*	如來地	296
114. *k'en-hsin* (?)	肯信	57, 89
115. *k'ung*	空	81, 106, 200, 201, 254, 256, 301
116. *k'ung-hua*	空花	297
117. *ko-chung i*	箇中意	105, 254
118. *kuan*	觀	81, 106, 163, 266
119. *kuei* (Buddhist sense)	歸	1, 159, 165, 172, 198, 250, 300
120. *kuei-i*	歸依	1
121. *kuei ch'ü-lai* (or *hsiu ch'ü-lai*)	歸去來（休去來）	124, 133, 282, 284
122. *kung-te*	功德	88
123. *kung-yang*	供養	159, 232
124. Kuo-ch'ing ssu	國清寺	40, 274
125. *lai-sheng*	來生	41
126. *lei-ch'en*	累塵	171
127. *li* (*fo*)	禮（佛）	63, 138, 159, 275
128. *li-ch'en i*	離塵衣	284
129. *li-tun* (*hsing*)	利鈍（性）	216

Term	Chinese	Poem Number
130. *liang-an*	兩岸	41
131. *liang-o* (?)	兩惡	225
132. *lien-hua* (see also *pai-lien*)	蓮花	70, 267
133. *liu-ch'ü*	六趣	261
134. *liu-ken*	六根	269
135. *liu-ko tsei*	六箇賊	248, 272
136. *liu-men*	六門	168
137. *liu-shih*	六時	275
138. *liu-tao*	六道	72, 204, 213, 234
139. *lo-ch'a*	羅刹	89, 118, 243
140. *lo-han*	羅漢	159
141. *lü*	律	230
142. *lun-hui*	輪迴	213, 252, 261
143. *mi* (*jen*)	迷（人）	83, 204, 252
144. *Mi-lo* (*fo*)	彌勒	275
145. *mo* (*Māra*)	魔	272
146. *mo-ni* (see also *chu*)	摩尼	198, 203
147. *na*	衲	197
148. *nai-ho*	奈河	74, 236
149. *na-mo*	南無	225, 275
150. *ni-wan*	泥丸	96
151. *nien*	念	74, 139
152. *nien-nien*	念念	214
153. *o-ch'ü*	惡趣	90
154. *o-tao*	惡道	255
155. *p'an-t'o* (*shih*)	盤陀（石）	175, 202, 266
156. *p'i-fu* (*Vipula*)	毗富	232, 280

Term	Chinese	Poem Number
157. *p'ing-teng*	平等	97, 159
158. *p'u-sa*	菩薩	88, 139, 243
159. *p'u-t'i*	菩提	162, 209, 258
160. *pa-feng*	八風	301
161. *pai-lien* (see also *lien-hua*)	白蓮	267
162. Pao-chih	保誌	172, 192
163. *pen-yüan*	本源	233
164. *pi-yen hu*	碧眼胡	244
165. *pu wang-ch'i*	不妄起	210, 296
166. *san-ch'e*	三車	189, 254
167. *san-chieh*	三界	197, 214, 233, 234, 246
168. *san-t'u*	三途	112, 197, 204, 255 (*san o-tao*), 283
169. *san-tu*	三毒	91, 209, 225, 272
170. *seng*	僧	63, 138, 159, 165, 232
171. *seng-chia-lan*	僧伽藍	172
172. *sha-men*	沙門	302
173. *shan-ken*	善根	299
174. *shan-tao*	善導	304
175. *shao-hsiang*	燒香	63, 159, 275
176. *Shao-shih* (mountain)	少室（山）	123
177. *shen-fo*	神佛	74, 275
178. *shih*	施	138

Term	Chinese	Poem Number
179. *shih-ch'an*	十纏	258
180. *Shih-chia fo*	釋迦佛	240
181. *shih-er pu*	十二部	152
182. *shih-fang*	十方	159, 254
183. *shih-hao*	十號	304
184. *shih-hsiang*	實相	167
185. *shih-o*	十惡	91
186. *shih-shan*	十善	261
187. Shih-kung (Shih-te)	拾公 （拾得）	40
188. *shih-tzu hou*	獅子吼	152
189. *ssu-i*	四依	172
190. *ssu-liang (shen — shan —, shu —)*	思量 （審~, 善~，熟~）	97, 114, 141, 151, 153, 168, 169, 190,
191. *ssu-she (= ssu-ta)*	四蛇 （＝四大）	212, 242, 244, 275, 272
192. *ssu-sheng*	四生	246
193. *ssu-t'ien*	四天	261
194. *sui-yüan*	隨緣	170, 196, 219
195. *t'an*	貪	38, 42, 75, 76, 84, 85, 86, 87, 94, 196, 234, 241, 243, 271
196. *t'an-chih*	彈指	225
197. *t'ien-chung t'ien*	天中天	258
198. *t'ien-lung*	天龍	159
199. *t'o*	脫	233
200. *t'u*	禿	232

Term	Chinese	Poem Number
201. *t'ung-tzu*	童子	117
202. *ta fa-wang*	大法王	159, 216
203. *ta-ch'ien*	大千	203
204. *Ta-chih-tu lun*	大智度論	43n, 266n
205. *ta-shih*	大士	172
206. *tao-ch'ang*	道場	131(?), 275
207. *ti shui huo feng* (= *ssu-ta*)	地水火風 （四大）	248
208. *ti-yü*	地獄	91, 95, 168, 213, 232, 234, 237, 241, 275, 283
209. *ts'an-k'uei*	慚愧	230
210. *tso* (as in meditation) (see also *ching-tso*)	坐	22, 25, 28, 49, 123, 147, 170, 176, 190, 202, 226, 266, 277, 281, 285, 293, 308
211. *tu*	度	245
212. *tuan-tso*	端坐	25, 231
213. *tz'u-pei*	慈悲	152, 159
214. *tzu-hsin*	自心	167, 245
215. *tzu-hsing*	自性	238
216. *tzu-tsai*	自在	163
217. *wan-ching*	萬境	210
218. *wan-hsiang*	萬象	203, 247, 277
219. Wan-hui	萬迴	172
220. *wang-hsiang ch'i*	妄想起	227
221. *wei-t'o* (*Vedas*)	圍陀	230

Term	Chinese	Poem Number
222. *wen-shu* (?)	文疏	232
223. *wo*	我	190, 230
224. *wu*	悟	41, 159, 232
225. *wu-ch'ang*	無常	84, 237, 261
226. *wu-chu*	無著	159
227. *wu-hsiang*	無相	159
228. *wu-hsin*	無心	226
229. *wu-lou*	無漏	301
230. *wu-ming*	無明	89, 233, 252, 275, 297
231. *wu-ni*	五逆	91
232. *wu-wei* (= *nirvāṇa*)	無為	159, 246
233. *wu-yin*	五陰	201, 272
234. *yeh* (*o-* — , *tsui-* —)	業（惡~, 罪~）	1, 89, 168, 188, 232, 236, 243, 251, 252, 261
235. *yen-fou* (*Jambudvīpa*)	閻浮	209
236. *yen-lao* (Yama)	閻老	283
237. *yin*	因	91, 188, 237
238. *yin-chih chien-yüeh*	因指見月	277
239. *yin-kuo*	因果	57, 72, 92
240. *ying-ping shuo-yao*	應病說藥	245
241. *yu-fang lü*	遊方履	106
242. *yüan* (see also *sui-yüan*)	緣	65, 95, 203, 214, 233, 296
243. *yüan-man*	圓滿	199

Term	Chinese	Poem Number
244. *yüeh* (as symbol of mind)	月	25, 51, 68, 81, 154, 165, 197, 199, 200, 201, 226, 227, 247, 277, 278, 281, 285, 290, 301, 308
245. Yün-kuang	雲光	159

Index to Sanskrit Phrases and Terms
(in the Poems and/or the Notes).

Term/Phrase	Location
1. *abhidharma*	152n
2. *agada*	193, 193n
3. *ālaya-vijñāna*	198n, 243n
4. Amitābha	225n
5. *anāgāmin*	172n
6. *anāsrava*	301n
7. *anitya*	237n, 261n
8. *anuttara*	304n
9. *āraṇya*	43n
10. *arhant*	159, 172n, 304n
11. *arūpaloka*	197n
12. *āsrava*	301n
13. *asuras*	204n
14. Aśvamukha	159n
15. *ātman*	248n, 97n, 204n, 230n
16. *avadāna*	152n
17. *avidyā*	233n
18. Bhagavān	304n
19. Bhāratavarṣa	209n
20. *bhūtatathatā*	77n, 155n, 161n, 167n, 232n, 246n, 309n
21. *bodhi*	162n, 209n, 258, 258n
22. Bodhidharma	244n
23. *bodhimaṇḍala*	275n
24. *bodhisattva*	34n, 139, 156n, 189n, 190n, 195n, 243n
25. Buddha	136, 138, 152, 156n, 159,

Term/Phrase	Location
	161, 162, 167, 178n, 189n, 192n, 195n, 198n, 199n, 212, 225, 240, 240n, 258n, 269, 275, 275n, 278n, 304n
26. buddha-kāya	1n
27. Buddha-lokanātha	304n
28. Buddha-nature	1n, 9n, 21n, 102n, 195n, 198n, 201n, 203n, 208n, 231n, 239n, 240n, 244n, 247n, 248n, 275
29. buddhapāla	162n
30. buddhatva	1n
31. cakravartī-rājan	261, 261n, 263n
32. candana	83m, 96n
33. catur-yoni	256n
34. daśākuśala	91n
35. devas	159, 204n
36. devātideva	258n
37. dharma(s)	90n, 152n, 172n, 189n, 210n
38. Dharma-king	90, 159, 162, 216
39. dharmakāya	161n
40. Dīpaṁkara	240, 240n
41. dveṣa	88n
42. Ekayāna	189n
43. evam	309n
44. gāthā	152n
45. gati	72n, 112n, 204n, 261n, 283n
46. geya	152n
47. Gośīrsa	159n
48. Hīnayāna	43n, 199n
49. indriya	296n
50. īśvara	221n
51. ītivṛttaka	152n
52. Jambudvīpa	209, 209n
53. jātaka	152n
54. kalpa	240n, 252
55. kāmaloka	197n
56. karma	1, 41n, 65n, 89, 89n, 112n, 168n, 188n, 236, 243n, 251, 268, 275n, 282n
57. karuṇā	152n

	Term/Phrase	Location
58.	*kāṣāya*	284n
59.	*kleśa*	34n, 65, 65n, 152n, 172n, 203n, 209n, 225n, 252, 252n, 255n, 282n, 291n, 301n
60.	*kṣānti*	88n
61.	*lakṣaṇa*	159n, 167n
62.	*lakṣaṇa-vyañjana*	304n
63.	Lokavid	304n
64.	*mahābhūta*	248n
65.	*mahāsattva*	172, 172n
66.	Mahāyāna	21n, 67n, 97n, 152n, 159n, 166n, 203n, 256n, 271n
67.	Maitreya	275
68.	*manas*	97n, 243n
69.	*maṇi*	198, 198n, 203, 203n
70.	*mano-vijñāna*	296n
71.	Māra	272
72.	*mithyā-dṛṣṭi*	74n
73.	*mithyā-mārga*	162n
74.	*moha*	88n
75.	Mount Sumeru (or Mount Meru)	119, 119n, 197n, 209n, 258, 258n
76.	Mount Vipula	232, 232n, 280, 280n
77.	*mukti*	188n
78.	*nāgas*	159
79.	*naivasaṁjñānāsaṁjñānāyatana*	214n
80.	*namaḥ*	225, 225n, 275n
81.	*nidāna*	152n
82.	*nimba*	65, 65n
83.	*nirvāṇa*	41n, 92n, 96, 96n, 145n, 159, 171n, 172n, 214n, 217n, 231n, 263n, 301n
84.	*Nirvāṇa-sūtra*	13n, 21n, 65n, 92n, 96n, 139n, 152n, 155n, 157n, 172n, 182n, 188n, 215n, 232n, 297n, 299n
85.	*pañcānantarya*	91n
86.	*pāramitā*	92n
87.	*Piṭaka*	199n

	Term/Phrase	Location
88.	*pratyaya*	296n
89.	*pratyeka-buddha*	189n
90.	*pravraj*	246n, 269n, 275n
91.	*preta*	204n
92.	Puruṣa-damya-sārathi	304n
93.	*rāga*	88n
94.	*rākṣasas*	89n, 118n, 243n
95.	*rūpaloka*	197n
96.	*sakṛdāgāmin*	172n
97.	Śākyamuni	240, 204n, 258n
98.	*śālavana*	155n
99.	*sama*	40n, 159n
100.	*samādhi*	190n
101.	*samatā*	40n, 97n
102.	*śamatha*	266n
103.	*saṁsāra*	41n, 213, 268n, 278n
104.	Samyak-saṁbuddha	304n
105.	*saṅghārāma*	172n
106.	*saptaratna*	261n
107.	Śāstā-deva-manuṣyānām	304n
108.	*śila*	159n, 230n, 302n
109.	*siṁhanāda*	152n
110.	*skandhas*	201, 201n, 272n
111.	*śrāvaka*	189n
112.	*srotāpanna*	172n
113.	*stūpa*	184
114.	Sugata	304n
115.	*śūnya* (or *śūnyatā*)	67n, 81n, 166n, 256n, 277n
116.	*Sūraṅgama-sūtra*	97n
117.	*sūtra*	139n, 152n, 172n, 275, 277n, 289n, 311
118.	Tathāgata	155n, 172, 188n, 238, 270, 296, 296n, 304n
119.	*tathāgata-dūta*	172n
120.	*tīrthikas*	92n
121.	*tri-sahasra-mahā-sahasra*	203n
122.	*triloka*	197n
123.	*udāna*	152n
124.	*upadeśa*	152n
125.	*upāya*	245n

	Term/Phrase	*Location*
126.	*vaipulya*	21n, 152n
127.	*vaśitā*	163n
128.	*Vedas*	230
129.	*vidyācaraṇa-saṁpanna*	304n
130.	*Vimalakīrti-sūtra*	54n, 156n
131.	*vinaya*	230
132.	*vipaśyanā*	266n
133.	*vīrya*	153n
134.	*vyākaraṇa*	152n
135.	Yama	283

Metaphors/Stories Associated with Specific Texts

	Metaphor/Story	*Location (Poem No.)*
1.	Pressed sugar cane as a metaphor for old age (*Nirvāṇa-sūtra*, Ch. 7: 2)	13
2.	Clarified butter as a metaphor for Buddha-nature (*Nirvāṇa-sūtra*, Ch. 7: 4)	21
3.	Crystalline sugar as metaphor for Mahāyāna scriptures (*Nirvāṇa-sūtra*, Ch. 8)	21
4.	The story of the elder who gives all away to his prodigal son (*Lotus-sūtra*, Ch. 4)	29
5.	The boat that transports believers between the two shores of *saṁsāra* and *nirvāṇa* as metaphor for Buddhist teachings and practices (*Nirvāṇa-sūtra*, Ch. 9)	41
6.	The "inexhaustible lamp" as metaphor for the continuing work of saving sentient beings (*Vimalakīrti-sūtra*, Ch. 4)	54
7.	A "mosquito biting an iron ox" as metaphor for something that will have no effect (*Pi-yen lu*, case 58)	63
8.	Seeds of the *nimba* as metaphor for *kleśa* as both cause and effect (*Nirvāṇa-sūtra*, Ch. 34)	65
9.	Explaining the color of milk to a	

Metaphor/Story	*Location (Poem No.)*
blind man compared to explaining *nirvāṇa* to heretics (*Nirvāṇa-sūtra*, Ch. 14)	92
10. Lazy and negligent people compared to thieves who throw away gold and shoulder off weeds (*Nirvāṇa-sūtra*, Ch. 9)	96
11. Practicing meditation without being rid of licentiousness compared to steaming sand to make rice (*Sūraṅgama-sūtra*, Ch. 6)	97
12. Meditating to realize one's Buddha-nature compared to polishing bricks to make mirrors (Ma-tsu's biography in the *Ching-te ch'uan-teng lu*, Ch. 5)	97
13. Experiencing Buddha-nature on one's own compared to determining with your own lips if something is hot or cold (*Wu-men kuan*, kōan 23)	98
14. Compassion is like a wild deer; anger is like the family dog (*Nirvāṇa-sūtra*, Ch. 14)	152
15. The nature of sentient beings is like the heart of the monkey (*Nirvāṇa-sūtra*, Ch. 29)	152
16. The tree born before the rest of the forest as metaphor for Tathāgata (*Nirvāṇa-sūtra*, Ch. 39)	155
17. A "hunter dressed in monk's robes" as a monk who breaks all the rules (*Nirvāṇa-sūtra*, Ch. 7)	157
18. The body as a house on the verge of collapse (*Nirvāṇa-sūtra*, Ch. 23)	182
19. The parable of the "burning house" (*Lotus-sūtra*, Ch. 3)	189, 254, 271
20. Grass grows up around the Buddha in meditation (*Kuan-fo san-mei hai ching*)	190

	Metaphor/Story	*Location (Poem No.)*
21.	The "priceless jewel" in our robes as metaphor for Buddha-nature (*Lotus-sūtra*, Ch. 8)	195, 201, 244, 283
22.	Life compared to a lonely tree on the edge of a cliff (i.e., on the brink of disaster (*Nirvāṇa-sūtra*, Ch. 38)	215
23.	The Zen way is the "Everyday Way" (*Wu-men kuan*, kōan 19)	226
24.	The body as a broken-down boat with real treasure inside, adrift at sea (*Nirvāṇa-sūtra*, Ch. 27)	231
25.	The three kinds of *karma* compared to "three mountains of iron" (*P'ang chü-shih yü-lu*)	243
26.	The "hair on a tortoise" and "horns on a hare" as metaphors for the completely unreal (*Nirvāṇa-sūtra*, Ch. 35)	297
27.	On the need for a raft to cross the waters of life (*Nirvāṇa-sūtra*, Ch. 20)	299
28.	On sentient beings being tossed and sunk by the waters of life and death as they seek to gather in lotus blooms (*Nirvāṇa-sūtra*, Ch. 29)	299

Bibliography

Editions Consulted

Ch'en Hui-chien. *Han-shan-tzu yen-chiu*. Taipei: Tung-ta t'u-shu, 1984.

Hakuin. *Kanzanshi sendai kibun*, in *Hakuin oshō zenshū*, Chapter 4. Tokyo: Ryūgin sha, 1934.

Han-shan, in *Ch'üan T'ang shih*, Ch. 860. Taipei: Ming-lun, 1971, Vol. 12, pp. 9063–9102.

Han-shan shih-chi, in *Tse-shih-chü ts'ung-shu ch'u-chi*. Chang Chün-heng, comp. 1926.

Han-shan-tzu shih-chi, in *Ssu-pu ts'ung-k'an, ch'u-pien* (reprints a Sung text from the collection of Mr. Chou of Chien-te).

Iritani Sensuke and Matsumura Takashi, ed. *Kanzanshi*, Vol. 13 in the series *Zen no goroku*. Tokyo: Chikuma Shoten, 1970.

Iriya Yoshitaka. *Kanzan*, in *Chūgoku shijin senshū*, Vol. 5. Tokyo: Iwanami Shoten, 1958.

Tseng P'u-hsin. *Han-shan shih-chieh*. Hua-lien: Tungching Temple, 1971.

Collected Articles on Han-shan

Chu Ch'uan-yü, ed. *Han-shan shih p'ing-ku*. Taipei: T'ien-i, 1982. 2 vols. Articles by Chao Tzu-fan, Hu Tun-yü, Wang Shao-sheng, and others. 7 articles in Vol. 1; 9 articles in Vol. 2.

Chung-kuo shih chi-k'an 3:3 (September 1972), "Han-shan shih chuan-hao," Vol. 1. Articles by Hu Tun-yü, Kao Yüeh-t'ien, I Chung-ta, and others (5 articles in all).

Chung-kuo shih chi-k'an 3:4 (December 1972), "Han-shan shih chuan-hao," Vol. 2. Articles by Hsü Tuan-fu, Chung Ling, Ch'en Ting-huan and others (8 articles in all).

Chung-kuo shih chi-k'an 4:1 (March 1973), "Han-shan shih chuan-hao," Vol. 3. Articles by Hu Tun-yü, Chao Tzu-fan, Kao Yüeh-t'ien, and others (6 articles in all).

Chung-kuo shih chi-k'an 4:3 (September 1973), "Han-shan shih chuan-hao," Vol. 4. Articles by Yü Chia-hsi, Ts'ao Ch'ien-i, Wang Shao-sheng, and others (9 articles in all).

OTHER STUDIES

Carré, Patrick. *Le Mangeur de brumes: l'oeuvre de Han-shan, poète et vagabond.* Paris: Phébus, 1985.

Chao Tzu-fan. *Han-shan ti shih-tai ching-shen.* Taipei, 1970.

Chung Ling. "Han-shan tsai tung-fang ho hsi-fang wen-hsüeh-chieh ti ti-wei." *Chung-yang jih-pao*, March 8, 1970.

Ch'en Hui-chien. *Han-shan-tzu yen-chiu.* Taipei: Tung-ta t'u-shu, 1984.

Ch'eng Chao-hsiung. *Han-shan-tzu yü Han-shan shih.* Taipei: Ta-lin, 1974.

Hu Shih. *Pai-hua wen-hsüeh shih.* Taipei: Wen-kuang, 1983.

Han-shan shih-chi. Taipei: Han-sheng, 1976. With articles by Chung Ling and Ch'en Ting-huan; the Chih-nan postscript; and other related materials.

Huang Po-jen. *Han-shan chi ch'i shih.* Taipei: Hsin wen-feng, 1980.

Jo Fan. "Han-shan-tzu shih-yün." *Yü-yen hsüeh lun-ts'ung*, 1963, pp. 99–130.

Pulleyblank, E. G. "Linguistic Evidence for the Date of Han-shan," in Ronald C. Miao, *Studies in Chinese Poetry and Politics*, Vol. 1. San Francisco: CMC, 1978, pp. 163–195.

Stalberg, Roberta. "The Poems of the Han-shan Collection." Unpublished Ph.D. dissertation, Ohio State University, 1977.

Wu Chi-yu. "A Study of Han-shan." *T'oung Pao* XLV (1957): 392–450.

Yü Chia-hsi. *Ssu-k'u t'i-yao pien-cheng.* Hong Kong: Chung-hua shu-chü, 1974.

Previous Translations

(Previous English translations—with the exception of that done by Red Pine—are indexed in Appendix II.)

Carré, Patrick. *Le Mangeur de brumes: l'oeuvre de Han-shan: poète et vagabond.* Paris: Phébus, 1985.

Idema, W. L., tr. *Hanshan, Gedichten van de Koude Berg: Zen-poezie.* Amsterdam: Arbeiderspers, 1977. (translation of 200 poems)

Jaeger, Georgette, tr. *Han Shan, ermite taoiste, bouddhiste, zen.* Brussels: Thanh-Long, 1985. (translation of about 100 poems)

Pimpaneau, Jacques. *Li Clodo du Dharma: 25 Poemes de Han-shan.* Paris, 1975.

Red Pine. *The Collected Songs of Cold Mountain.* Port Townsend, WA: Copper Canyon Press, 1983. (complete English translation)

Schumacher, Stephan. *Han Shan: 150 Gedichte vom Kalten Berg.* Düsseldorf and Köln, 1974.

Snyder, Gary. "Cold Mountain Poems." *Evergreen Review* 2:6 (Autumn 1958): 68–80. Reprinted in *Riprap and Cold Mountain Poems.* San Francisco: Four Seasons Foundation, 1965.

Tobias, Arthur, Sanford, James, and Seaton, J. P., translators, *The View from Cold Mountain.* Buffalo, NY: White Pine Press, 1982. (translation of 34 poems)

Waley, Arthur. "27 Poems by Han-shan." *Encounter* 3:3 (September 1954): 3–8.

Watson, Burton. *Cold Mountain: 100 poems by the T'ang poet Han-shan.* New York and London: Columbia University Press, 1970.

Wu Chi-yu. "A Study of Han-shan." *T'oung Pao* XLV (1957): 392–450.

List of Works Cited in Notes

Acker, William. *Some T'ang and Pre-T'ang Texts on Chinese Painting.* Leiden: E. J. Brill, 1954.

Birch, Cyril, ed. *Anthology of Chinese Literature.* New York: Grove Press, 1965.

Birch, Cyril, tr. *Stories From a Ming Collection.* New York: Grove Press, 1958.

Bodde, Derk. *Festivals in Classical China.* Princeton: Princeton University Press, 1975.

Chan-kuo ts'e. Ssu-pu pei-yao edition.

Chan, Wing-tsit. *A Source Book in Chinese Philosophy.* Princeton: Princeton University Press, 1963.

Chan, Wing-tsit, tr. *The Way of Lao Tzu.* Indianapolis: Bobbs-Merrill, 1963.

Chang Yü-shu, et al. *P'ei-wen yün-fu.* Taipei: Shang-wu (Commercial Press), 1983.

Ch'en Ch'i-yu. *Han-fei-tzu chi-shih.* Taipei: Shih-chieh shu-chü, 1963.

Ch'en, Kenneth. *Buddhism in China: A Historical Survey.* Princeton: Princeton University Press, 1964.

Cheng Hsiao-chieh, Cheng Pai-hui-chen, and Thern, Kenneth Lawrence. *Shan Hai Ching: Legendary Geography and Wonders of Ancient China.* Taipei: Committee for Compilation and Examination of the Series of Chinese Classics, 1985.

Chin shu. Peking. Chung-hua shu-chü, 1974.

Ch'u-hsüeh chi (see Hsü Chien).

Chü Ju-chi. *Chih-yüeh lu.* Taipei: Hsin wen-feng, 1983.

Ch'u-tz'u so-yin: Ch'u-tz'u pu-chu. Taipei: Chung-wen, 1979.

Ch'un-ch'iu ching-chuan yin-te. Shanghai: Ku-chi, 1983.

Cleary, Thomas, and J. C., tr. *The Blue Cliff Record.* Boulder, Colo.: Shambhala, 1977. 3 vols.

Conze, Edward. *Buddhism Wisdom Books: The Diamond and the Heart Sutra.* New York: Harper Torchbooks, 1972.

Crump, J. I. *Songs From Xanadu: Studies in Mongol-Dynasty Song-Poetry (San-ch'ü).* Ann Arbor: Center for Chinese Studies, 1983.

Crump, J. I., tr. *Chan-kuo Ts'e.* San Francisco: Chinese Materials Center, 1979.

Dumoulin, Heinrich. *A History of Zen Buddhism.* New York: McGraw-Hill, 1963.

Eoyang, Eugene. "The Solitary Boat: Images of Self in Chinese Nature Poetry." *Journal of Asian Studies* XXXII:4 (August 1973), pp. 593–621.

Feuchtwang, Stephan. *An Anthropological Analysis of Chinese Geomancy.* Taipei: Southern Materials Center, 1982.

Fo-tsu t'ung-chi. T.2035.

Frodsham, J. D. *The Murmuring Stream: The Life and Works of the Chinese Nature Poet Hsieh Ling-yün (385–433). Duke of K'ang-Lo.* Kuala Lumpur: University of Malaya Press, 1967.

Fung Yu-lan. *A History of Chinese Philosophy,* Vol. II (tr. Derk Bodde). Princeton: Princeton University Press, 1953.

Girardot, Norman. *Myth and Meaning in Early Taoism.* Berkeley: University of California Press, 1983.

Graham, A. C., tr. *The Book of Lieh-tzu.* London: John Murray, 1960.

Han-fei-tzu chi-shih (see Ch'en Ch'i-yu).

Han shu. Peking: Chung-hua shu-chü, 1962.

Han Wu ku-shih. Lu Hsün ch'üan-chi. Shanghai: Jen-min wen-hsüeh, 1973.

Harvard-Yenching Institute Sinological Index Series: Supplement No. 10 (A Concordance to Yi Ching). Taipei: Ch'eng-wen, 1973.

Harvard-Yenching Institute Sinological Index Series: Supplement No. 16 (A Concordance to the Analects of Confucius). Taipei: Ch'eng-wen, 1972.

Harvard-Yenching Institute Sinological Index Series: Supplement No. 20 (A Concordance to Chuang Tzu). Cambridge, Mass.: Harvard University Press, 1956.

Harvard-Yenching Institute Sinological Index Series: Supplement No. 23 (A Concordance to Hsiao Ching). Taipei: Ch'eng-wen, 1966.

Hawkes, David, tr. *Cao Xuegin: The Story of the Stone,* Vol. I. New York: Penguin Books, 1973.

Hawkes, David, tr. *The Songs of the South,* London: Penguin Books, 1985.

Henricks, Robert G. "The Hero Pattern and the Life of Confucius." *Journal of Chinese Studies* 1:3 (October 1984), pp. 241–260.

Henricks, Robert G. *Philosophy and Argumentation in Third-Century China: The Essays of Hsi K'ang.* Princeton: Princeton University Press, 1983.

Hightower, Robert. *The Poetry of T'ao Ch'ien.* Oxford: Clarendon Press, 1970.

Hou Han shu. Peking: Chung-hua shu-chü, 1965.

Hsi-ching tsa-chi, in *Ku-chin i-shih*. Taipei: Shang-wu (Commercial Press), 1969.

Hsi Chung-san chi. *Ssu-pu pei-yao* edition.

Hsin T'ang shu. Peking: Chung-hua shu-chü, 1975.

Hsü Chien, et al. *Ch'u-hsüeh chi*. Peking: Chung-hua shu-chü, 1962.

Hsü-t'ang lu. T.2000.

Hu Shiu-ying. *An Enumeration of Chinese Materia Medica*. Hong Kong: The Chinese University Press, 1980.

Huang Fu-mi. *Kao-shih chuan*. *Ssu-pu pei-yao* edition.

Hucker, Charles. *A Dictionary of Official Titles in Imperial China*. Stanford: Stanford University Press, 1985.

Hui Chiao. *Kao-seng chuan ch'u-chi*. Taipei: Taiwan yin-ching ch'u, 1970.

Hurvitz, Leon, tr. *Scripture of the Lotus Blossom of the Fine Dharma (The Lotus Sutra)*. New York: Columbia University Press, 1976.

I-shih chuan, in *Yü-han shan-fang chi-i-shu pu-pien*.

I-wen lei-chü (see Ou-yang Hsün).

Jui-ying ching. T.185.

Kaltenmark, Max, tr. *Le Lie-sien Tchouan: Biographies légendaires des Immortels taoîtes de l'antiquité*. Pékin: Centre d'études sinologiques de Pékin, 1953.

Kandel, Barbara. *Taiping Jing: The Origin and Transmission of the 'Scripture on General Welfare'—the History of an Unofficial text*. Hamburg: Gesellschaft für Nature und Völkerkunde Ostasiens, 1979.

Karlgren, Bernhard, tr. *The Book of Documents*. Stockholm: Museum of Far Eastern Antiquities, Bulletin 22, 1950.

Karlgren, Bernhard, tr. *The Book of Odes*. Stockholm: Museum of Far Eastern Antiquities, 1950, p. 23.

Ko Hung. *Pao-p'u-tzu*. *Ssu-pu pei-yao* edition.

Ko Hung. *Shen-hsien chuan*. *Li-tai chen-hsien shih-chuan*. Taipei: Tzu-yu (Freedom Press), 1970.

Kuo Mao-ch'ien. *Yüeh-fu shih-chi*. Peking: Chung-hua shu-chü, 1979.

Lai, Whalen, and Lancaster, Lewis R., ed. *Early Ch'an in China and Tibet*. Berkeley: Berkeley Buddhist Studies Series, 1973.

Lao-tzu. Ssu-pu pei-yao edition.

Lau, D. C., tr. *Confucius: The Analects.* New York: Penguin Books, 1979.

Legge, James, tr. *The She King (The Chinese Classics,* Vol. 4). Taipei: Wen-hsing shu-tien, 1966.

Legge, James, tr. (modernized edition by Clae Waltham). *Shu Ching: Book of History.* Chicago: Henry Regnery, 1971.

Li Fang, et al., ed. *T'ai-p'ing kuang-chi.* Taipei: Wen-shih-che, 1981.

Liao, W. K., tr. *The Complete Works of Han Fei Tzu: A Classic of Chinese Legalism.* London: Arthur Probsthain, 1939.

Lieh-hsien chuan. Li-tai chen-hsien shih-chuan.

Lieh-nü chuan. Ssu-pu pei-yao edition.

Lieh-tzu. Ssu-pu pei-yao edition.

Liu Hsiang. *Shuo-yüan. Ssu-pu pei-yao* edition.

Loehr, Max. *The Great Painters of China.* Oxford: Phaidon Press, 1980.

Loewe, Michael. *Ways to Paradise: The Chinese Quest for Immortality.* London: George Allen & Unwin, 1979.

Luk, Charles. *Ch'an and Zen Teaching,* Series Two. London: Rider & Company, 1961.

Mao-shih cheng-i. Shih-san-ching chu-shu edition. Peking: Chung-hua shu-chü, 1979.

Mao-shih yin-te. Taipei: Hung-tao wen-hua shih-yeh, 1971.

Maspero, Henri. *Taoism and Chinese Religion* (tr. from the French by Frank A. Kierman, Jr.). Amherst: University of Massachusetts Press, 1981.

Mather, Richard. "The Mystical Ascent of the T'ient'ai Mountains: Sun Ch'o's Yu-T'ien-T'ai-Shan Fu." *Monumenta Serica* 20 (1961), pp. 226–245.

Mather, Richard, tr. *Shih-shuo Hsin-yü: A New Account of Tales of the World (by Liu I-ch'ing with commentary by Liu Chün).* Minneapolis: University of Minnesota Press, 1976.

McRae, John. *The Northern School and the Formation of Early Ch'an Buddhism.* Honolulu: University of Hawaii Press, 1986.

Miao-fa lien-hua ching (The Lotus-sūtra). T.262.

O'Hara, Richard. *The Position of Woman in Early China: According to the Lieh Nü Chuan "The Biographies of Eminent Chinese Women."* Washington, D.C.: The Catholic University of America Press, 1945.

Ou-yang Hsün. *I-wen lei-chü.* Shanghai: Ku-chi, 1965.

Owen, Stephen. *The Poetry of The Early T'ang.* New Haven: Yale University Press, 1977.

P'ei-wen yün-fu (see Chang Yü-shu).

Pi-yen lu. T.2003.

P'u-chi. *Wu-teng hui-yüan.* Taipei: Hsin wen-feng, 1983.

Rawlinson, Andrew. "The Ambiguity of the Buddha-nature Concept in India and China," in Lai and Lancaster, ed., *Early Ch'an in China and Tibet.*

Read, Bernard. *Chinese Materia Medica: Turtle and Shellfish Drugs, Avian Drugs, A Compendium of Minerals and Stones.* Taipei: Southern Materials Center, 1977.

Read, Bernard. *Chinese Materia Medica: Animal Drugs.* Taipei: Southern Materials Center, 1976.

Read, Bernard. *Chinese Materia Medica: Insect Drugs, Dragon and Snake Drugs, Fish Drugs.* Taipei: Southern Materials Center, 1977.

Read, Bernard. *Chinese Medicinal Plants from the Pen Ts'ao Kang Mu.* Taipei: Southern Materials Center, 1977.

Reps, Paul, tr. *Zen Flesh, Zen Bones: A Collection of Zen and Pre-Zen Writings.* New York: Doubleday & Company, 1957.

Robinson, Richard H. "The Sutra of Vimalakirti's Preaching." Unpublished manuscript.

Rotours, Robert des. *Le Traité des Examens: Traduit de la Nouvelle Histoire des T'ang (Chap. XLIV, XLV).* Paris: Librairie Ernest Leroux, 1932.

Rushton, Peter. "An Interpretation of Hsi K'ang's Eighteen Poems, Presented to Hsi Hsi on His Entry Into the Army." *Journal of the American Oriental Society* 99:2 (April–June 1979), pp. 175–190.

San-kuo chih. Peking: Chung-hua shu-chü, 1959.

Saso, Michael. *The Teachings of Taoist Master Chuang.* New Haven: Yale University Press, 1978.

Schafer, Edward H. *Pacing the Void: T'ang Approaches to the Stars.* Berkeley: University of California Press, 1977.

Schafer, Edward H. *The Golden Peaches of Samarkand: A Study of T'ang Exotics.* Berkeley: University of California Press, 1963.

Schafer, Edward H. *The Vermilion Bird: T'ang Images of the South.* Berkeley: University of California Press, 1967.

Seidel, Anna. "Imperial Treasures and Taoist Sacraments: Taoist Roots in the Apocrypha," in Strickmann, Michel, ed., *Tantric and Taoist Studies in Honour of R. A. Stein: Mélanges Chinois et Bouddhiques*, Vol. XXI (1983), pp. 291–371.

Seng Chao. "Pao-tsang lun." T.1857.

Shan-hai ching. Ssu-pu pei-yao edition.

Shang-shu K'ung chuan. Ssu-pu pei-yao edition.

Shen-hsien chuan, in *Li-tai chen-hsien shih-chuan.* Taipei: Tzu-yu, 1970.

Shen Nung pen-ts'ao ching. Ssu-pu pei-yao edition.

Shih-chi. Peking: Chung-hua shu-chü, 1959.

Shih-i chi, in *Ku-chin i-shih.*

Shih Tao-yüan. *Ching-te ch'uan-teng lu.* Taipei: Chen-shan-mei, 1968.

Shou-leng-yen ching (The Sūraṅgama-sūtra). T.945.

Soothill, William Edward, and Hodous, Lewis. *A Dictionary of Chinese Buddhist Terms.* Kaohsiung: Fo-kuang, 1982.

Strickmann, Michel. *Le Taoïsme du Mao Chan: Chronique d'une Révélation.* Mémoires de l'institut des hautes études chinoises, Vol. XVII, 1981.

Stuart, G. A. *Chinese Materia Medica: Vegetable Kingdom.* Taipei: Southern Materials Center, 1979.

Ta-chih tu-lun. T.1509.

Ta-pan nieh-pan ching (The Nirvāṇa-sūtra). T.374.

Ta-pan nieh-pan ching (The Nirvāṇa-sūtra). T.375.

T'ai-p'ing kuang-chi (see Li Fang).

Ting Fu-pao. *Ch'üan Han san-kuo Chin nan-pei-ch'ao shih.* Taipei: Shih-chieh shu-chü (World Publishing Co.), 1969.

Tsan-ning, et al., ed. *Sung Kao-seng chuan (Kao-seng chuan san-chi).* Taipei: Yin-ching-ch'u, 1961.

Tu Kuang-t'ing. *Hsien-chuan shih-i,* in *T'ai-p'ing kuang-chi.*

Twitchett, D. C. *Financial Administration under the T'ang Dynasty*. Cambridge: The University Press, 1970.

Twitchett, Denis, ed. *The Cambridge History of China*: Volume 3, *Sui and T'ang China, 589–906*. Cambridge: Cambridge University Press, 1979.

Waley, Arthur, tr. *The Analects of Confucius*. New York: Vintage Books, 1938.

Waley, Arthur, tr. *The Book of Songs*. New York: Grove Press, 1937.

Wang Kuo-wei, edited. *Shui-ching chu chiao*. Shanghai: Jen-min, 1984.

Ware, James R., tr. *Alchemy, Medicine and Religion in the China of A.D. 320: The Nei P'ien of Ko Hung*. New York: Dover Publications, 1966.

Watson, Burton. *Chinese Lyricism: Shih Poetry from the Second to the Twelfth Century*. New York: Columbia University Press, 1971.

Watson, Burton. *Chinese Rhyme-Prose: Poems in the Fu Form from the Han and Six Dynasties Periods*. New York: Columbia University Press, 1971.

Watson, Burton. *Courtier and Commoner in Ancient China: Selections from the History of the Former Han by Pan Ku*. New York: Columbia University Press, 1974.

Watson, Burton. *Records of the Historian: Chapters from the Shih Chi of Ssu-ma Ch'ien*. New York: Columbia University Press, 1969.

Watson, Burton. *The Complete Works of Chuang Tzu*. New York: Columbia University Press, 1968.

Wei-mo-chieh so-shuo ching (*The Vimalakīrti-sutra*). T.475.

Welch, Holmes. *Taoism: The Parting of the Way*. Boston: Beacon Press, 1957.

Wen-hsüan. Taipei: Cheng-chung. 1985.

Wen-hsüan so-yin. Taipei: Cheng-chung. 1985.

Werner, E. T. C. *Chinese Weapons*. Los Angeles: Ohara Publications, 1972.

Wilhelm, Richard (tr. into English by Baynes, Cary F.). *The I Ching (or Book of Changes)*. Princeton: Princeton University Press, 1950.

Wu-men kuan. T.2005.

Yampolsky, Philip B., tr. *The Platform Sutra of the Sixth Patriarch*. New York: Columbia University Press, 1967.

Yang Yung. *Shih-shuo hsin-yü chiao-chien*. Hong Kong: Ta-chung shu-chü, 1969.

Yang Yung. *T'ao Yüan-ming chi chiao-chien*. Hong Kong: Wu-hsing chi-shu-chü, 1971.

Yen-shih chia-hsün. Ssu-pu pei-yao edition.

Yü Ying-shih. "Life and Immortality in the Mind of Han China." *The Harvard Journal of Asiatic Studies* 25 (1964–65), pp. 80–122.

Yün-chi ch'i-ch'ien. Cheng-t'ung Tao-tsang, Vols. 36–38. Taipei: I-wen, 1977.

Index

(Chinese and Sanskrit Buddhist terms
are indexed separately in Appendix IV)

abbey, 339
abbots, 133
age of great peace, 63
alabaster orchards, 301
alchemical potions, 52
alchemical practice, 410
alms, 204, 228
Amitābha, 7, 311
An Lu-shan rebellion, 254, 420
Ananda, 149
ancient megaliths, 52
ancient tombs, 46, 304
ant, 297
ape, 375
appearance and form, 375
appearance and speech, 10, 171
appointment, 10, 171, 182
arrow, 184, 258, 323, 339
ash of a lamp, 277
ashes and dust, 299, 379
ass, 173, 188
autumn(s), 35, 95, 271, 278; and
    springs, 381

ballads and songs, 172

bamboo, 62, 135, 251; groves, 146;
    pipes, 343; screen, 42; shoots
    of, 74
basket, 291, 393
bay, 91
beautiful brow, 49
beautiful maid, 48
beautiful men, 144
beautiful pearls, 357
beautiful sing-song girls, 59
beautiful woman/women, 47, 50,
    101, 392
beautiful youth, 91, 194
bird(s), 17, 32, 35, 51, 54, 62, 64,
    70, 186, 195, 215, 235, 254, 306,
    332, 351, 356, 393; evil, 105;
    sick, 357
bird's body, 169
bird's trails, 32
biscuits, 153; and cakes, 84
blessings field, 319
blessings fields clothes, 373
blind ass, 275
blind boy, 13, 143, 171
blind man, 385
bloom(s), 74, 278, 398, 399

blossoms, 100, 165, 223, 392
blue beetles, 182
Blue Cliff Record, 110, 246, 247
blue cliffs, 273
blue clouds, 137
blue-eyed barbarian, 336
Blue Maid, 16, 174, 175
blue phoenix, 83
blue-phoenix furs, 82
blue sky, 234, 239, 240, 281, 384
Blue Waves, 104
bluebottle flies, 42, 43, 76
bluish-green creepers, 364
boat, 81, 256; and oars, 94; lotus-
    gathering, 82; rotten wood,
    112; unattached, 256
Bodhidharma, 93, 134, 186, 305, 336
bodhisattva(s), 73, 99, 205, 225,
    266, 267, 276, 334
bodhisattva's path, 139
body, 55, 92, 112, 140, 225, 267,
    272, 277, 283, 305, 339, 340,
    341, 342, 344
bones, 55, 92, 210, 289, 320, 379, 382
Book of Changes, 129, 216
Book of Documents, 66, 129, 216, 404
Book of History, 213
Book of Poetry, 216
Book of Songs, 68, 129, 404
books, 36, 40, 51, 64, 167, 182, 194,
    225, 258, 290, 315, 337, 400
bottles and urns, 210
Bottom Village, 192
boulders, 18, 65, 288, 406
bracelet, 297
bracken, 127
bramble(s), 66, 216, 250
bramble door, 67, 271, 304
breath, 55, 128
breathing exercises, 11, 58, 366
briars and thorns, 263
bricks, 149, 419
brocades, 76
broken-down tub, 318
brook(s), 58, 288, 306
bubbles, 135

Buddha(s), 6, 19, 63, 67, 109, 116,
    122, 141, 149, 150, 157, 202,
    204, 221, 228, 247, 266, 270,
    276, 280, 281, 296, 300, 330,
    337, 353, 366, 372, 377, 406,
    407; teaching of, 35, 57
Buddha-body, 31
Buddhahood, 134, 233
Buddha's knowledge and views,
    238
Buddha's teachings, 220
Buddhism, 6, 112, 114, 178, 197,
    226, 266, 310, 316, 317, 352,
    360, 363, 383, 390
Buddhist(s), 3, 4, 6, 7, 8, 11, 16, 18,
    21, 23, 24, 25, 31, 63, 98, 161,
    162, 225, 278, 306, 328, 347,
    354, 366, 374, 402, 421; books,
    355; clergy, 14, 178; cosmology,
    279, 338; criticism of geomancy,
    345; faith, 67; image(s), 115,
    148; monk(s), 246, 403; notions
    of karma, 170; parlance, 265;
    saying, 337; scriptures, 73;
    term(s), 127, 224; truths, 245;
    virtues, 220; way, 81, 122, 318;
    writings, 317
bug in a bowl, 325
bullock carts, 266
burdock, 321, 322
burning house, 266, 348; lord, 368
butterflies, 74, 338; and bees, 54; of
    gold, 108

cages, 47
calamus, 197; isle, 196
calisthenics, 11, 366
candana, 133, 148
candle(s), 15, 93, 369
candy, 57
cane, 306
Cantonese, 385
cap-clasps, 210
cap of cane, 16
carp, 169

carpe diem, 98
carriage(s), 38, 263, 372
cart(s), 73, 218, 335
cassia beams, 83
cassia rafter, 399
cassia trees, 115
cat, 13; gray spotted, 227; lame, 88–89
catamite, 84
cave, 54, 60, 232, 362; of five shades, 369
cavern heaven, 358
cedar, 148
cemetery, 9, 91. *See also* graveyards
censors, 226
census reports, 129
Chan-kuo Ts'e, 103, 183, 258
Chang, 287, 387
Chang I, 268
Chang Seng-yu, 270, 420
Chang Tao-ling, 340
Chao, 59, 287
Chao-chou, 24, 312
Chao Fei-yen, 83
chariot(s), 36, 357
Chekiang, 22
chen-kuan, 4
Cheng Hsüan, 404
cherries, 195
Chia I, 335
Chiang Hsü, 35
chicken, 388
Chien-ming, 419
chignon(s), 106, 108
Chih I, 80
Chih-nan, 3, 22, 25
Chih Tun, 306
Chih-yen, 4, 22
Chih-yüeh lu, 24
Chin shu, 21, 144, 259
Chin dynasty, 165
chin straps, 331
Ching-te ch'uan-teng lu, 22, 23, 24, 246
Cho River, 340
Chou and Shao, 401, 402

Chou dynasty, 43, 308; poetry of, 111
Chou the Perfected of Purple Yang, 247
chrysanthemums, 254
Chu Mai-ch'en, 167
Chu Tao-ch'ien, 306
Chu Tao-i, 402
Chu Tao-sheng, 402
Chuang-tzu, 21, 35, 37, 42, 88, 119, 156, 168, 209, 250, 344, 378
Chung family, 144
Chung-li Ch'un, 145
Chung Tzu-ch'i, 405, 410
cicadas, 406, 407
cinnabar, 271
Cinnabar Mound, 111, 273, 274, 358
city park rats, 303
civil service examinations, 385. *See also* examinations
clarified butter, 57
Classic of Filial Piety, 213
classics, 8, 9, 167, 194, 404
clay, 265
cliff(s), 19, 32, 54, 60, 66, 86, 243, 278, 281, 283, 288, 299, 351, 376, 380, 381, 411; blue, 273; emerald-green, 350; empty, 363; no-outflows, 401; rocks, 367; stone, 285; verdant, 52
cliff rocks, 367
clogs, 288
cloud ladder, 263, 264
clouds, 17, 35, 47, 165, 186, 223, 267, 273, 288, 339, 342, 350, 355, 394; and thunder, 60, 215; black, 341; blue, 273; drifting, 133; mountain, 251; of delusion, 115; of ignorance, 114, 342, 350; pink, 58; rose-colored, 116, 162; vapor and, 86. *See also* white clouds
coarse linen kerchiefs, 378
coarse woolen robe, 366
coffins, 42
Cold Cliff(s), 3, 23, 80, 234, 375, 393, 401

Cold Mountain, 3, 22, 25, 70, 167, 178
cold spring, 384
cold wind, 252
commanderies, 38
common, 103, 347; and vulgar, 407; crowd, 314; customs, 212; dumb men, 319; man, 129; people, 123, 333; words, 385
commoners, 72
complexion(s), 13, 48, 55, 392; peachy, 241; rosy, 398
concubine(s), 83, 94
Confucian(s), 159, 378
Confucianism, 317
Confucius, 51, 60, 93, 113, 132, 144, 156, 158, 159, 166, 184, 207, 217, 243, 264, 308, 332, 378
Consciousness-only School, 150, 335
coral, 83, 91
cosmic mountain, 279
cottage, 343; of weeds, 266
cotton-fur robes, 232, 277, 305; coat, 288
court, 67, 232
court ladies, 12
courtyard(s), 52, 115, 206, 239
covers and bonds, 389
cow, 198
crackpot, 8
crane(s), 47, 79, 166, 237, 304, 339, 355, 388
crane's knee, 385, 386
creepers, 251, 364
crossbow pellet, 180
crow(s), 104, 105, 406, 407; and kites, 42
crystal, 357
crystalline sugar, 57
cuckoos, 104, 105
cypress, 210, 271, 272; and pine, 146
Cypress Beam Terrace, 370
Ch'an, 5. *See* Zen
Ch'ang-an, 9, 91, 187, 191, 254, 274, 420

Ch'ang-lin, 167
Ch'ao Fu, 306, 378
Ch'i, 113, 246; and Ch'u, 164
Ch'in, 103, 254, 340; and Wei, 164
Ch'in Kao, 340
Ch'in Shih-huang-ti, 370
Ch'ing, 385
Ch'u, 101, 111, 183, 192
Ch'u-hsüeh chi, 144
Ch'u-tz'u, 10, 21, 32, 68, 88, 105, 115, 116, 117, 157, 199, 273
Ch'ü Yüan, 32, 68, 69, 105, 116
Ch'üan T'ang shih, 3, 12, 20, 26
Ch'un-ch'iu, 129, 216

daisies, 209, 250
daisy fields, 92
death(s), 42, 46, 57, 71, 73, 90, 120, 125, 127, 128, 154, 169, 212, 263, 275, 287, 290, 356, 361, 377, 379, 399; early, 113
debater, 161
deep wood(s), 37, 105, 156, 391
deer, 220, 390–91; carts, 266
demon(s), 31, 109, 140, 179, 287, 334; of ignorance, 397
deserted city, 46
Destiny, 308. *See* fate
dew, 34, 162, 292, 341
diamond, 229, 387
Diamond-sutra, 205
diced fish, 289
Dīpaṁkara, 330
divine immortal, 340
divine oranges, 38
divined/divining, 32, 127, 157, 198; with milfoil, 129
dog(s), 103, 153, 173, 177, 178, 241, 263, 307; family, 220; fierce, 177
dog's heart, 241
dogwood, 126; wine, 125
donkey(s), 104, 105, 117, 173, 249
donkey shit, 372
dragon(s), 269, 270
dragon fish, 169

Dragon King, 280
dragon palace, 280
dream(s), 38, 39
dregs, 48
drinking wine, 180, 308
drugs, 400, 403; of long life, 55
duck, 157, 289
duckweed, 216, 346
Duke Chang, 191
Duke of Chou, 166, 402
Duke of Shao, 402
dust, 35, 100, 133, 210, 244, 249,
    297, 316, 352, 378, 380, 383,
    390; and the vulgar, 195; blan-
    ket of, 325; in the glow, 135;
    particles, 135
duster, 134
dustpan and broom, 249
dust-whisk, 134
dusty world, 162

Earth, 143, 368, 369
Earthly Immortals, 340
east, 8, 40, 41, 53, 75, 82, 98, 101,
    111, 144, 169, 186, 216, 239,
    245, 282, 287, 348, 350; house
    to the, 75
eastern cliff, 395
Eastern inn, 14, 48
Eastern sea, 91, 100, 168, 201
Eastern Tai, 71
editing pen, 315
eggplant, 24
egrets, 52
eight directions, 53
eight festive days, 368
eight winds, 401
elixir, 340; of immortality, 370
embroidered quilts, 59
emerald-green cliffs, 350
emerald-green flow, 284
emerald-green mountain streams,
    364
emerald-green peaks, 380
emerald-green pool, 390

emerald lake, 95
Emperor Ai of the Han, 203
Emperor Ching, 40
Emperor Ch'eng, 83
Emperor Hui of the Chin, 144
Emperor Ming of the Wei, 184
Emperor of Ch'in, 370
Emperor Shun of the Han, 185
Emperor Wen, 40
Emperor Wu, 40, 246
Emperor Wu of the Chin, 166
Emperor Wu of the Han, 370
Emperor Wu of the Liang, 246, 247,
    270, 420
Emperor Yüan of Liang, 91
Empress Wu, 246
empty cliffs, 363
empty name, 32, 33, 379
enlightenment, 12, 16, 18
Erh of Han, 49
essence, 55, 128
Everyday Way, 312
evil destinies, 141. *See* three paths
examination(s), 9, 10, 13, 182, 197;
    civil service, 77, 385
Examinations Board, 171
exile, 67
eyeballs, 125

Fa-yün kung, 246, 420
fall, 14, 16, 39, 50, 58, 98, 254;
    stream, 381; wind(s), 48, 392
family and friends, 39, 195
family and kin, 39
Fan Li, 198
farm, 35; boy, 260
farmer(s), 8, 156, 180, 239
fast-flowing stream, 368
fast-flying arrow, 346
fate, 10, 13, 171, 234, 256, 277, 278,
    304, 308, 347, 362
father and mother, 51
fathers and sons, 38
feather cloak, 340
feathered clothes, 47

feathered men, 273
feathers, 78, 79
Feng-kan, 3, 4, 5, 7, 8, 24, 80
ferns, 124
feudal rank, 185
Few Homes (Mt. Shao-shih), 186
field(s), 64, 240, 304, 352, 358, 373;
     and gardens, 8, 9, 51, 395; of
     rocks, 113; of wheat, 36
filial, 9, 213; devotion, 39; son, 9,
     36
finger, 19, 20
fire and smoke, 266
fish(es), 52, 54, 64, 124, 167, 168,
     261, 309, 339; and birds, 343;
     and beasts, 176; and dragons,
     313; fresh, 303
fish and meat, 14, 122, 147
fish pond, 36
fisherman/men, 51, 68, 105
fisherman's songs, 69
five aggregates, 369
five-character poems, 367
Five Classics, 9, 129
five desires, 399
five elements, 66, 283
Five Hundred Arhats, 24
Five Peaks, 169, 273, 274
Five Perversions, 142
five planets, 340
five sacred mountains (peaks), 169,
     352
five senses, 396
five shades, 62, 83
five tones, 405
flower(s), 49, 50, 51, 53, 57, 98,
     106, 107, 116, 361; /spots, 317
fog, 19, 44, 66, 96, 133, 162, 236,
     251
forest(s), 186, 224, 357, 364; care-
     taker, 224; and springs, 234
forester's snare, 47
Four Brights, 358
four constituent elements of reality,
     342
four directions, 384

four elements, 369
four forms of birth, 338
Four Heavens, 356, 357
Four Immortals, 245, 247, 420
four island continents, 292
four seasons, 53, 368
four snakes, 369
four supports, 245, 246, 420
fox, 179, 354
frankincense, 271, 272
frogs, 74
frost, 135, 258; and dew, 163
fruit, 393; and wine, 267
Fu Hsi, 247, 402
funeral, 42
funeral bier, 267
furs, 393

garlic buds, 125
garlic sauce, 289, 290
gentleman/gentlemen, 8, 60, 72, 77,
     132, 146, 184, 233, 264, 308, 381
geomancy, 345
ghost(s), 55, 109, 304, 339, 340, 345
gibbons, 127, 215
glory and honor, 244
goat carts, 266
goblins, 269
god(s), 13, 14, 120, 146, 148, 156,
     267, 269, 352, 353; and Bud-
     dhas, 122, 372
Goddess of Frost, 16, 175
gold, 168, 179, 241, 244, 250, 317,
     357, 410; and silver, 331; bridle
     of, 99, 107; cage, 47; seals, 226
Gold Thread (golden thread), 124,
     290
golden bridle, 391
Golden Gates, 86, 280
golden hairpins, 74, 83
golden oriole, 392
Golden Terraces, 370
goose, 47
gourd in the tree, 86–87
granary rice, 76

grass(es), 18, 65, 130, 223, 234, 267,
341, 351, 391; and trees, 211;
and swamps, 66
grave(s), 46, 92, 146, 210, 212, 277,
326, 345, 394, 403, 413
gravestone, 413
graveyard, 120, 146
Great Goose Pagoda, 274
Great Plan, 66
greed, 14, 15, 31, 124, 277, 310, 369
greedy people, 137
green bear mat, 82, 83
green forest, 399
green grass(es), 90, 267, 400
green hawks, 155
green hills, 314, 381, 403
green peak(s), 186, 195
Green Pearl, 343
green ridge, 375
green shoots, 291
green water, 68, 254
green willow, 57
grindstones, 176

hairpins, 331; of gold, 74, 83, 98
Hakuin, 21, 26, 40, 41, 73, 85, 230,
267, 335
Han, 100
Han-fei tzu, 177
Han shu, 21, 129, 176, 335
Han-tan, 59, 84
Han Wu-ti, 40, 370
hares, 9, 155, 183
hawk(s), 9, 307
Heaven, 45, 66, 96, 104, 143, 156,
157, 186, 213, 247, 293, 308,
319, 328, 362; and Earth, 42,
234, 243, 268
Heavenly Immortals, 340
Hell (hell), 122, 141, 142, 147, 169,
230, 239, 278, 287, 297, 319,
323, 327, 331, 374, 382
Hell's torments, 373
hemp, 356
herbs, 11, 226, 366

Herd Boy, 196
hibiscus, 49, 50, 94
histories, 9, 194
honey, 57, 388
hook, 184
horse(s), 46, 57, 99, 331; and carts,
64; flower-plucking, 82; prized,
89; thousand-li, 60; "treading
snow," 203; worn-out, 117
Hou Han shu, 21, 38, 129, 159, 172,
185
hound, 183
Hsi-ching tsa-chi, 83
Hsi Hsi, 165
Hsi K'ang, 165, 391
Hsi Yün, 388
Hsiang Yü, 41
Hsiao ching, 21, 214
Hsieh Ling-yün, 32, 33
Hsien, 254, 420 (the capital)
Hsien-ching, 254
Hsien-yang, 254
Hsin t'ang shu, 21, 171
hsiu-ts'ai, 171, 385, 421
Hsiung-nu, 138
Hsü Kao-seng chuan, 22
Hsü Ling-fu, 22, 25
Hsü Number Five, 212
Hsü the Sixth, 147
Hsü-wu of Ch'i, 160
Hsü Yu, 37, 87, 378, 400
Hsüan-tsang, 150
Hsüan-tsung, 94
Hu Shih, 4, 5, 22, 23
Hua-liu, 13, 88
Hua-ting, 237
Hua-yen, 112
Huai-jang, 150, 419
Huang and Lao, 56
Huang-lao, 144
Huang Po, 388
Huang-ti, 56, 144, 145
Hui-neng, 5, 25, 205, 419
Hui-shih, 88
Hui-yen, 402
Hui-yüan, 402

hun, 92
hungry ghost, 120, 141, 169, 349,
    382
hunter, 226

I (ching), 21, 60, 129, 216
I-wen lei-chü, 38, 149, 156
ice, 19, 44, 77, 136, 154, 408
immortal(s), 13, 14, 39, 46, 47, 79,
    91, 115, 128, 155, 213, 226, 273,
    301, 304, 339, 340, 359, 400,
    402; arts, 370; books, 52; elixir,
    339; and gods, 79, 241; regis-
    ters of, 128; soul, 340
immortality, 14, 39, 111, 115, 273,
    274, 325, 339, 370
imperial law, 31
Imperial Records, 10, 129
impermanence, 135, 327
incense, 228
insects, 323
Iriya Yoshitaka, 6, 20, 23
Isles of the Blessed, 370
ivory beds, 258

jackal, 323
jade, 13, 15, 48, 99, 108, 156, 174,
    210, 392; discs, 42, 156; girdles,
    98; insignia, 174
Jade Emperor, 71
jagged peaks, 68
Jambudvipa, 292
Juan Chi, 59
Jui-tsung, 5

Kan Pao, 343
Kao-seng chuan, 3, 22, 23, 24, 246,
    306, 402
Kao-ti, 32
Kashmir, 85
Kāśyapa, 116
kerchief of birch bark, 288
King Chao of the Chou, 83

King Chou Hsin of the Yin, 258
King Ch'eng, 402
King Hsiang of Ch'u, 156, 192, 250
King Hsüan, 145
King Mu of the Chou, 88, 170
King Wen of the Chou, 329
King Wu, 43
King Wu of the Chou, 213
kings of Wu and Yüeh, 168
king's carriage, 36
kingfisher-blue screens, 358
kingfisher feathers and plumes, 196
kingfisher-green, 22, 306
Ko Hung, 39, 100, 109
koan(s), 7, 230, 312
kolanut tree, 62
Ku K'ai-chih, 86, 270
Kuan-yin, 270
Kung-shu Pan, 264
Kuo-ch'ing (Temple), 3, 4, 8, 11, 24,
    25, 80, 274, 371
K'ung, 166

Lady Kuo, 259
lamb, 101, 354
Lamplighter Buddha, 330
Lao-tzu, 56, 92, 144, 145, 179, 207,
    225, 231, 247, 263, 264
lay masses, 383
laymen, 317
lead ore, 179
leaving (left) home, 11, 48, 338, 372
leeks, 291
Li, 287
Li-chi, 129, 216, 315
Li-chou, 4, 22
Li Ho, 24
Li Hsün, 340
Li Po, 12
Li Shang-yin, 407
Li Shao-chün, 370
Li Shih-min, 309, 421
Li-yüeh, 370
Liang (dynasty), 38, 230, 245, 246,
    247, 269, 420, 421

Liang Huang, 388, 421
Liang Wu-ti, 82, 270
lice, 383
Lieh-hsien chuan, 340
Lieh-nü chuan, 36, 145, 160
Lieh-tzu, 49, 164, 405
Lin-ch'üan, 230
Ling-yu, 24
lion's position, 179
lion's roar, 220
Liu Hsiang, 184
Liu the Third, 212
Lo Pin-wang, 407
Lo-yang, 9, 24, 71, 82, 106; streets
    of, 24, 91
long life, 9, 11, 115, 211, 293, 395;
    minerals and herbs, 366; search
    for, 125
loom, 9, 51, 153, 196, 200
Lord, 156, 157, 329, 341, 389
Lord Heaven, 347
Lord of the Cart, 9, 36
lotus blossoms, 118, 363
lotus flowers, 330, 399
Lu, 378
Lu Chi, 39
Lü-ch'iu Yin, 3, 4, 5, 22, 24, 25
Lu-erh, 169, 170
Lu family girl, 82
lü-shih, 5, 19, 385. *See also* regulated
    verse
Lu T'an-wei, 270
Lun-yü, 21, 60
lunar lodging, 130
lute, 36, 252, 392, 405, 410

Ma-ku, 100
Ma-tsu, 6, 150, 419, 421
magpie(s), 38, 407
Mahāsattva Fu, 245, 247, 420
Maitreya, 373
malaria and miasmas, 198
mallows, 393
Manchurian Snow Pheasant, 83
Mandarin ducks, 94, 108, 165

Mañjuśrī, 7, 24
Mao Chang, 404
Mao Heng, 404
Mao-ling, 370
master(s), 18, 20, 24, 150, 158, 236,
    269, 287, 319, 329, 384
Master Chih-kung, 269, 270
Master Chu of T'ao, 198
Master Han-shan, 255
Master K'ung Ch'iu, 60
Master Mao, 404
Master Meng, 164
Master Sang-hu, 156
Master Shih, 80
Master Tsou's wife, 84
Master Tung, 203
Master Yang's crane, 166
Master Wan-hui, 245, 246, 420
Master White Hare, 39
Master Yellow Stone, 340
Master Yellow Turban, 339, 340
meat, 98, 124, 204, 228, 230, 242,
    289, 329, 354, 365, 366; and
    wine, 206; soup, 289. *See also*
    fish and meat
meditation, 18. *See* sitting (in medi-
    tation)
Medlar broth, 125
melons, 39
Mencius, 191, 233
Meng-ch'ang chün, 258
Meng K'o, 191
metal, 265; or stone, 293
Methusaleh, 141
Mi Heng, 47
mice, 88
Ming, 385
Ming-huang, 388, 421
mirror, 20, 24, 149, 150, 205, 283,
    301
mist(s), 14, 17, 54, 96, 114, 162, 165,
    236, 312, 347, 363; and clouds,
    380; and fog, 278; and smoke,
    136; and wind, 395; mountain,
    273; spring, 48
Mo-ch'ou, 82

mole, 37, 209
mole crickets and ants, 42
monastery, 7, 186, 366
monastic discipline, 403
monastic life, 317
monastic vows, 11
money, 219, 228, 229; and wealth,
    260
Mongolian goat, 169
monk(s), 11, 24, 103, 109, 134, 204,
    226, 228, 230, 236, 247, 317,
    319, 338; and nuns, 374
monk's robe(s), 226, 278, 383
monkey(s), 52, 220, 221, 235
moon, 17, 19, 20, 39, 49, 61, 92, 96,
    97, 100, 115, 130, 131, 186, 223,
    236, 278, 281, 282, 283, 286,
    313, 314, 339, 355, 358, 360,
    376, 384, 390; autumn, 95;
    bright, 115, 380, 411; cold, 355;
    full, 115, 236; lonely, 401;
    round, 376
moon cape, 339
moonlight, 163
moral rules, 317
morning dew, 293
morning mushroom, 344
mosquito, 109, 110
moss, 18, 65
Mount Heng, 169
Mount Hua, 169
Mount Sumeru, 180, 352
Mount T'ai, 169
Mount Vipula, 319, 320
mountain(s), 32, 44, 65, 114, 115, 186,
    215, 218, 236, 241, 252, 274,
    277, 279, 301, 306, 314, 320,
    339, 344, 350, 355, 360, 364,
    379, 390, 406, 408; and hills,
    82; and sea, 57; and streams,
    162, 295; and woods, 378; blos-
    soms, 54; cliffs, 286; families,
    390; fruit(s), 52, 64, 180, 243;
    lakes, 195; pass, 116; peak, 316;
    pool, 393; roots, 393; songs,
    351; stream, 70, 380; wood, 250

Mountain School, 390
mourners, 42, 43, 76, 206
mourning, 42, 132
Mr. Cheng, 404
Mr. Kuei-ku, 268
Mr. Liu, 15, 16, 174, 175
Mr. Lu, 82
Mr. Tu, 84
Mr. Wang, 421
Mrs. Lan, 15, 16
Mt. Meru, 292
Mt. Shou-yang, 42, 43
Mt. T'ai, 71
mulberry(ies), 82, 100, 198; groves,
    102; trees, 201
mule, 123
mushrooms and thistles, 115
musk, 372
mustard seed, 180, 352

Nai-ho, 122, 326
Nan-ch'üan, 312, 421
neighbors, 8, 35, 101, 390
Neo-Confucians, 347
net, 38, 184
Never Grieve, 82
Ni K'uan, 167
nine heavens, 53
nine rules, 66
nine virtues, 66
nine wildernesses, 169
Nineteen Old Poems, 33, 46, 58,
    70, 94, 96, 130, 146, 196, 201,
    213, 293, 304
no-outflows, 401
North, 169, 198, 216, 287
Northern Mang, 71
Northern sea, 119
nourishing life, 366
nun(s), 338, 374

obstacles, 17
ocean, 292, 313, 318, 352; and tides,
    314

office, 77, 172
official(s), 132, 167, 168, 171, 187, 210, 419; appointment, 10; caps, 331; documents, 31; employment, 194; examinations, 10
Old lady Chang, 249
Old lady Chia, 144
Old Liu, 218
Old man Yin, 218
old pines, 351
old rat, 365
one cloud, 284
one hundred feet, 184
one hundred men, 224
one hundred rivers, 98
one hundred thousand foot cliff, 282
one hundred victory technique, 138
one hundred years, 58, 82, 135, 201, 220, 224, 254, 257, 420
one mind, 20, 25, 205, 238, 239, 384
one thousand clouds, 381
one thousand domains, 254
one thousand li, 60, 78
one thousand lives, 275
one thousand mountains, 273
one thousand sages, 232
one thousand sons, 357
one thousand streams, 252
one thousand years old, 282
one wheel, 19
oranges, 38–39
oriole, 392
orchid islet, 165
orchid rooms, 83
ordained, 11
other shore, 112, 302. *See also* shore(s)
owl, 105, 137
ox(en), 73, 102, 163, 230, 323, 356; and plows, 373
Oxhead, 228, 230

Pa songs, 191
Painted rafters, 399
pai-ting, 10

palace, 59
Pao Chao, 46
Pao-chih, 230, 245, 246, 270, 421
Pao-p'u-tzu, 39, 109
parrot(s), 47, 49
Parrot Isle, 252
path(s), 18, 19, 34
pathways, 186
paulownia, 62
pavilion(s), 97, 184
peach(es), 13, 14, 48, 79, 125, 196; and plums, 197; apotropaic qualities of, 125; bitter, 78, 79; blossoms, 100
peak(s), 18, 32, 34, 54, 60, 114, 127, 218, 252, 274, 283, 288, 299, 350, 384; jagged, 351; lofty, 375; precipitous, 306; sacred, 71
pear, 13, 14, 48
pearl(s), 13, 48, 49, 120, 280, 285, 286, 301, 336, 341, 357, 369, 375; of the black dragon, 157
Pei-mang, 9, 71, 91
Pen-chi, 25
pepper and salt, 289
perch, 168
Perfected of T'ung-po, 247
Personnel Board, 419
pheasant, 144
phoenix, 62, 63, 83
Phoenix Pond, 165
Pi-yen lu, 110, 247
pig(s), 14, 15, 123, 323; meat, 118
piglet, 289
pigweed, 288
pillars and beams, 45
pillow, 395, 400
pine(s), 18, 34, 56, 65, 90, 127, 181, 235, 252, 273, 306, 360; and bamboo, 314; and creepers, 211; and cypress, 146; forest, 399; old, 351; tall, 58
pitch and tone, 62
plantain, 180
Platform Sutra, 25, 240
plow, 194

plums, 74, 197; withered, 223
Po Chü-i, 12
Po I and Shu Ch'i, 43, 127, 308
Po-ya, 410
polishing bricks, 149, 419
polishing this tile, 150
pond, 36, 127, 165
poor, 81, 187, 198, 216, 248, 290,
    309, 345, 347; ass, 173; scribe,
    169, 182
poplar(s), 16, 174, 175
poverty, 163, 222, 227, 244, 248,
    387; and low station, 262
Preface (Lü-ch'iu Yin's), 3, 4, 5, 22,
    24, 25
priceless jewel, 275, 276, 283, 336
Prince Ch'iao, 213
prodigal son, 67
profit and fame, 136
Profound Drugs, 339
Pu-shang, 217
Pulleyblank, 6–9, 21, 24, 101–2, 131,
    133, 136, 149, 151, 158, 162, 165,
    180, 183, 196, 229, 231–34, 238–
    39, 242–43, 245, 253, 255, 257,
    262, 266, 269, 277, 282, 284,
    297–301, 305, 313–14, 316, 319,
    321, 326–31, 336–38, 340–41,
    343–44, 349–50, 352, 356, 360–
    61, 364, 366, 369, 371, 373, 375,
    379, 381, 383, 389, 393, 394,
    396–97, 409, 412–13, 419–20
puppet, 388, 421
Pure Land, 311, 407, 421
purple, 24; and red, 331; brocade,
    108; fungus, 55, 393
P'ei the Perfected of Purity and the
    Void, 247
P'eng-lai, 78, 79, 91
P'eng-tsu, 39, 141
p'i-p'a, 49
P'i-p'a Valley, 252
p'o, 92

Queen of Ch'i, 145

rabbit-horns, 397
raft, 278, 399
rain, 18, 65, 223, 248, 299, 302, 341,
    355
rainbow, 273
rank, 72, 185
raw slices of fish, 289
rays of the sun, 292, 316
Record of Rites, 129, 216, 315
recluse(s), 35, 37, 51, 105, 113, 195,
    236, 304, 306, 308, 364, 378,
    395, 400, 402
red, 241; carp, 340; cinnamon tree,
    395; dust (realm of), 167, 203,
    267, 400; sashes, 226
Red Wall, 273, 274
refined sugar, 57
regulated verse, 65, 385, 386, 405
reincarnation, 11
rhinoceros horn, 125
rice, 149, 176, 187, 248, 296, 343, 356,
    374; jar, 227, 365; stalk, 143
rich, 14, 15, 24, 222, 309; dog, 173;
    kids, 76, 169; women, 49
riches and rank, 83; and wealth,
    146; and women, 77
river(s), 37, 82, 186, 326, 400, 405;
    fast-moving, 93
River of Heaven, 196
road(s), 18, 19, 34, 44, 56, 65, 79,
    312, 375, 406; in the clouds, 362;
    of perversion, 233; through the
    clouds, 350; to Han-shan, 34
    (*See also* way to Han-shan); to
    the immortals, 273
robbers and thieves, 315
rock(s), 32, 235, 243, 250, 271, 282,
    284, 306, 363, 368, 400, 408;
    bed, 312
roots, 180; and shoots, 226
rose of Sharon, 35
round chisel, 13, 88
ruddy glow, 91

sacred melon(s), 38, 39

sacred prayers, 319
sacred terrace, 329
sage(s), 24, 270, 293, 300; and worthies, 229
Śākyamuni, 330, 353
śālavana trees, 224
Samantabhadra, 7
saṃsāra, 18, 297, 365, 377
San-kuo chih, 21, 39, 42, 163, 167
sand(s), 148; on the shore, 165
sandalwood, 133
Sandy Mound, 370
sausage, 15, 118
scholar(s), 11, 64, 67, 161, 167, 194, 247, 315, 378; impoverished, 153
scholar-official, 77
scorpion, 73
screen(s), 47, 239, 415
scribe, 419
scriptures, 21, 389
sea, 280, 313, 358, 379
season(s), 14, 58, 115, 375; of green, 129
seasonal, 14, 90; change, 279
Secretariat, 165
sediments, 147
semen, 128
Seng Chao, 357
Seng-yu, 269, 270, 420, 421
sentient beings, 310, 313, 320
Seven Jewels, 356, 357, 360
Shan-hai ching, 169
Shan Tao, 421
Shan T'ao, 391
Shang, 213
Shang-ch'ing, 86
Shang-yü, 32
shang-yüan, 4
Shao-lin Monastery, 186
sheep, 183
Shen-hsien chuan, 100
Shen-hui, 419
Shen Nung pen-ts'ao ching, 55, 197
Shen Yüeh, 59
shepherds, 51

Shih-chi, 21, 41, 129, 191, 198, 340
Shih (ching), 21, 43, 68, 69, 129, 164, 199, 216, 250, 392, 404
Shih Ch'i-nu, 343
Shih-feng, 5, 22, 23
Shih-ning, 32
Shih-shuo hsin-yü, 166, 208, 259, 306, 343, 400
Shih-te, 3, 5, 7, 8, 22, 24, 80, 295, 413
shoots, 16, 74, 174, 175, 226, 254, 291, 377, 399
shore(s), 81, 96, 112, 278, 302, 313, 318, 340
Shu, 66, 129, 213, 216, 309, 404, 421
Shuo-yüan, 184
shuttle, 51, 153, 196, 200; and loom, 249
silver, 241; bed, 59; poplars, 146
silverfish, 315
silk, 189, 241, 362; raw, 76; soft white, 293
silken slippers, 83
silkworms, 74
sitting (in meditation), 48, 127, 150, 243, 284, 305, 316, 411
Six Arts, 161, 216
six brothers, 335
six consciousnesses, 335
six destinies, 287, 297
six doors, 239
six doorways, 240
Six Dynasties, 21
six extremities, 66, 67
six kinds of rebirth, 356
six klesas, 220
six roots, 366
six sense organs, 240
six senses, 335, 342, 366, 369
six paths, 120, 323
six thieves, 341, 369
six times, 372, 374
six ways, 287, 297
Sixth Patriarch, 205
sky, 17, 19, 96, 114, 121, 304, 350, 376; clear, 237, 283

sky-flower clothes, 397
sleet, 96
snow, 17, 18, 70, 96, 114, 143, 223,
    408
sojourner, 278
souls, 230, 253
South, 169, 198, 216, 287, 407
Southern Ch'i, 32
southern continent, 292
Southern Court, 10, 182, 419
southern fields, 107
Southern Land, 199
Southern raised path, 82
Southern School of Zen, 5
Southern sea, 119
Southern Sect, 419
Southern-style flowers, 241
sparrow(s), 13, 68, 69, 171, 184, 307
sparrow hawk, 104, 105
spirit(s), 31, 128; and gods, 372;
    and ghosts, 319; and soul, 258
spring(s), 14, 18, 32, 35, 54, 70, 106,
    107, 254, 271, 278, 306, 361,
    366, 392, 410; and autumn(s),
    99, 344; colors and hues, 74;
    seasonal, 90
Spring and Autumn Annals, 129, 216
Ssu-ma Lun, 343
Ssu-ming, 390
star hats, 340
starry cap, 339
stars, 281, 358
State messenger, 155
steaming sand, 149
stingy, 209
stinking cedar, 35
stone bed, 390
Stone Bridge, 86, 301
stone caves, 312
stone cliffs, 285
storax, 83
straw, 390; door, 127; hut, 195
stream(s), 17, 18, 38, 39, 65, 81, 93,
    94, 131, 196, 198, 243, 268, 299,
    321, 325, 350, 362, 363, 399,
    400, 401, 402; sourceless, 80;

sparkling, 54; tree by the, 129;
    valley, 64
student(s), 40, 197
Su Ch'in, 268
suburbs and walls, 304
sugar cane, 14, 25, 48
Sui, 3, 6, 9, 23, 385
Sumeru, 279, 352
summer, 19, 44, 58, 100, 122, 133,
    375; cicada, 344; months, 180
sun, 17, 18, 44, 59, 66, 67, 70, 90,
    92, 94, 135, 141, 251, 299, 358,
    363, 377, 385, 393, 401, 408;
    and moon, 42, 222, 232, 340;
    evening, 108, 211; morning, 92,
    195; setting, 94, 211
sun's rays, 316
Sun Ch'o, 86, 274, 301, 302, 359, 390
Sun Ch'u, 400
Sun Ch'üan, 43
Sun Hsiu, 343
sunflowers, 393
Sung, 72, 177, 264
Sung Ch'iung, 39
Sung Yü, 101, 192
Supreme Purity, 86
swallows, 96, 97
swans, 79
swine and sheep, 323
sword(s), 40, 138; of wisdom, 225
swordsmanship, 41, 161

ta-li, 5
tailorbird, 37, 105
Tao (the), 179, 207, 231, 263, 264,
    342
Tao-ch'iao, 3
Tao-te ching, 92, 225
Tao-tzu, 269, 420
Taoism, 86, 169, 317, 342;
    organized, 340
Taoist(s), 11, 13, 22, 25, 58, 180,
    247, 340, 359, 366; adepts, 340,
    403; arts, 169; books on immor-
    tality, 129; clergy, 31; encyclo-

pedia, 128; foods of long life, 197; immortality, 43; immortals, 39; incantation, 31; long life practices, 56, 111, 128; monks and nuns, 162; practice of *nei-tan*, 340; priest, 47; quest for immortality, 79; statecraft, 144; sacraments, 31; ways to immortality, 98
tax reform, 188
taxation (T'ang system of), 119
taxes, 119
temple(s), 270, 340, 353; hair, 61, 71, 108, 200, 215, 301
Temple of the One King, 85
Ten Cords, 352, 353
ten directions, 348
Ten Evils, 142
Ten Good Traits, 356, 357
Ten Names, 406
ten thousand affairs, 127, 399
ten thousand ages, 293
ten thousand axe and knife scars, 268
ten thousand beginnings, 377
ten thousand dharmas, 294
ten thousand feet, 362
ten thousand forms, 19, 20, 285, 339, 376
ten thousand layers, 288
ten thousand li, 96, 138, 400
ten thousand realms, 294
ten thousand shoots, 377
ten thousand streams, 381
ten thousand things, 53, 141
ten thousand tiers, 236
Ten Titles, 406
ten volumes, 315
thatch, 393; cottage, 248
thatched eaves, 163
thatched hut, 64
thief (thieves), 332, 373; of delusion, 225
thirty, 14, 99; li, 208; locations, 343; thousand days, 213; years, 11, 14, 48, 93, 182, 400

thorns, 264
thousand li horse, 60; stallion, 157
three carts, 266, 348
three evil destinies, 349, 382
three evil gatis, 169
three evil paths, 382
three flavors, 48
Three Histories, 9, 129
Three Jewels, 371
three kinds of karma, 335
three months, 49, 50
three mountains of iron, 334, 335
three paths, 35, 169, 170, 278, 287
three poisonous snakes, 310
three poisons, 139, 142, 292, 310, 369
Three Principles, 161
three realms, 278, 279, 298, 321, 322, 323, 324, 338
Three Schools, 316
Three Teachings, 317
three vital powers, 128
three-winged boat, 60
Ti-yen, 84
tiger(s), 174, 211, 235, 390, 402
Tiger Brook, 401, 402
Tiger Mound, 401, 402
Tiger Mound Temple, 402
tiger's head pillows, 258
tile(s), 15, 77, 102, 136, 150, 174, 419; roof, 257
toad, 186
tomb(s), 46, 210, 304
tortoise-hair, 397
tortoises, 73
tower(s), 97, 184; shining moon, 96
transmigration, 297, 356
traps and nets, 184
traveller(s), 17, 46, 53, 114, 186, 292, 351, 374
tree(s), 54, 278, 309; of white jade, 301; or rocks, 323
tristia, 10
trousers, 307
Tsan-ning, 3, 5, 24, 25
Tso chuan, 21, 46, 111, 113, 258

Tu Fu, 12
Tu Kuang-t'ing, 5, 22, 25
Tufted Ducks, 94
tumbleweed, 46
Tung-fang Shuo, 191
Tung Hsien, 203
tun-wu, 5
turban(s), 260; high head, 420; of
    silk, 378
turtle, 169
Two Forms, 347
Tzu-chang, 217
Tzu-ch'i, 410
Tzu-hsia, 217, 264, 308
Tzu-kung, 113
Tzu-lu, 244
T'ai-chou, 3, 4
T'ai-kung, 249
T'ai-p'ing kuang-chi, 5, 22, 23, 230
T'ai-p'ing tao, 340
T'ang, 3, 4, 5, 6, 7, 9, 12, 19, 22,
    23, 24, 25, 47, 49, 57, 72, 77,
    94, 119, 171, 187, 188, 226, 229,
    236, 246, 254, 259, 260, 274,
    385, 388, 405, 420
T'ang-hsing, 3, 4, 5, 22
T'ang T'ai-tsu, 402
T'ang T'ai-tsung, 309, 421
T'ao Ch'ien, 8, 24, 34, 35, 180, 187,
    190, 308
T'ao Hung-ching, 32, 247
T'ien-t'ai, 3, 4, 5, 20, 22, 23, 25, 32,
    80, 96, 112, 127, 238, 255, 273,
    274, 288, 295, 301, 302, 314,
    358, 359, 362, 390; county, 274;
    range, 237, 274, 358; School,
    180, 281, 352
Ts'ang-lang, 105
Ts'ao Chih, 48, 97, 99, 149, 203
Ts'ao Jui, 184
Ts'ao O, 208
Ts'ao-shan, 25
Ts'ao Shu, 187
Ts'ao Ts'ao, 163, 208
Ts'ao-tung school/sect, 25, 329
Ts'ui yin, 159

unfilial sons, 228
unpolished rice, 366
Upper East Gate, 146
Utter Darkness Stream, 86

vagrants, 176
vale, 45
valley(s), 17, 18, 34, 64, 65, 66, 215,
    273, 284, 288, 306, 363; and
    dales, 351; and hills, 224; mist,
    127; streams, 251, 360
vase, 265
Vedas, 316
vegetarian fare, 393
vermilion, 395
Vermilion Bird Street, 187
Vermilion Sparrow, 187
Vinaya, 316
vines, 235, 395
Void, 19, 130, 237, 282, 283, 340,
    348, 376

Wang, 287, 387
Wang Chi, 400
Wang Ch'iao (Wang Tzu-ch'iao), 38
Wang Fan-chih, 22
Wang Tzu-ch'iao, 247, 402
Wang Wei, 12
Wang Yen, 259
Wang Yüan, 100
wasp's waist, 385, 386
water and ice, 154
water beetles, 182
water buffaloes, 24
Water Immortal, 340
Watson, 5, 16, 25, 33, 35, 37, 41,
    42, 43, 46, 58, 69, 96, 108, 119,
    130, 146, 156, 167, 168, 178, 191,
    196, 201, 209, 213, 250, 262,
    274, 293, 344, 390
waves, 94, 156, 157, 268, 318; bil-
    lowy, 112; blue, 104; karma's,
    140; water and, 112, 140

Way (the), 12, 17, 19, 65, 133, 135,
148, 159, 202, 225, 236, 238,
245, 247, 253, 312, 314, 328,
352, 377, 383
Way of Heaven, 179
way to Han-shan, 44, 65, 70, 406
wealth, 32, 102, 130, 198, 241, 323,
372; and goods, 188; and
honor, 36, 308; and power, 343;
and rank, 36, 77, 136, 226, 308,
331, 347
wealthy and ranked, 187
wealthy ladies, 47
wealthy men, 66
weasel, 88
weaving, 121, 200
Weaving Girl, 196
weeds, 52
Wei, 163
Wei Chieh, 144
Wei Ch'üan, 144
Wei clan, 144
Wei Kuan, 144
Wen-hsüan, 6, 21, 32, 33, 35, 46, 47,
48, 58, 86, 94, 97, 101, 130, 146,
187, 192, 196, 201, 274, 301
west, 8, 40, 53, 75, 98, 101, 144, 169,
216, 239, 245, 282, 287, 348, 350
West Mountain, 308
West River, 168
western hills, 211
western land(s), 47, 169
Western lodge, 14, 48
wheat fields, 146
whip, 57; coral, 91
white bones, 210
white candana, 148
white clouds, 17, 18, 32, 55, 61, 65,
68, 104, 111, 195, 234, 235, 237,
278, 306, 312, 314, 350, 375,
380, 390, 395, 409, 411; and
pink, 360
white crane(s), 42, 78, 143
white duster, 133
white-haired old hags, 241
White Hare, 38, 39

white horse, 9, 99, 107, 155
white lotus blooms, 364
white ox, 368
white ox cart, 368
white rocks, 410
White Snow, 191, 406
White Snow in the Spring, 192
wick, 277
wildcat, 88, 169
wild deer, 220
wild ducks, 38, 156
Wild Goose Pagoda, 273
wild tumeric, 83
willow(s), 16, 57, 175, 195; drooping, 96
wind(s), 14, 18, 34, 36, 58, 65, 70,
87, 90, 100, 107, 210, 215, 223,
235, 251, 273, 297, 299, 302,
314, 318, 341, 342, 347, 378;
and frost, 113, 198, 224; strong,
94; violent, 257
wine, 98, 163, 177, 178, 206, 276,
293, 319, 366; dipper of, 180;
goblets of, 180; jug, 181
winter(s), 32, 132, 171, 176, 194,
366, 375; and springs, 295; and
summer, 132
wistaria, 52; vines, 273
witches and spooks, 241
wolf, 323, 324
women and wealth, 373
woodcutter(s), 51
woods, 17, 64, 113, 115, 244, 278,
351; secluded, 114
wren(s), 36, 104, 105
writing, 41
writing and judgment, 10, 171
Wu Chi-yu, 4, 21, 22, 24
Wu En, 390
Wu-men kuan, 312
wu-nien, 5, 23
Wu-t'ai shan, 24
Wu Tao-tzu, 270, 420
Wu-teng hui-yüan, 24
Wu-ti, 230
Wu Tse-t'ien, 260

Wu Tzu-hsü, 113

Yama, 382
Yang, 58
Yang Hsiu, 207, 208
Yang Hu, 166
Yang Kuei-fei, 94
Yang-shan, 306
Yang Yu-chi, 258
Yao, 37, 400; and Shun, 250, 378;
    wilderness, 169
Yellow Bark, 188, 189
yellow bills, 184
Yellow Clouds, 254
Yellow Emperor, 56
yellow gold, 410
yellow leaves, 406
Yellow oak, 388
yellow ochre pen, 315
Yellow pine, 271, 272
Yellow River, 111, 346
yellow scrolls, 182
Yellow Springs, 53, 90, 93, 98
Yellow Turban revolt, 340
Yen, 242
Yen-rouge, 241

Yen Yüan, 159
Yin, 39; and Yang, 347
Yü, 66
Yü Fan, 42, 76
Yü Hsin, 38, 64
Yü-ling Tzu-chung, 36
Yü Po-ya, 405, 410
Yüan Shu, 39, 268
yüeh-fu, 6, 24, 57, 59, 79, 91, 98, 203
Yüeh-fu shih-chi, 21, 79, 82, 91, 98,
    99, 155, 160, 203
Yün-chi ch'i-ch'ien, 128
Yün-kuang, 229, 230
Yung-chia, 32

Zen, 5, 6, 7, 11, 18, 19, 20, 24, 25,
    65, 81, 114, 116, 127, 152, 282,
    302, 329, 342, 377, 384, 421;
    circles, 419; frame of mind, 312;
    master(s), 102, 134, 150, 312,
    388, 419, 421; message, 384;
    quest for enlightenment, 236,
    350; phrase, 102; schools, 110;
    temple, 274; tenet, 238; texts,
    336, 342; tradition, 246; words,
    384